Why the Electoral College
Is Bad for America

Why the Electoral College Is Bad for America

Second Edition

GEORGE C. EDWARDS III

Yale UNIVERSITY PRESS

NEW HAVEN AND LONDON

Published with assistance from the foundation established in memory of Philip
Hamilton McMillan of the Class of 1894, Yale College.

Yale University Press books may be purchased in quantity for educational, business,
or promotional use. For information, please e-mail sales.press@yale.edu
(U.S. office) or sales@yaleup.co.uk (U.K. office).

Set in Garamond type by Keystone Typesetting, Inc.
Printed in the United States of America.

Library of Congress Cataloging-in-Publication Data
Edwards, George C.
    Why the electoral college is bad for America / George C. Edwards. — 2nd ed.
        p.   cm.
    Includes bibliographical references and index.
    ISBN 978-0-300-16649-1 (pbk. : alk. paper)
1. Electoral college—United States. 2. Presidents—United States—Election. I. Title.
JK529.E38 2011
324.6'3—dc22   2011000061

A catalogue record for this book is available from the British Library.

This paper meets the requirements of ANSI/NISO Z39.48-1992
(Permanence of Paper).

10 9 8 7 6 5 4 3 2 1

To those who have fought to fulfill James Madison's view that "the vital principle of republican government is . . . the will of the majority"

Contents

Preface

On February 24, 2005, Russian President Vladimir Putin and President George W. Bush held a joint press conference in Bratislava. A reporter asked Putin about the antidemocratic direction in which he was taking his country. Putin responded, "I'd like to draw your attention to the fact that the leaders of the regions of the Russian Federation will not be appointed by the president. Their canvases will be presented, will be submitted to regional parliaments that are elected through secret ballot by all the citizens. This is, in essence, a system of the electoral college, which is used, on the national level, in the United States, and it is not considered undemocratic, is it?"

The fact that the leader of Russia, who has demonstrated a distinct lack of appreciation for democracy, used the electoral college as a rationale to defend the less than democratic elections in his own country is in itself disconcerting. The fact that he had a point is even more so.

I have been a student of the presidency for nearly four decades. Until the election of 2000, I never paid much attention to the manner in which we selected the president, often referred to as the most powerful person in the world. I was less upset that George W. Bush won election than about *how* he won. I could not reconcile the victory of the person finishing second in the popular vote with my democratic values.

As a result, I began looking at the electoral college literature, seeking a rationale for such an incongruous outcome. I could not find one. In the process, however, I discovered among advocates of the electoral college an insensitivity to democratic norms and a wide range of justifications for the electoral college's violations of them. On their face, all these justifications seemed to be contrary to fact.

Upon closer inspection, I found that defenders of the electoral college based their assertions of the system's virtues on a series of faulty premises. They virtually never engaged in rigorous reality checking, provided systematic data to support their claims, or referred to the vast relevant literature on politics and elections. Instead, they simply *assumed* their claims to be true.

This is no way to evaluate the election of the president. As a result, I undertook to make a more rigorous analysis of the electoral college than had been done before. The positive reception to the first edition of the resulting volume, both in the academy and among journalists, has been gratifying. So has the fact that the book has proved useful to electoral reformers. After eight years and two presidential elections, it is appropriate to offer a second edition. I have refined and reorganized my arguments, provided additional data, and responded to new assertions by defenders of the electoral college.

In Chapter 1 I raise questions about the electoral college, and in Chapter 2 I explain how it works. Chapters 3 and 4 show how the electoral college violates democratic norms, particularly political equality. In the next chapter I explore the origins of the electoral college, asking whether we can find justification for it in the intentions of the framers. In Chapter 6 I examine the claims made by advocates of the electoral college that it protects the interests of states, especially small states, and of racial and ethnic minorities. In Chapter 7 I focus on yet other claims made by defenders of the electoral college, namely that it is essential for maintaining the harmony and cohesion of the Republic. In the next chapter, I analyze whether the electoral college is necessary to prevent the fragmentation and polarization of the party system. In the final chapter, I review alternatives to the electoral college and explore the consequences of adopting direct election of the president.

I am grateful to a number of people and institutions for their help in this project. William Frucht of Yale University Press encouraged and facilitated this revision. Dan Heaton did an outstanding job with copyediting and page proofs. Gary McDowell and the Institute of United States Studies at the University of London gave me a supportive environment in which to write the first edition, and Texas A&M University provided the same for writing this second edition. As always, my wife, Carmella, is the one who makes all my work possible.

Chapter 1 Raising Questions

Perhaps the most important legacy of the 2000 presidential election is that it demonstrated the critical role of the electoral college. It was the electoral college, not the Supreme Court's decision in *Bush v. Gore,* that actually determined the outcome of the election. If we selected presidents as we select virtually every other elected official in the United States, Al Gore would have been president—no matter how many chads clung to ballots in Florida.

Having the runner-up in the popular vote win the presidency raised yet again the question of our mechanism for selecting presidents. Should the candidate receiving the most votes win the election? Supporters of the electoral college saw no problem in the outcome of the Bush-Gore race. Those wishing to reform the electoral college, however, saw the outcome of the election as violating central tenets of democracy: political equality and majority (or at least plurality) rule.

The country's surface acceptance of the election result masked deeper concerns about the new president's legitimacy. The first Gallup poll of Bush's tenure found that he had the highest level of disapproval of any new president since polling began.[1] Similarly, Gary Jacobson reported that the public's initial reception of Bush reflected the widest partisan differences for any newly elected president in polling history. In the twenty-eight Gallup and CBS/*New York Times* polls taken before September 11, 2001, Bush's approval ratings averaged 88 percent among self-identified Republicans but only 31 percent among Democrats. Independents averaged 50 percent. This 57-point difference between party identifiers indicates an extraordinary polarization in the wake of the resolution of the 2000 election.[2]

Even after two and a half years and a sharp increase in his approval following the 9/11 attacks, 38 percent of the public, including a majority of Democrats and half of Independents, did not consider George W. Bush the legitimate winner of the 2000 presidential election.[3] As Thomas Patterson put it, to say that the system works is to judge its soundness "by the public's willingness to tolerate its distortions."[4]

No president should have to govern with so many questioning his legitimacy. Gerald Ford decided against a recount in the very close election in 1976, telling his staff, "I lost the popular vote. It would be very hard for me to govern if I won the presidency in the Electoral College through a recount." As James Baker, Ford's campaign manager and later Bush's lead advocate in the Florida recount, concluded: "He was right, of course."[5]

But the electoral college wasn't a problem only in 2000.

THE 2008 ELECTION

The presidential election of 2008 was historic in several senses. The election of an African American was a source of pride for much of the nation—and the world. For many, the rejection of the George W. Bush presidency and the election of large Democratic majorities seemed to portend an era of reform and progress. But the process itself was also significant.

Barack Obama rejected public funding of his general election campaign, choosing instead to finance his effort with donations from millions of people who were excited about his candidacy. This decision gave him great flexibility, as he had by far the largest campaign war chest in the history of presidential elections. He spent more than $700 million running for president, including more than $250 million in October 2008 alone.[6]

Obama had another advantage: the Republican Party was particularly unpopular. George W. Bush's presidency was closing with two intractable wars and a financial crisis, leaving him very low in the polls. In early November, Bush's approval rating in the Gallup Poll stood at 27 percent.[7] Only 26 percent of the public identified as Republicans, while 38 percent identified as Democrats.[8]

In other words, conditions were ripe for the Democratic presidential candidate to be competitive in more states than in 2004 or 2000. Obama had both the means and the motive to campaign broadly across the country, taking his case to the American people.

Such a campaign is exactly what supporters of the electoral college expect presidential candidates to run. They argue that with each state guaranteed a specific number of electoral votes, and with all but two states choosing to cast their votes as a unit, the electoral college forces major-party candidates to pay attention to all regions of the country and build broad coalitions by winning a wide geographic distribution of states. The winner's coalition must mirror the nation. One proponent asserts that presidential candidates "tour the nation, campaigning in all states and seeking to build a national coalition."[9] Moreover, advocates claim, the electoral college ensures that presidential candidates will be attentive to state-based interests, especially those of states with small populations.

So what did Barack Obama and John McCain, his Republican opponent, actually do in the 2008 general election? Did they campaign across the nation, paying special attention to small states?

Table 1.1 shows the campaign stops in each state. Rather than campaigning across the nation and trying to win as many votes as possible, the candidates' travel was highly concentrated. Obama and McCain appeared in the competitive small states of New Mexico, Nevada, and New Hampshire, but they never went to *any* of the seventeen other states with six or fewer electoral votes or campaigned in Washington, DC. Of the next nine smallest states (those with seven to nine electoral votes each), the candidates visited only Iowa and Colorado. Between them, the two presidential candidates personally campaigned in only five of the twenty-nine smallest states.

They also bypassed Washington, Massachusetts, New Jersey, Georgia, California, Texas, and Illinois. New York saw only a single McCain event, when he had to be there for other reasons. McCain campaigned in Arizona, Minnesota, Maryland, and Tennessee, but Obama did not.

Despite the extraordinary resources available to him, Barack Obama

Table 1.1
Candidate Campaign Appearances in States, 2008 Election

State	Electoral Votes (2008)	Candidate Campaign Appearances		
		Presidential Candidates	Vice Presidential Candidates	Total
Wyoming	3	0	0	0
Alaska	3	0	3	3
Vermont	3	0	0	0
District of Columbia	3	0	0	0
North Dakota	3	0	0	0
Delaware	3	0	3	3
South Dakota	3	0	0	0
Montana	3	0	1	1
Rhode Island	4	0	0	0
Idaho	4	0	0	0
Hawaii	4	0	0	0
New Hampshire	4	8	8	16
Maine	4	0	1	1
Nevada	5	7	6	13
New Mexico	5	9	3	12
Nebraska	5	0	0	0
Utah	5	0	0	0
West Virginia	5	0	1	1
Arkansas	6	0	0	0
Kansas	6	0	0	0
Mississippi	6	0	0	0
Iowa	7	5	5	10
Oregon	7	0	0	0
Oklahoma	7	0	0	0
Connecticut	7	0	0	0
South Carolina	8	0	0	0
Kentucky	8	0	0	0
Colorado	9	13	11	24
Alabama	9	0	0	0
Louisiana	9	0	0	0
Arizona	10	1	0	1
Minnesota	10	2	1	3

Table 1.1

Continued

		Candidate Campaign Appearances		
State	Electoral Votes (2008)	Presidential Candidates	Vice Presidential Candidates	Total
Maryland	10	1	0	1
Wisconsin	10	9	5	14
Tennessee	11	1	0	1
Washington	11	0	2	2
Missouri	11	8	14	22
Indiana	11	5	5	10
Massachusetts	12	0	0	0
Virginia	13	14	15	29
Georgia	15	0	0	0
North Carolina	15	8	11	19
New Jersey	15	0	0	0
Michigan	17	11	6	17
Ohio	20	39	42	81
Illinois	21	0	0	0
Pennsylvania	21	33	27	60
Florida	27	31	26	57
New York	31	1	0	1
Texas	34	0	0	0
California	55	0	0	0

Sources: Data collected by author.

Note: A visit to a state to vacation, spend time at home or work, appear on a national television program, or prepare for debates does not count as a campaign visit unless the candidate actually campaigned while in the state. When the presidential candidate and his running mate appeared together, the visit was recorded as an appearance for both the presidential candidate and the vice presidential candidate.

campaigned in only fourteen states, representing only 33 percent of the American people, during the entire general election. John McCain campaigned in nineteen, representing 50 percent of the public.[10] There was no such thing as a national campaign, and small states got little attention. According to Joel Benenson, Obama's lead pollster in 2008, the Obama general election effort did not even include national polling. "We created a sample of battleground states," he said. "As we tested ideas and messaging, we were focused on the voters we had to influence. We wasted no resources."[11]

The campaigns of vice presidential candidates Joseph Biden and Sarah Palin were hardly different. Each campaigned in eighteen states, including the competitive small states of New Mexico, Nevada, and New Hampshire. Palin added a single visit to Maine and her home state of Alaska, while Biden went to Montana, West Virginia, and his home state of Delaware. Aside from Iowa and Colorado, they bypassed the rest of the twenty-nine smallest states—as well as Arizona, Maryland, Tennessee, Massachusetts, Georgia, New Jersey, Illinois, New York, Texas, and California.

Each candidate avoided entire regions of the country. Democrats had little incentive to campaign in the heavily Republican Great Plains and Deep South, and Republicans had little incentive to visit most of the Northeast and the West Coast. As Obama's campaign manager wrote,

> Most of the country—those who lived in safely red or blue states—did not truly witness the 2008 presidential campaign. The real contest occurred in only about sixteen states, in which swing voters in particular bumped up against the campaign at every turn—at their doors; on their phones; on their local news, TV shows, and radio programs; and on the Internet. In these states, we trotted out the candidate and our surrogates, built large staffs and budgets to support our organizational work, and mounted ferocious and diversified advertising campaigns. They were the canvas on which we sketched the election.[12]

It is not surprising, then, that fewer than 1 percent of the candidates' ads were national.[13]

Did Obama and McCain center their campaigns on interests focused in the states in which they did campaign? No. Their stump speeches and advertisements, although seen by only a fraction of the public, addressed issues of national concern such as the wars in Iraq and Afghanistan, the financial crisis and the economy, health care, education, and energy.

If the candidates did not take their cases to most of the country and largely ignored state interests and small states in particular, perhaps they made private pledges to support interests of the states in which they did not campaign. There is no evidence of any such pledges, however. More-over, it did not make any sense for the candidates to make such pledges. For example, the candidates ignored most of the country, including a great swath of the sixteen states of Idaho, Utah, Wyoming, Montana, North and South Dakota, Nebraska, Kansas, Oklahoma, Texas, Arkansas, Louisiana, Mississippi, Alabama, Georgia, and South Carolina. John McCain did not make private pledges in these states, because he had no need to. He was going to win them anyhow.

Barack Obama made no private pledges to these states either, knowing they were a lost cause. He could not call, say, Texas Republican Governor Rick Perry or Louisiana Republican Governor Bobby Jindal with private pledges and expect that the political leaders of these Republican states would somehow secretly help a Democratic candidate. And *private* pledges were not going to help win the votes of the broad electorate.

Another dimension of the 2008 election bears scrutiny. What if John McCain's electoral strategy had been successful? The seven states in which he suffered the narrowest losses were Colorado, Florida, Indiana, New Hampshire, North Carolina, Ohio, and Washington. If we shifted just enough votes from Obama in each of those states to make McCain the winner, he would have taken exactly 270 electoral votes. (In four states—Indiana, Missouri, Montana, and North Carolina—he would have won all the electoral votes while winning less than a majority of the popular vote.) McCain would still have received only 46 percent of the vote compared with Obama's 52 percent, a difference of more than eight million votes. Yet the electoral college would have made John McCain the president.

Defenders of the electoral college claim that forcing presidential candi-dates to seek broad support helps maintain national harmony and provides the president a mandate for governing. We have already seen that the candidates do not seek broad support. Nevertheless, we can ask whether Barack Obama received broad public support in winning the 2008 election and whether he received a meaningful mandate for governing.

Did the electoral college ensure that the winner received the broad backing of the American public? In 2008, 89.1 percent of the public voted for the presidential candidate of the party with which they identified, the second-highest level in the history of the American National Election Studies (ANES), which go back to 1952. Only the 89.9 percent party line voting in 2004 surpassed this level. Moreover, Obama's electoral coalition contained the smallest share of opposite-party identifiers, just 4.4 percent, of any president elected since the advent of the ANES series.[14]

It is not only that Republicans and Republican-leaning independents did not support Obama. They did not just oppose him; they despised and feared him. By election day, they perceived a huge ideological gulf between themselves and the Democratic candidate and viewed him as untrustworthy, a radical leftist with a socialist agenda.[15]

Jay Cost calculated both unweighted and weighted (with each state factored according to its share of the nationwide popular vote) averages of Obama's share of the vote in each state plus the District of Columbia to arrive at the standard deviation of votes. The greater the standard deviation, the more the states varied around the average, meaning that their differences were greater and thus that there was more polarization. He found that partisan polarization was the highest it has been in sixty years.[16]

Other measures also reveal this schism. Although the 2008 election was less close than the previous two, Obama still lost twenty-two states. More states deviated from the winner's share of the nationwide vote (about 52.9 percent for Obama) by 10 percentage points or more than in any election of the previous sixty years (Figure 1.1).[17] A few—Vermont, Rhode Island, Hawaii, and the District of Columbia—were polarized in favor of Obama. Most of the polarized states, however, voted for McCain. The majority of them form a belt stretching from West Virginia, Kentucky, and Tennessee through Alabama, Mississippi, Louisiana, and Arkansas over to Oklahoma, Kansas, and Nebraska. In addition, Wyoming, Idaho, Utah, and Alaska were strongly in the Republican camp. Few of these states had ever voted so heavily against a victorious Democrat.

When President Obama took office, he enjoyed a 68 percent approval level, the highest of any newly elected president since John F. Kennedy. For all of his hopes about bipartisanship, however, his early approval ratings were the most polarized of any president in the past four decades. By February 15, less than a month after Obama took office, only 30 percent of Republicans approved of his performance in office, while 89 percent of Democrats and 63 percent of Independents approved.[18] Three weeks into his term, the gap between Democratic and Republican approval had already reached 59 percentage points—and Obama never again drew 30 percent approval among Republicans. By the one hundred–day mark of

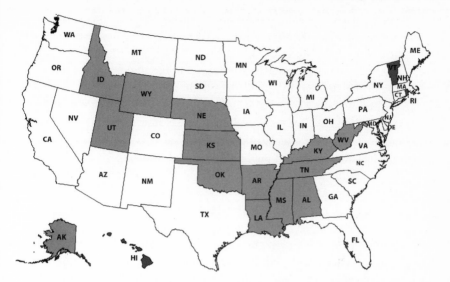

Figure 1.1. States with polarized election results in the 2008 presidential election. Light gray indicates polarized voting for McCain; dark gray indicates polarized voting for Obama.

his tenure, 92 percent of Democrats but only 28 percent of Republicans approved of his performance, a 64-point difference.[19] Gallup reported that there was an average gap of 65 percentage points between Democrats' and Republicans' evaluations of the president in his first year, greatly exceeding the previous high of 52 percentage points for Bill Clinton.[20]

Nor did Obama receive a mandate to govern. He won the presidency with nearly 53 percent of the popular vote, the first time a Northern Democrat had won a majority of the popular vote for president since Franklin D. Roosevelt's victory in 1944—and only the third time any Democrat had won a popular majority in the intervening sixty-four years. Democrats won additional seats in both houses of Congress, and the election of the first African American president generated an enormous amount of favorable press coverage. Furthermore, the new president had emphasized change, not continuity, in his campaign and promised bold new initiatives.[21] It was easy to overinterpret his mandate for change.

There was no mandate, however. An ABC News/ *Washington Post* poll taken shortly before his inauguration found that although most people felt

Obama had a mandate to *work* for major policy changes, 46 percent of the public felt he should compromise with Republicans in doing so.[22] This, of course, was a recipe for gridlock.

Subsequent events showed how little support the president had. Republicans did not defer to him, and the public opposed many of his major initiatives. With the exception of limits on executive pay, which were popular when George W. Bush occupied the White House, regulating the highly unpopular large financial institutions and food safety regulatory reform, which had always received public support, and repealing "don't ask, don't tell," which the public had backed for several years before Obama took office, no major Obama initiative enjoyed widespread public support. The president could not muster majority backing for his policies regarding the Troubled Assets Relief Program, the bank and automaker bailouts, health care reform, climate change, or his overall handling of the economy, the deficit, or foreign policy. Those who voted for him were the most unlikely to support the war in Afghanistan. The public also clearly opposed closing the prison at Guantánamo Bay and transferring its inmates to the United States.[23]

In 2008 the electoral college did not work at all as its defenders said it would. Instead of encouraging candidates to take their cases to the entire country and pay special attention to small states, it distorted the electoral process and gave the candidates strong incentives to ignore most of the country, especially the smallest states. It did not guarantee victory to the candidate receiving the most votes. It did not ensure national harmony or provide the winner a broad coalition and a mandate to govern but instead failed to prevent extreme polarization and provided only tenuous support for the new president.

A NEED TO REEVALUATE

Given the electoral college's sometimes antidemocratic results and its failure to fulfill its advocates' claims for it, one might think that there would be substantial informed debate about the unique manner in which Americans select their presidents. But there is not.

Two aspects of discourse on the electoral college are especially striking. First, the supporters of the electoral college rarely join the issue. Reformers argue that the electoral college violates political equality as epitomized in the principle of one person, one vote—one of the most fundamental tenets of democracy. Given the country's commitment to democracy and the importance of equality in American life, one might anticipate that supporters of the electoral college would respond to attacks on it with principled arguments. But they rarely do. Instead, they typically simply dismiss such concerns and focus on what they see as the system's advantages.

A second striking aspect is the nature of the discussion. Supporters argue—often passionately, sometimes hysterically—that the electoral college has a wide range of advantages for the American polity. These benefits are said to include protecting the interests of small states and strategically placed minorities, preserving federalism, encouraging the two-party system, and protecting against voter fraud. These assertions certainly deal with important issues and require careful examination, especially when, on their face, many of them appear quite mistaken.

It is disconcerting, then, to find that supporters of the electoral college are extraordinarily insouciant about their claims on its behalf. They virtually never marshal data systematically or evaluate supposed benefits rigorously. Nor do they cite relevant literature. Instead, they make assertions.

Yet there are ways to test claims. For example, do candidates really pay attention to small states? We can find out. Is the electoral college really a fundamental pillar of federalism? Let us examine the federal system and see. Is the winner-take-all system in the electoral college the critical institutional underpinning of the two-party system? Researchers have been studying party systems for years.

Talking past each other is not a useful means of evaluating constitutional provisions for selecting the president. The purpose of this book is to join the issue: to focus directly and systematically on the core questions surrounding the electoral college and assess whether it warrants a role in American democracy.

Chapter 2 How the Electoral
College Works

Before we can evaluate the electoral college, we must understand
how it works. The popular election every fourth November is
only the first step in a complex procedure that should culminate
in the formal declaration of a winner two months later. In fact,
under the Constitution, the November election is not for the
presidential candidates themselves but for the electors who subsequently choose a president. All that the Constitution says of this
stage of the election process is that "each state shall appoint, in
such manner as the legislature thereof may direct, a number of
electors, equal to the whole number of Senators and Representatives to which the state may be entitled in Congress." (Readers
who wish to read the constitutional provisions relating to presidential elections may consult the Appendix.)

How Many Electors Are There?

Each state's representation in the electoral college is equal to its
representation in Congress. As a result, every state is guaranteed a
minimum of three electoral votes: two matching the number of

Table 2.1
Electoral Vote Allocation by State, 2012

State	Electoral Votes	State	Electoral Votes
Alabama	9	Montana	3
Alaska	3	Nebraska	5
Arizona	11	Nevada	6
Arkansas	6	New Hampshire	4
California	55	New Jersey	14
Colorado	9	New Mexico	5
Connecticut	7	New York	29
Delaware	3	North Carolina	15
District of Columbia	3	North Dakota	3
Florida	29	Ohio	18
Georgia	16	Oklahoma	7
Hawaii	4	Oregon	7
Idaho	4	Pennsylvania	20
Illinois	20	Rhode Island	4
Indiana	11	South Carolina	9
Iowa	6	South Dakota	3
Kansas	6	Tennessee	11
Kentucky	8	Texas	38
Louisiana	8	Utah	6
Maine	4	Vermont	3
Maryland	10	Virginia	13
Massachusetts	11	Washington	12
Michigan	16	West Virginia	5
Minnesota	10	Wisconsin	10
Mississippi	6	Wyoming	3
Missouri	10		

Source: U.S. Census Bureau, 2010.

its U.S. senators, and one or more corresponding to the number of representatives it has in the U.S. House of Representatives. In the twenty-first century, with fifty states in the Union, the electoral college consists of 538 persons: 435 corresponding to the number of representatives, 100 to the number of senators, and an additional 3 for the District of Columbia under the Twenty-third Amendment to the Constitution. Table 2.1 shows the number of electoral votes for each state in the 2012 presidential election.

Following each census, Congress adjusts these totals, reallocating the number of members of the House of Representatives to reflect state-by-state population changes. The decennial reapportionment of electors, however, does not account for significant population shifts that often occur in the course of a decade. For this reason, a state's congressional apportionment—and hence its electoral vote—tends to lag behind population shifts. Because each census takes place in the first year of a decade (1790, 1800, 1990, 2000, and so on), each reapportionment takes effect, at the earliest, two years later.

When a presidential election falls in the same year as a census, the apportionment of a full decade earlier governs the allocation of electoral votes. In the election of 2000, for example, the allocation of electoral votes actually reflected the population distribution of 1990, a decade earlier. The increase or decrease in a state's population since 1990 was not reflected in that state's electoral vote apportionment until the 2004 election. As a result, George W. Bush received six fewer electoral votes than he would have had the results of the 2000 census determined states' electoral votes in the 2000 election.

Who Nominates the Electors?

States use a variety of methods to select presidential electors. The most common procedure is for state conventions of the parties to nominate the electors. In most other states and the District of Columbia, the state party's central committee makes the nominations.[1]

Who Are the Electors?

The Constitution says merely that "no Senator or Representative, or person holding an office of trust or profit under the United States, shall be appointed an elector." The founders wished to prevent members of Congress and federal officials from having a role in the election of the president—at least in the first instance—to avoid the bribery and intrigue they feared might result. The framers intended that electors would be distinguished citizens, and such they were in some early elections.

As early as 1826, however, a Senate select committee observed that electors were "usually selected for their devotion to party, their popular manners, and a supposed talent for electioneering."[2] In 1855, in contrast, some asserted that the electors in Alabama and Mississippi were among the state's ablest men and went among the people to instruct, excite, and arouse them on the issues of the campaign.[3]

Today, few voters know their state's electors. Rather than the assembly of wise and learned elders assumed by its creators, the electoral college is largely a collection of party loyalists and donors. As one well-known 1968 elector, the best-selling author James Michener, candidly put it, "My finest credentials were that every year I contributed what money I could to the party."[4] It appears that such rewards have often been reserved for citizens and party workers in the twilight of their lives. Thomas O'Connor, for example, was ninety-three when he was elected president of the Massachusetts electoral college in 1960.

The 2004 electors from Minnesota ranged in age from fifty-two to eighty-three and included a retired businessman, a retired electrician, an attorney, a retired civil rights leader, a union business agent, a St. Cloud city council member, a retired nurse, a retired teacher, a marketing consultant, and a homemaker and volunteer.[5] A study of the 2000 election found that the electors, especially the Republican electors, were likely to be white males, with high levels of political activity.[6]

In 1936 the Democratic Party of New York State attempted to use its list of electors for political purposes by placing several prominent trade unionists, including International Ladies' Garment Workers' chief David Dubinsky, on its electoral slate to attract the labor vote to Franklin D. Roosevelt. At the time, some expressed fears that allocating elector slots on the basis of class, racial, and religious appeals might "Tammany-ize" electoral slates.[7] These fears appear to be unwarranted, however, for it is rare for states to list the names of electors on their ballots.

Some small measure of prestige for their service is the sole reward for electors; the only payment electors normally receive is a small per diem allowance (if that) on the day they cast their votes.[8]

Electors may be individually obscure, but their names are public. Each state must send the National Archives a Certificate of Ascertainment, which lists the names of the electors for the presidential candidates.[9]

Who Elects the Electors?

The Constitution permits each state to select electors "in such manner as the legislature thereof may direct."[10] As Justice John M. Harlan observed in *Williams v. Rhodes* (1968), during the first four decades of the United

States, states selected electors "by the legislature itself, by the general electorate on an at-large and district-by-district basis, partly by the legislature
and partly by people, by the legislature from a list of candidates selected by
the people, and in other ways."[11]

In the first presidential election, in 1788, the legislatures in five states
selected the electors without a popular vote. The New York legislature
could not agree on a method of selecting electors and so selected none at
all. The other states elected electors in districts or in statewide elections. In
1792 there were fifteen states, in nine of which the state legislators chose the
electors. In 1796 there were sixteen states, and once again the state legislatures in nine of them chose the electors.

As time passed, many saw legislative selection of electors as corrupt and
were put off by the inevitable bargaining and payoffs that occurred.[12] By
1824 only six state legislatures appointed electors, and the number dropped
to two in 1828. From 1832 through 1860, only South Carolina continued this
practice. With the exception of the newly reconstructed state of Florida in
1868 and the newly admitted state of Colorado in 1876, the people of the
states have chosen the electors in statewide elections since the Civil War.

Should any state legislature wish, however, it has the right under the
Constitution to take the choice of the electors from the people and either
do the job itself or deputize another body to make the selection. In the
words of a Senate committee in 1874, "The appointment of these electors is
thus placed absolutely and wholly within the legislatures of the several
States. They may be chosen by the legislature, or the legislature may provide that they shall be elected by the people of the State at large, or in
districts; . . . and it is, no doubt, competent for the legislature to authorize
the Governor, or the Supreme Court of the State, or any other agent of its
will, to appoint these electors."[13]

The Supreme Court quoted this language approvingly in a landmark
case, *McPherson v. Blacker* (1892), in which a group of Michigan citizens
challenged the right of that state's legislature to shift to a district system for
the elections of 1892. The Court rejected the appeal, finding that the word
"appoint" in the Constitution conveys the "broadest power of determination" to the legislatures. The state legislatures, the Court said, have "plenary power" over appointing electors, and could even refuse to provide for
the appointment of any electors at all if they so chose. Moreover, the public
has no constitutional right to vote for electors. "The Constitution does not

provide that the appointment of electors shall be by popular vote, nor that the electors shall be voted for upon a general ticket, nor that the majority of those who exercise the elective franchise can alone choose the electors . . . . In short, the appointment and mode of appointment of electors belong exclusively to the States under the Constitution."[14]

The Court's opinion echoed a statement made years earlier, during a House debate in 1826. Representative Henry R. Storms of New York asserted that nothing in the Constitution prevented a state legislature from vesting the power to choose presidential electors "in a board of bank directors—a turnpike commission—or a synagogue."[15]

In *Bush v. Gore* (2000), the Supreme Court made the point once again, declaring that "the individual citizen has no federal constitutional right to vote for electors for the President of the United States unless and until the state legislature chooses a statewide election as a means to implement its power to appoint members of the electoral college."[16]

After the election of 1960, segregationist forces in the Louisiana legislature suggested revoking the choice of the regular Democratic electors already elected by the people and substituting a new slate of electors who would oppose John F. Kennedy's election. Despite the strong conservative sentiment in the legislature, however, the motion was withdrawn before it could come to a vote. If the motion had passed, opponents could probably have successfully challenged it in the courts because it would have violated the congressional requirement that the electors be chosen on a uniform date—which had already passed. However, a move by a legislature to choose the electors itself before the nationally established date for choosing the electors would not be open to a similar challenge.

Despite the sweeping language of *McPherson v. Blacker,* there are some legal and political limitations on the discretion of state legislatures in establishing the mechanisms for selecting electors. In *McPherson,* the Supreme Court recognized that if a state permits the people to choose the electors, then the Fourteenth Amendment protects citizens from having their vote denied or abridged. The Supreme Court has also upheld congressional enactments designed to prevent fraud or regulate campaign expenditures in connection with presidential elections.[17]

It would probably never occur to most state legislatures to take the power of appointment of presidential electors directly unto themselves. Even if the temptation presented itself, fear of retribution at the polls would restrain them. The governor of a state, moreover, would probably veto a legislative act abolishing popular election for presidential electors. In referendum states, a law abolishing popular election could be referred to the people, where it would almost certainly be defeated. Citizens could use initiative measures in a similar way.[18] Nevertheless, in a disputed election, as in 2000 in Florida, the temptation for a legislature to attempt to resolve the issue by directly choosing the electors would be real.

Ohio at one point had a set of laws that made it both impossible for independent candidates for elector to obtain a place on the ballot and difficult for a new party or a small existing party to gain a place on the state ballot. In *Williams v. Rhodes* (1968), the Supreme Court found that the Ohio laws violated the right of individuals to associate for the advancement of their political beliefs and the right of voters to cast their votes effectively.[19] As Michael Glennon points out, this decision ignored the problem that people do not have a right to vote for electors and in no way suggests overruling *McPherson*.[20]

When Do We Elect Electors?

The Constitution provides that Congress may determine the date for selecting electors and mandates that the date chosen be uniform throughout the United States.[21] Before 1845 Congress refrained from setting a specific day for the election of the electors. The 1792 law that spelled out procedures for presidential election stipulated only that the electors must be chosen within the thirty-four days preceding the first Wednesday in December every fourth year. Congress apparently refrained from setting a specific date for two reasons. First, such a date would be inconvenient for state legislatures that directly chose the electors and would need more than a single day to complete their debates and action. In addition, states' rights advocates argued that Congress should not place unnecessary restrictions on the states.[22]

In 1845, however, Congress established a uniform national election date: the first Tuesday after the first Monday in November.[23] The date was especially appropriate for an agrarian society, for it fell after most of the autumn harvest had been gathered but before the rigors of winter set in. This date has been observed in every subsequent presidential election. Congress selected Tuesday because it allowed a full day's travel between Sunday, which was widely observed as a strict day of rest, and election day.

In most rural areas, the only polling place was at the county seat, frequently a journey of many miles on foot or horseback. The first Tuesday after the first Monday was chosen to eliminate November 1, All Saints' Day—a holy day of obligation for Roman Catholics—as a possible election day.

How Do We Elect Electors?

The virtual anonymity of the presidential elector has been reinforced in recent years by the use of the presidential elector "short ballot" in the November election, apparently spurred by the desire to simplify the vote count and by the spread of voting machines. Instead of facing a ballot or voting machine with long lists of elector candidates, the voter sees the names of each party's presidential and vice presidential candidates. Unless voters are well versed politically, they have no way of knowing that they are actually voting for presidential electors rather than directly for president and vice president.

Before 1920, in every state, electors appeared on the ballot. Voters could pick and choose among elector candidates, even selecting electors for more than one candidate. By 1940, however, fifteen states employed the presidential short ballot. The number increased to twenty-six in 1948; by 1992, forty-two states and the District of Columbia prescribed it by law. Today, only North Dakota, South Dakota, Arizona, Idaho, Oklahoma, and Louisiana list electors on the ballot. Even where electors appear on the ballot, voters must select one slate and cannot choose among electors for different candidates. The last time a state let voters pick and choose individual electors from different slates was Vermont in 1980.[24]

One beneficial result of the short ballot is that it reduces the chances of voter confusion in marking ballots. History abounds with examples of spoiled ballots resulting from voter confusion over how to vote for electors. In the 1904 presidential election in Florida, the names of the twenty candidates for elector, five from each of the four parties that qualified, were printed in a close column, one name below the other, with no line or space separating the party nominees. Nor did the ballot carry any emblem or name to indicate which party each candidate for elector represented. The Democratic voter had to mark the first five electoral candidates, the Republican numbers six through ten, the Populist numbers eleven through fifteen, and so on. Naturally, a large number of voters were muddled, and 4,300 of Florida's 39,300 voters failed to mark all the electors of their parties.[25] Similarly, in Maryland in 1904, some 2,000 Republican voters marked only the square for the first Republican elector, thinking that that square represented a vote for all eight Republican elector nominees. The result was that the Republicans received only one instead of all eight Maryland electoral voters.[26]

One of the most serious voter mix-ups of modern times occurred in Ohio in 1948. The state normally employs the short ballot, with the names of the Republican and Democratic electors not appearing on the ballot. Henry Wallace's Progressive Party was unable to qualify as a regular party for the general election ballot, however, so the Wallace electors appeared on the ballot as individual names. Thousands of voters were confused by the double system and voted for some Wallace electors as well as marking ballots for Thomas Dewey or Harry Truman. More than 100,000 Ohio presidential ballots were invalidated for this reason. The confusion may well have determined the outcome in the state, which Truman won by a margin of only 7,105 votes.[27]

Under the general ticket ballot, the voter chooses one entire elector slate as a unit, and there is no chance for a split result: some electors elected from one slate and some from another. But where a voter can vote for individual electors, there is a chance for a divided result, as happened in New York in 1860; California in 1880, 1892, 1896, and 1912; North Dakota, Oregon, and Ohio in 1892; Kentucky in 1896; Maryland in 1904 and 1908; and West Virginia in 1916.[28] In 1960 Alabamans selected five electors pledged to John F. Kennedy and six unpledged electors, who ultimately voted for Senator Harry Byrd.

How Do States Allocate Their Electoral Votes?

Since the advent of Jacksonian democracy, the states have almost exclusively used the winner-take-all method for allocating their electors to candidates. (I discuss the implications of this practice in Chapter 3.) Under this system, electors are chosen "at large" (on a statewide basis), and the party with the most votes receives all the state's electoral votes.

The district division of electoral votes was common early in the nineteenth century but disappeared by 1836. Since 1832, three states have reverted to the district system. The first instance occurred in 1892 in Michigan, where Democrats were temporarily in control of the legislature and sought to divide the state's electoral votes so that they would not go en bloc to the Republicans, who normally had a voting majority in the state. Each of the state's twelve congressional districts became a separate elector district, and two additional "at large" districts, one eastern and one western, were established for the votes corresponding to Michigan's two senators. The plan was successful in dividing the Michigan electoral vote: nine electoral votes went for the Republican presidential ticket and five for the Democratic ticket in that year's election. The national outcome was not close enough to be influenced by the Michigan return, however. It was this Michigan plan that the Supreme Court refused to invalidate in *McPherson v. Blacker.*

Two more recent experiments with the district plan continue today. In 1969 Maine resurrected the district division of electoral votes by adopting a plan, which went into effect as of the presidential election of 1972, allowing for the determination of two of its four votes on the basis of the presidential popular vote in its two congressional districts. The other two electoral votes go to the popular vote winner of the entire state. As of the 2008 election, however, an actual division of Maine's electoral votes three to one (the only division possible) has not occurred. In 1992 Nebraska followed the lead of Maine and adopted a similar district determination of three of its five electoral votes, first to go into effect with the 1992 presidential election. In that election, as in the subsequent three presidential elections, each of the state's three congressional districts went solidly for the Republican nominee. In 2008, however, Democrat Barack Obama won one electoral vote in Nebraska, while Republican John McCain received the other four.

When Do Electors Cast Their Votes?

The Constitution, in Article II and the Twelfth Amendment, requires that the electors shall meet "in their respective states" to vote by ballot for president and vice president. Congress is given the power to determine the day of voting, "which day shall be the same throughout the United States." Aside from limiting the inconvenience of traveling to the nation's capital in the early days of the Republic, this system of simultaneous elections in each state was adopted, according to one of the delegates to the Constitutional Convention, in the hope that "by apportioning, limiting and confining the electors within their respective states . . . intrigue, combination and corruption would be effectively shut out, and a free and pure election of the

President of the United States made perpetual."[29] The founders had apparently hoped that the electors would be unaware of, and thus not influenced
by, the actions of their counterparts in other states.

Even in the first election, of course, the curiously naive hope for absolutely independent action by the electors in the various states was not
fulfilled. But the form of election that the Constitution's framers prescribed
has remained unchanged for more than two centuries, and on a specified
day every fourth year a separate group, or "college," of electors meets in
each state capital to vote for president. In 1792 Congress decreed that the
day should be the first Wednesday in December. This provision remained
in effect until 1877, when Congress shifted the date to the second Monday
in January, reportedly to allow a state more time to settle any election
disputes.[30] Congress set the current date of the first Monday after the second Wednesday in December in 1934 following ratification of the Twentieth Amendment, which shifted Inauguration Day forward from March 4
to January 20.[31]

How Do Electors Vote?

On the appointed day in December, the electors convene, in most states at
noon. The meeting usually takes place in the state capitol in the legislative
chambers, the executive chambers, or the office of the secretary of state.
Under federal law, the governor of the state must by this time have sent to
the National Archives in Washington, DC, a Certificate of Ascertainment
reporting the names of the electors from each party and the number of
popular votes cast for them, specifying the electors who were elected by the
voters. A state official presents copies of these certificates to the electors
when they convene, and the governor or secretary of state generally makes
a short speech welcoming the electors to their august duty.[32]

At times, however, some of the electors fail to appear for their great day.
Congress, in a law first passed in 1845, has authorized the states to provide
for filling of elector vacancies. In almost every state today, the electors
themselves are authorized to choose replacements. Although states have
discretion in filling vacant elector positions, federal law requires that any
controversy or contest concerning the appointment of electors must be
decided under state law at least six days before the meeting of the electors.[33]

Sometimes replacement electors are found by scouring the hallways of
the state capitol for likely candidates. This process was followed by the

Michigan electoral college in 1948, when only thirteen of the nineteen chosen electors—all pledged to Thomas Dewey and his running mate, Earl Warren—appeared. One of the substitutes recruited on the spot, however, a Mr. J. J. Levy of Royal Oak, had to be restrained by his colleagues from voting for Harry Truman and his running mate, Alben Barkley. "I thought we had to vote for the winning candidate," Levy was quoted as saying.[34] Sometimes it has been necessary to designate substitute electors because federal officeholders have been improperly chosen as electors, in violation of the Constitution.

Although they have but one function—to vote for a president and a vice president—the electors in many states go through an elaborate procedure of prayers, election of temporary and permanent chairpersons, speeches by state officials, appointment of committees, and the like. In a speech accepting the chairmanship of the Ohio electoral college (for the fifth time) in 1948, Alfred M. Cohen said: "Our task is purely perfunctory if we are faithful to the trust confided in us." Cohen had apparently developed little love of the institution he often headed, however, because he told his colleagues that he favored abolishing the system altogether in favor of direct popular voting for president.[35]

In 1976, while Wisconsin's electoral votes were being collected and tabulated, Wisconsin governor and electoral college chairman Patrick Lucey invited a political scientist in the audience to speak to the electoral college. The resulting remarks were severely critical of the electoral college as an institution, which the speaker described as "little more than a state by state collection of political hacks and fat cats." Instead of being insulted by these words, the Wisconsin electors adopted a resolution calling for the abolition of their office and the electoral college system.[36]

The Twelfth Amendment provides specifically that the electors shall vote "by ballot" separately for president and vice president (at least one of the candidates must be from another state). The "ballot" requirement has been interpreted to require paper ballots. Although it might seem that it would also require a secret vote, in fact, voting is not secret in many states. In some states, electors vote by signed ballot, in others by oral announcement, and in yet others by unsigned ballot accompanied by a public announcement of how each has voted.[37]

In 1800, one New York elector, Anthony Lispenard, insisted on his right to cast a secret ballot. It was reported, however, that Lispenard intended to forsake Thomas Jefferson and cast his double vote for vice presidential running mate Aaron Burr and someone else—a maneuver that would have given Burr the presidency. Jefferson's supporters then brought the prestigious statesman De Witt Clinton into the meeting, and his presence had such an impact that the participants showed each other their ballots before placing them in the ballot box. Lispenard hesitated but finally exhibited his ballot, marked properly for Jefferson and Burr.[38] Actual use of the secret written ballot, as one observer has noted, "is an anti-democratic provision which may cause a blunder, and could be easily used to cover a crime. An agent of the people should never be permitted to act secretly in transacting their business, except in cases where the public safety may require."[39]

Before the Twelfth Amendment, each elector cast two undifferentiated votes for president. The candidate who won the most votes, provided this total was at least a majority of the number of electors, was elected president, and the runner-up was elected vice president. This system, which failed to anticipate the emergence of political parties and unified party tickets of president and vice president, led to a tie vote between Jefferson and Burr in the election of 1800. A constitutional crisis and contingent election in the House of Representatives followed (this episode is discussed in Chapter 4).

More mischief was brewing in 1803. The Federalists threatened to cast their electoral votes for the second person on the Democratic-Republican ticket in the election of 1804, thereby denying Jefferson reelection as president. This maneuver would force the Democratic-Republican electors to scatter their second votes so that Jefferson could receive the most votes. The Federalists then might be able to elect their candidate for the presidency to the vice presidency.[40] (Jefferson had served as vice president under his political opponent John Adams from 1797 to 1801.) The Twelfth Amendment, which specified separate votes for president and vice president, remedied this anomaly of the original system.

After balloting separately for president and vice president, the electors send signed Certificates of Vote and Certificates of Ascertainment listing their choices by registered mail to the president of the Senate in Washington. This constitutional requirement has been amplified by statute to safeguard against loss of the first copy. The secretary of state of each state keeps two copies, two copies go to the archivist of the United States, and one copy is sent to the chief judge of the local federal district court.[41] The electors then adjourn, and the electoral college ceases to exist until the next presidential election.

Congressional Counting of Electoral Votes

Once the electors have balloted and the certificates of their votes have been forwarded to Washington, the scene shifts to Congress, where the votes are to be counted. The Twelfth Amendment to the Constitution provides simply that "the President of the Senate shall, in the presence of the Senate and House of Representatives, open all the certificates and the votes shall then be counted." In 1792 Congress provided that the joint session for counting the votes should take place on the second Wednesday in February. Since the passage of the Twentieth Amendment, the date has been January 6 at 1 P.M. (Congress occasionally sets a different date for the electoral vote count session, particularly in years when January 6 falls on a Sunday.) The count takes place in the chamber of the House of Representatives, with the vice president of the United States, in his role as president of the Senate, presiding.

Over the years, the president of the Senate's role has been reduced to little more than presiding at the joint session and breaking the seals on the ballots. He opens the electoral vote certificates from each state, in alphabetical order. He then passes the certificates to four tellers (vote counters), two appointed by each house of Congress, who announce each state's votes and add up the national tally. Objections, if any, must be presented in writing and must be signed by at least one senator and one representative. The president of the Senate then has the honor of announcing the names of the new president and vice president of the United States—assuming that there has been a majority electoral vote (since 1964, 270 of 538).

There may be a touch of melodrama in such announcements. In modern times, the sitting vice president has frequently been a candidate for president. Vice President George H. W. Bush had the privilege of announcing his own election as president in January 1993. By contrast, Vice Presidents Richard Nixon (1961), Walter Mondale (1981), and Al Gore (2001) had the less pleasant task of officially announcing their own losses and the victory of their opponents.

HOW DOES CONGRESS HANDLE DISPUTED VOTES?

Throughout the nineteenth century, major controversies regarding the electoral college procedure centered on the technicalities of the vote count in Congress. By one theory, the president of the Senate has authority to count the votes; by another, the two houses present in joint session have the responsibility for counting; by still another theory, the Constitution is silent on who actually should do the counting.[42]

The question was of great importance because of a number of disputed electoral votes. Whoever is responsible for counting votes may be able to disqualify disputed electoral votes or to decide among them in the event of double returns from a state. During the first two decades of the nineteenth century, it was the unquestioned custom for the president of the Senate "to declare the votes."

Thomas Jefferson was president of the Senate as well as his party's nominee for the presidency as Congress counted the electoral votes for the election of 1800. When he opened the envelope containing Georgia's four electoral votes, the ballot paper was, in the words of Bruce Ackerman, "blatantly irregular." He refused to call the defects of the Georgia ballot to the express attention of the House and Senate and counted the Georgia votes—for himself. Without these votes, the resulting contingent election that occurred in the House of Representatives (discussed in Chapter 4)—under the rules of the original Constitution—would have included three Federalist candidates: John Adams, Charles Cotesworth Pinckney, and John Jay. This is the only time in U.S. history when the president of the Senate has used his vote-counting power in such a consequential fashion.[43]

In Jefferson's defense, we can note that everyone understood that Georgia's electoral votes should have gone to him, and there was no time to send a fact-finding mission to Georgia, given the miserable winter roads at that time. Moreover, one could argue that Jefferson simply shifted the burden of raising objections to the Federalists. He had acted in the same fashion (although he was not vice president at the time) in 1796, when he did not challenge four electoral votes from Vermont that gave Adams the edge in the election.[44]

From 1821 onward, however, the Senate president's authority was undercut, and in the Reconstruction period, Congress itself exercised the power to judge disputed returns. Major nineteenth-century ballot controversies centered on whether a state was fully admitted to the Union at the time its electoral ballots were cast (Indiana in 1817, Missouri in 1821, Michigan in 1837); whether certain southern states were properly readmitted to the Union when they sought to cast electoral votes immediately following the Civil War; and which ballots should be counted when a state submitted two sets of returns. Congress rejected electoral votes on technical grounds after the elections of 1820 and 1832, votes cast for Horace Greeley in 1872 because he was deceased when the electors voted, and a vote cast on the wrong day following the election of 1880.[45]

Some of the objections raised during the century bordered on the trivial. In 1856 Wisconsin's electors met and voted one day later than the date set by Congress because of a blizzard that prevented their assembling on the proper date. The certificate of their vote was transmitted to the president of the Senate with an explanation of the circumstances that precluded their meeting on the appointed day. Although Wisconsin's vote would not have changed the national result, spirited argument began when the presiding officer in the joint session of Congress announced the count of the tellers, "including the vote of Wisconsin." The arguments were ruled out of order, but the two houses withdrew to their chambers for two days of bitter and inconclusive argument over whether the Constitution was inexorable in its requirement of the casting of the electoral vote on a single day. Among the most arbitrary actions of Congress was its vote in 1873 to exclude the electoral vote of Arkansas because the certificate of returns bore the seal of the secretary of state instead of the state's great seal—an article that the state did not possess at the time![46]

THE ELECTORAL COUNT ACT OF 1887

In passing the Electoral Count Act of 1887, Congress finally established a procedure for use in disputed vote cases—one still largely in force today. The statute represented an effort by Congress to avoid the issue of disputed electoral votes after the controversial election of 1876, in which Republican Rutherford B. Hayes narrowly defeated Democrat Samuel J. Tilden.

The law permits Congress to reject those electoral votes not "regularly given." However, it shifts the onus of decision in disputed vote cases to the states by providing that if a state has established a mechanism to resolve disputes, the decisions of the state officials would be binding on Congress. The statute provides that state law "shall be conclusive, and shall govern in the counting of electoral votes," if the state law meets three conditions. It must (1) be "enacted prior to the day fixed for the appointment of electors"—that is, before election day in November; (2) provide for the state's "final determination" of any controversy about an elector's appointment; and (3) require that the final determination be made six days before the meeting of the electors in the state in mid-December.

States may not, in effect, change the rules after the game is over. The thrust of the federal statue is that if electors are selected under one set of state rules, those rules continue to apply for federal electoral purposes even if the state changes them in midgame. This point became significant during the protracted battle over Florida's electoral votes in 2000. Republicans charged that the Democrats were seeking to change the rules of counting disputed ballots after the election was over.

The report of the committee handling the 1887 legislation explained that the act provided that state courts should determine whether a vote from that state is legal. It also provided that "the two Houses shall be bound by this determination." The committee concluded that "it will be the State's own fault if the matter is left in doubt."[47]

To accomplish the goal of state, rather than congressional, determination of the winning slate of electoral votes from a state, the Electoral Count Act created a "safe harbor" for states that resolved disputes concerning their electoral votes in a timely manner. This section appears in Title 3, Section 5 of the U.S. Code:

> If any State shall have provided, by laws enacted prior to the day fixed for the appointment of the electors, for its final determination of any controversy or contest concerning the appointment of all or any of the electors of such State, by judicial or other methods or procedures and such determination shall have been made at least six days before the time fixed for the meeting of the electors, such determination made pursuant to such law so existing on said day, and made at least six days prior to said time of meeting of the electors, shall be conclusive, and shall govern the counting of the electoral votes as provided in the Constitution, and as hereinafter regulated, so far as the ascertainment of the electors appointed by such State is concerned.

The Election of 2000

The "safe harbor" provision played a critical role in determining the outcome of the 2000 presidential election. Shortly after the election, it was clear that Vice President Al Gore had won 267 electoral votes, 3 short of the 270 necessary to win election. Governor George Bush of Texas had won 246 electoral votes. Florida's 25 electoral votes—essential for either candidate to win a majority in the electoral college—were the focus of an extraordinary political and legal battle. The nation witnessed impassioned debates over counting absentee ballots, interpreting hanging chads on punch card ballots, and litigating the legitimacy of poorly designed butterfly ballots. Both sides went to the courts to seek judicial decrees to structure the recounts in the incredibly close race.

The Florida Supreme Court ordered a recount, and the case ultimately made its way to the U.S. Supreme Court. A key issue was whether the safe harbor provision set a firm deadline beyond which any recounts could not proceed. On December 12, 2000, the Supreme Court handed down its decision in *Bush v. Gore*.[48] The Court ruled, first, that the recount ordered by the Florida Supreme Court violated the equal protection clause of the Constitution and therefore was invalid. Second, the Court ruled that it was infeasible to remand the case back to the Florida Supreme Court with instructions to resolve the equal protection issue, because doing so would cause the state to miss the December 12 deadline stipulated in the Electoral Count Act of 1887. In effect, the Court held that under the Electoral Count Act, Florida would have to meet the deadline in order not to lose the opportunity for its electoral votes to be cast. Thus the Court brought the Florida recount to a halt, thereby handing the presidency to George W. Bush.

Bush v. Gore remains a controversial decision. Several authors have concluded that the Electoral Count Act intended the safe harbor provision to provide but one of several mechanisms by which a state could ensure that its electors' votes would be counted. Rather than intending the safe harbor to set a firm deadline that states would not dare miss, they argue, Congress intended the provision to provide a rule of evidence to be used by Congress in considering disputes. It provided additional rules of evidence in subsequent sections of the act so that if a state missed the safe harbor date, it could still expect to have its votes counted.[49] Scholars have also found that the coalition that enacted the act in 1887 rejected proposals for federal court involvement in the resolution of disputes concerning electors.[50] As we shall see, Congress counted Hawaii's electoral votes in 1960 even though it did not determine the winner in the state until after the safe harbor date.

Refusing to Count Votes

Congress may refuse to count votes from a state only if the two houses decide concurrently that the certification is invalid or that the electoral votes were not "regularly given" by the certified electors. The law strictly limits debate on disputed electoral votes. No one can speak for more than five minutes or more than once, and the total debate is limited to two hours in each house. After that, each chamber must vote on the matter.

Congress's counting and certification of electoral votes has become a mostly ceremonial act since the celebrated battle over the returns of the 1876 election—with two exceptions. When the House and Senate met in joint session on January 6, 1969, to count the 1968 electoral votes, Senator Edmund Muskie, the Democratic vice presidential nominee, along with six other senators and thirty-eight representatives, objected to a vote for George Wallace of Alabama cast by Republican elector Dr. Lloyd W. Bailey. Bailey was a faithless elector from North Carolina, which had voted for Richard Nixon for president. Ironically, Muskie was fighting to preserve an electoral vote for the opposing Richard Nixon–Spiro Agnew ticket.

Under the terms of the 1887 statute, the two bodies then moved to separate deliberations on the disputed electoral vote, with a rejection of the vote by both House and Senate necessary to invalidate it. Throughout the debate in both houses, there was general dismay about the possibility of electors casting unexpected votes; there was also a feeling, however, that after-the-fact congressional challenges were not the appropriate mechanism for eliminating this evil. Both the House (229 to 160) and the Senate (58 to 33) rejected the challenge to Bailey's vote. The result of the debates in both houses on January 6, 1969, however, was to give considerable new impetus in 1969 and 1970 to intense but ultimately stymied congressional attempts to abolish or modify the electoral college through the constitutional amendment process.[51]

Congress was again counting electoral votes in joint session on January 6, 2005. Representative Stephanie Tubbs Jones of Ohio and Senator

Barbara Boxer of California interrupted the ritual roll call of each state's certificate of electoral votes, contending that Ohio's results were not "regularly given," citing voting irregularities in the state. The presiding officer, Vice President Dick Cheney, followed legal guidelines and sent lawmakers to their respective chambers so that each house could debate the matter for two hours. In the end, each chamber voted overwhelmingly to uphold Ohio's votes.[52]

Receipt of Two Certificates from the Same State

The nation's experience in the period before 1887 led Congress to be especially concerned in the Electoral Count Act with resolving the issue of two lists of electors and votes being presented to Congress from the same state. The statute addresses three circumstances in which two lists are presented. First, Congress must accept the list of electors who it determines were appointed pursuant to the state election statute. If lists are offered by two state authorities, each of which arguably made determinations provided for under the law, the act specifies that agreement of both houses of Congress is necessary to resolve the question of which state authority is the lawful agent of the state to make the decision (and thus which electors' votes to accept). If no state authority has determined the winning slate of electors, the statute requires that both houses of Congress agree to accept the votes of one set of electors. The two houses may also agree not to accept the votes of electors from that state.[53]

When the two houses disagree, then the statute states that Congress will count the votes of the electors whose appointment was certified by the governor of the state. It is probable but not certain that this contingency for split votes in the House and Senate applies only to the scenarios in which the House and Senate cannot decide between two determinations allegedly made under the state contest law, or where no determinations have been made under state law, rather than where there is only one determination under a state election contest law and procedure.

Since 1887 Congress has had to choose between competing slates of electors only once. Following the 1960 presidential election, the governor of Hawaii first certified the electors of Vice President Nixon as having been appointed and then, due to a subsequent recount that determined that Senator John Kennedy had won the Hawaii vote, certified Kennedy as the winner. Both slates of electors had met on the prescribed day in December, cast their votes for president and vice president, and transmitted them according to the federal statute. This was the case even though the recount apparently was not completed until December 28. The president of the Senate, Vice President Nixon, suggested "without the intent of establishing a precedent" that Congress accept the latter and more recent certification of Senator Kennedy so as "not to delay the further count of electoral votes." Congress agreed to Nixon's proposal by unanimous consent.[54]

WHAT HAPPENS IF THE PRESIDENTIAL CANDIDATE OR PRESIDENT-ELECT DIES?

Under the United States' multistage process of electing a president—stretching from the day that the national party conventions nominate candidates to the day in January that a new chief executive is inaugurated—a number of contingencies can arise through the death, disability, or withdrawal of a prospective president or vice president during the period between nomination and inauguration.[55]

A Nominee Dies Between the Convention and Election Day

The first contingency may arise if a nominee were to die between the adjournment of the convention and the day in November when the electors are officially chosen. No law covers this contingency, although both the Democratic and Republican parties have adopted procedures to cover the eventuality. Essentially, the parties' national committees will select a new nominee.[56]

Should they be called on to fill a vacancy caused by the death of a presidential candidate, the national committees may well select the vice presidential nominee as the candidate for president and substitute a new candidate for vice president, but such an action is not certain. They may choose to nominate the candidate who finished second in the race for the presidential nomination. If the death of a candidate took place just before election day—especially if he or she were one of the major presidential candidates—Congress might decide to postpone the day of the election, allowing the national party time to name a substitute contender and the new candidate at least a few days to carry his or her campaign to the people.

At no time in our history has a presidential candidate died before election day. In 1912, however, Vice President James S. Sherman, who had been nominated for reelection on the Republican ticket with President William H. Taft, died on October 30. No replacement was made before election day, but thereafter the Republican National Committee met and instructed the Republican electors (only eight had been elected) to cast their vice presidential votes for Nicholas Murray Butler.[57]

In 1860 the man nominated for vice president by the Democratic National Convention, Benjamin Fitzpatrick of Alabama, declined the nomination after the convention had adjourned. By a unanimous vote, the Democratic National Committee named Herschel V. Johnson of Georgia to fill the vacancy.[58] The Democratic vice presidential nominee in 1972, Senator Thomas F. Eagleton, resigned a few weeks after being nominated after it had been revealed that he had twice been hospitalized and had received electroshock therapy for depression. The Democratic National Committee hastily assembled and selected Sargent Shriver of Massachusetts as his replacement.

A Candidate Dies Between Election Day and the Day Electors Vote

The second major contingency may arise if a presidential or vice presidential candidate dies between election day and the day that the electors actually meet in December. Theoretically, the electors would be free to vote for anyone they pleased. But the national party rules for the filling of vacancies by the national committees would still be in effect, and the electors would probably respect the decision of their national committee on a new nominee. Again, the elevation of the vice presidential candidate to the presidential slot would be likely but not certain. One potential problem at this stage is that a faithful elector, perhaps complying with a state statutorily mandated pledge, would vote for the decedent even though precedent suggests that such votes might not be counted by the Congress.[59]

The only time that a candidate has died in this period was in 1872, when the defeated Democratic presidential nominee, Horace Greeley, died on November 29—three weeks after the election and a week before the electors were to meet. Sixty-six electors pledged to Greeley had been elected, and they met to vote on the very day Greeley was laid in his grave. Sixty-three of them scattered their votes among a variety of other eminent Democrats, but three Greeley electors in Georgia insisted on marking their ballots for him despite his demise. Congress refused to count these votes in the official national tally.[60]

A President- or Vice President–Elect Dies Between the Day Electors Vote and the Day Congress Counts Electoral Votes

A third contingency may occur if the president- or vice president–elect dies between the day the electors vote in mid-December and January 6, the day that the electoral votes are counted in Congress. There would probably be debate about whether the votes cast for a dead man could be counted, but most constitutional experts believe that the language of the Twelfth Amendment gives Congress no choice but to count all the electoral votes cast, providing that the "person" voted for was alive when the ballots were cast.[61] The U.S. House committee report endorsing the Twentieth Amendment sustains this view. Congress, the report said, would have "no discretion" in the matter and "would declare that the deceased candidate had received a majority of the votes."[62]

Section 3 of the Twentieth Amendment, which states, "If, at the time fixed for the beginning of the term of the President, the President elect shall have died, the Vice President elect shall become President," would seem to be the operative law in such an instance. When the vice president–elect took office as president, he would be authorized under the Twenty-fifth Amendment to nominate a new vice president. Similarly, if the vice president–elect should die before the count in Congress, he or she would still be declared the winner, and the new president would be able to nominate a replacement.

Yet what if we cannot rely on the presumption that a presidential or vice presidential designate who has received a majority of the electoral votes is officially the president-elect or vice president–elect before Congress counts the electoral votes? If there is no official president- or vice president–elect until the electoral votes are counted and announced by Congress on January 6, then we lack clear constitutional or statutory direction for selecting a new president.[63]

A President- or Vice President–Elect Dies Between the Day Congress Counts Electoral Votes and Inauguration Day

The death either of the president- or vice president–elect between the day Congress counts and certifies the electoral votes and Inauguration Day, January 20, raises yet another contingency. If the president-elect dies, the Twentieth Amendment provides that the vice president–elect becomes president. The president would then fill the resulting vacancy after being inaugurated by nominating a new vice president, who must be confirmed by majorities of both houses of Congress under the Twenty-fifth Amendment. In the event of the death of the vice president–elect, the Twenty-fifth Amendment similarly authorizes the new president to nominate a vice president, subject to the approval of Congress. No president-elect has ever died in this period. But on February 15, 1933, a week after his election had been declared in joint session of Congress and three weeks before his inauguration, President-elect Franklin D. Roosevelt barely escaped a would-be assassin's bullets in Miami.

No Candidate Qualifies by Inauguration Day

In the event that neither a president nor a vice president qualifies on Inauguration Day, January 20, then the Twentieth Amendment and the Presidential Succession Act of 1947 would go into effect. This statute places the Speaker of the House, the president pro tempore of the Senate, and then the various cabinet officials in line for the presidency, providing that they are constitutionally qualified and accept the office.

The Speaker (or someone else in the line of succession) would serve only as acting president until a president is qualified but would have to resign from the House (or the Senate in the case of the Senate pro tempore) to serve in that capacity. A Speaker or senator might not wish to resign to serve only in a caretaker role for a short time. The cabinet officials in the line of succession would be from the outgoing administration. Many may find both of these situations less than satisfactory.

Finally, the Twentieth Amendment authorizes Congress to pass a law to provide for the death of any of the persons from whom the House might choose a president or the Senate might choose a vice president. Congress has not enacted such a law, however.

The electoral college established in the Constitution is an extraordinarily complex mechanism for selecting a president. Subsequent state and national laws drawn to implement the electoral college system have only added to the complexity—and the risks of a malfunction. There is a large number of potential trouble spots, and the potential for violating democratic norms is great.

The allocation of electoral votes among the states may not accurately represent the citizens resident in those states. Electors are not wise elites, and they may make errors or violate their charges when casting their votes. As we will see in the next chapter, the allocation of electoral votes within states can distort the wishes of the voters.

Disputed elections results open a Pandora's box of problems. The laws required to implement the electoral college are open to multiple interpretations and may well involve Congress and the courts in partisan wrangling over which candidate won a state. Their decisions may misrepresent the public's wishes.

Other aspects of the electoral college reveal its antediluvian nature. The absence of a right to vote in presidential elections is certainly inconsistent with our notions of democracy in the twenty-first century. Similarly, the selection of the ultimate choosers of the president—electors—by party committees is contrary to our notions of transparency and popular participation. Allowing a state legislature to choose the winning slate of electors of a state makes a mockery of popular selection of the president.

The distinguished historian of the founding period Carl Becker put it well:

> If the motives of the founding fathers in devising the electoral system were of the highest, it must be said that their grasp of political realities, ordinarily so sure, failed them in this instance. Of all the provisions of the federal Constitution, the electoral college system was the most unrealistic—the one provision not based solidly on practical experience and precedent. It was in the nature of an academic invention which ignored the experience in the vain expectation that, in this one instance for this high purpose, politicians would cease to be politicians, would divert themselves of party prejudice, and class and sectional bias, and be all for the time being noble Brutuses inspired solely by pure love of liberty and the public good.[64]

Chapter 3 The Electoral College and Political Equality

The electoral college does not provide a straightforward process for selecting the president. Instead, it can be extraordinarily complex and has the potential to undo the people's will at many points in the long journey from the selection of electors to counting their votes in Congress. Congress may find it difficult to choose justly between competing slates of electors. It is even possible, although highly unlikely, that a state legislature could take the choice of the electors away from the people altogether. The electoral college poses an even more fundamental threat to American democracy, however.

POLITICAL EQUALITY

Political equality lies at the core of democratic theory. It is difficult to image a definition of democracy that does not include equality in voting as a central standard for a democratic process. Robert Dahl, the leading democratic theorist, argues that in a democracy, "every member must have an equal and effective opportunity to vote, and all votes must be counted as equal." A constitution for democratic government, he adds, "must be in conformity with one elementary principle: that all members are to be treated (under the constitution) as if they were equally qualified to participate in the process of making decisions about the policies the association will pursue. Whatever may be the case on other matters, then, in governing this association all members are to be considered as *politically equal.*"[1]

It is difficult to find a contemporary theorist who argues that some people's votes should count more than other people's votes.[2] James S. Fishkin, for example, maintains that political equality is an essential condition for democracy.[3] Jon Elster argues as a matter of first-order political theory that democracy *is* "simple majority rule, based on the principle of 'one person, one vote.'"[4]

That a nation should have political equality is impossible to *prove*. Such an assertion expresses a moral judgment about human beings, that the good of anyone is intrinsically equal to that of anyone else. This *intrinsic equality* treats all persons as if they possess equal claims to life, liberty, and the pursuit of happiness and other fundamental goods and interests.[5] The authors of the Declaration of Independence finessed the issue of proving that "all men are created equal"—a radical notion at the time—by simply declaring it a "self-evident" truth (the first one they proclaimed).

Yet there are reasons why a nation should adopt political equality as the basic principle of a state.[6] First, there are ethical and religious grounds—the notion that we are all equally God's children. Joseph Schumpeter argued that political equality has traditionally been defended on the basis of Christian belief. He writes that the "intrinsic value of the individual soul" is "a sanction . . . of 'everyone to count for one, no one to count for more than one'—a sanction that pours super-mundane meaning into articles of the democratic creed."[7]

Political equality is also a prudent approach to the distribution of power. Even if you were privileged, your status could change, and you might be hurt if voting power were inequitable. In John Rawls's famous thought experiment, he imagines what principles of governing a group of reasoners might choose if they were shrouded in the famous "veil of ignorance" and thus unaware of their political or social identities. He asserts that they would choose political equality, and few have challenged this part of his argument.[8]

Political equality is also the alternative for distributing voting power that is most likely to receive public support. Because no one ever proposes to count some votes more than others, public opinion polls rarely pose a question dealing with political equality in voting. An exception is the electoral college itself. As the Gallup Poll reported in 2001, "There is little question that the American public would prefer to dismantle the Electoral College system, and go to a direct popular vote for the presidency. In Gallup polls that stretch back over 50 years, a majority of Americans have continually expressed support for the notion of an official amendment of the U.S. Constitution that would allow for direct election of the president."[9] In both 2000 and 2004, Gallup found that 61 percent of the public wished to amend the Constitution so that the candidate who receives the most total votes nationwide wins the election.[10]

If members of Congress were to pass a law that established a system that counted the votes of citizens in certain states more than the votes of citizens of other states, there can be little doubt that those members supporting such a law would have brief legislative careers.

Finally, as Dahl, points out, there is no plausible and convincing alternative to political equality. Who would argue that some persons are more worthy than others or that some people's good is more worthy than that of others? Such an argument would, as Justice Hugo Black declared in *Wesberry v. Sanders* (1964), "run counter to our fundamental ideas of democratic government."[11]

Everyone knows that the Republic the founders created deviated in important ways from the democratic principle of political equality. To point this out does not constitute an argument on behalf of political inequality, however. Rather, such an assertion raises the question of whether in the twenty-first century it is possible to justify political inequality. We must understand the degree and consequences of political inequality to evaluate properly whether to continue it.

Most of the Constitution's violations of political equality were compromises designed to obtain the support of each state in order to launch the new nation. It does not follow that these compromises are inviolate. Some are more important than others. As Dahl put it almost half a century ago, "I do not mean to suggest that the Connecticut Compromise should be undone; but I do mean to say that it is rather muddleheaded to romanticize a necessary bargain into a grand principle of democratic politics."[12]

A central theme of American history is in fact the democratization of the

Constitution. What began as a document characterized by numerous restrictions on direct voter participation has slowly become much more
democratic. The Constitution itself offered no guidelines on voter eligibility, leaving it to each state to decide. As a result, only a small percentage
of adults could vote; women and slaves were excluded entirely. Of the
seventeen constitutional amendments passed since the Bill of Rights, five
have focused on the expansion of the electorate. The Fifteenth Amendment (1870) prohibited discrimination on the basis of race in determining
voter eligibility (although it took the Voting Rights Act of 1965 to make the
amendment effective). The Nineteenth Amendment (1920) gave women
the right to vote (although some states had already done so). The Twenty-
third Amendment (1961) accorded the residents of Washington, DC, the
right to vote in presidential elections. Three years later, the Twenty-fourth
Amendment prohibited poll taxes (which discriminated against the poor).
Finally, the Twenty-sixth Amendment (1971) lowered the voter eligibility
age to eighteen.

Not only are more people eligible to vote, but also voters now have more
officials to elect. The Seventeenth Amendment (1913) provided for direct
election of senators.

Even those who gave us the Constitution came to have doubts about its
violations of political equality. James Madison, the most influential of all
the delegates to the Constitutional Convention, was writing as early as
1792 in the *National Gazette* about the importance of "establishing political
equality among all" and arguing that no group should have influence out
of proportion to its numbers.[13] Forty-one years later, he was still at it,
writing in 1833 that republican government is the "least imperfect" form of
government and "the vital principle of republican government is . . . the
will of the majority."[14]

Because political equality is central to democratic government, we must
evaluate any mechanism for selecting the president against it. To begin this
assessment, we examine how the electoral college translates popular votes
into electoral votes—the votes that count.

THE TRANSLATION OF POPULAR VOTES INTO ELECTORAL VOTES

A popular misconception is that electoral votes are simple aggregates of
popular votes. In reality, the electoral vote regularly deviates from the

popular will as expressed in the popular vote—sometimes merely in curious ways, usually strengthening the electoral edge of the popular vote leader, but at times in such a way as to deny the presidency to the popular preference. Popular votes do not equal electoral votes—the former express the people's choice, while the latter determine who is to be the people's president.

As reported and generally understood in the United States, the *popular vote* is the sum of the votes cast by the people on election day for each slate of electors in each state—Republican, Democratic, or minor party. If a state requires that an elector slate be chosen as a unit, the common practice in recent decades, then the popular vote represents the number of ballots cast for that slate. If a state should insist that its citizens vote separately for presidential electors, however, each elector is likely to have a slightly different total vote. In this case, the modern practice is to credit the presidential candidate with the number of votes received by the highest-polling elector pledged to him in that state.[15] The national popular vote total for a particular candidate thus consists of the total of the votes cast for the most popular elector pledged to him or her in the various states.

With rare exceptions, this system of counting provides an accurate picture of the national will. In some instances, however, a candidate's national vote has been artificially reduced when state party rules or state laws prevented a slate of electors pledged to him from qualifying. In 1860 no electoral slate was pledged to Lincoln in ten of the thirty-three states then in the Union. In 1912 the only way for California voters to cast ballots for President Taft was to write in the names of thirteen elector candidates, since Theodore Roosevelt's Progressives had seized the Republican slot. In 1948 and again in 1964, the Dixiecrat and unpledged elector movements controlled the Alabama Democratic Party machinery and appropriated the Democratic electoral slate for their own purposes. The Alabama voter had no way to register a vote for the national Democratic nominees in those years.

Because the national popular vote has no role in selecting the president, there is no one officially assigned responsibility to arrive at the total, and thus there is no official figure at the time of the election. Since the election of 1920, the clerk of the House of Representatives has provided the closest we have to an official national popular vote. The clerk's office compiles the certified votes from each state and publishes them several months following a presidential election. More careful efforts to record election results can be found in Congressional Quarterly's *Guide to U.S. Elections* and Jerrold G. Rusk's *Statistical History of the American Electorate*.[16] In this volume, I rely primarily on these two sources for election results.

Whatever the popular vote, it is the electoral votes that count, and the percentages of electoral votes candidates receive nationally often differ substantially from their percentages of the popular vote. Four factors are at the heart of this disparity: (1) the winner-take-all (or unit-vote) system in force in most states; (2) the two electoral votes accorded to each state corresponding to its two U.S. senators; (3) the skewed relationship between the number of people who actually vote in a state and the number of electoral votes the state casts; and (4) the size of the House of Representatives.

The Winner-Take-All (Unit-Vote) System

All states except Maine and Nebraska have adopted a system in which *all* electoral votes are awarded to the candidate who receives the most popular votes in that state. In this winner-take-all (or unit-vote) system, the electoral votes allocated to a state based largely on its population are awarded as a bloc to the plurality winner of the state. In effect, the system assigns to the winner the votes of the people who voted *against* him or her.

The operation of the winner-take-all system effectively disenfranchises voters who support losing candidates in each state. In the 2000 presidential election, nearly three million people voted for Al Gore in Florida. Because George W. Bush won 537 more votes than Gore, however, he received *all* of Florida's electoral votes. As a result of this process of allocating electoral votes, a candidate can win some states by very narrow margins, lose other states by large margins (as Bush did by more than one million votes in California and New York in 2000), and so win the electoral vote while losing the popular vote. Because there is no way to aggregate votes across states, the votes for candidates who do not finish first in a state play no role in the outcome of the election.

For every other office in the country—every governor, every legislator, on both the state and the national level—we aggregate the votes for the candidates across the entire constituency of the office. Only for the presidency do we fail to count the votes for the candidate who does not win a subsection of the constituency.

In a multiple-candidate contest (as in 1992, 1996, and 2000), the winner-take-all system may suppress the votes of the *majority* as well as the minority. In the presidential election of 1996, less than a majority of votes decided the blocs of electoral votes of twenty-six states. In 2000 pluralities rather than majorities determined the allocation of electoral votes in eight states, including Florida and Ohio. In each case, a minority of voters determined how *all* of their state's electoral votes would be cast.

In 1992, in a three-candidate contest, 2,072,698 of Florida's voters, 39 percent, cast their ballots for Bill Clinton, and another 1,053,067 state voters, or 20 percent, chose Ross Perot, but Florida's twenty-five electoral vote slate went as a bloc to George H. W. Bush on the basis of his popular vote plurality of 2,173,310, just 41 percent of the state vote. Fifty-nine percent of Florida's voters, 3,125,765 citizens, preferred Clinton or Perot but received no electoral votes reflecting their preferences. Although 62 percent of the voters in Arizona supported other candidates, all of Arizona's electoral votes went to Bush on the basis of his state popular vote of only 38 percent. Conversely, in California, Bush won 3,630,574 votes, or 33 percent of the state total, and Perot 2,296,006, or 21 percent. Nevertheless, Clinton, with 46 percent of the state popular vote, received 100 percent of the state's fifty-four electoral votes.[17]

The winner-take-all system not only disenfranchises millions of Americans (distorting majority rule in the process, as we will see), it also distributes influence in selecting the president unequally. Large states enjoy a theoretical advantage in being more likely than small states to cast the pivotal bloc of electoral votes in the electoral college, and thus a citizen of a large state is hypothetically more likely to be able to cast the vote that will determine an election.[18] As George Rabinowitz and Elaine MacDonald have concluded, "In presidential elections, some citizens, by virtue of their physical location in a given state, are in a far better position to determine presidential outcomes than others . . . . Extreme inequities exist between the power of citizens living in different states."[19]

We saw in Chapter 2 that the Constitution is silent on the issue of the distribution of a state's electoral votes. The states themselves decide whether to award their electoral votes in a winner-take-all fashion (all but two states currently do so). We cannot lay the blame on the states rather than the electoral college for distortions that result from the winner-take-all system, however. It is only because of the electoral college that the potential for a winner-take-all system exists, and a constitutional amendment is required to prohibit its use.

In the early years of the Republic, states experimented with a variety of methods of distributing their electoral votes. The leading statesmen of both parties, including Alexander Hamilton, Thomas Jefferson, James Madison, James Wilson, Albert Gallatin, James Bayard, Rufus King, Nathaniel Macon, John Quincy Adams, Andrew Jackson, Martin Van Buren, Robert Hayne, Daniel Webster, and many others, supported a version of the district plan. The essence of such plans was to divide each state into a number of districts equal to the number of its electoral votes. The voters in each district would determine which candidate would receive that district's electoral vote. (Some versions of the plan provided for two of the state's electoral votes to be decided by the state at large.) As Madison put it, the district system "was mostly, if not exclusively, in view when the Constitution was framed and adopted."[20]

Almost all the states approved such a plan and the Senate passed it as a constitutional amendment. The district plan never became law, however, because of the opposition of the predominant party in many states. From the beginning, partisan advantage drove states' decisions about means of selecting electors.[21] The dominant party in a state favored the winner-take-all system precisely because it distorted the popular will and allowed the majority to reap all the benefits of the state's electoral votes. According to Madison, other states adopted the winner-take-all system "as the only expedient for baffling the policy of the particular States which had set the example."[22] As Lucius Wilmerding put it, the winner-take-all system "owes its establishment to the ferocity of party politics and the demoralizing institutions of faction."[23]

We can examine 1799–1800 to illustrate the point. Federalists won eight of the nineteen House districts in Virginia 1798. The next year, the Virginia legislature scrapped the district system for allocating electors that it had used in previous elections in favor of the winner-take-all format. In Massachusetts the Federalists responded by transferring the choice of electors from districts to the state legislature (which they controlled). In New York, Federalists defeated a Republican plan for allocating electoral votes by districts, certain they would win control of both houses of the legislature and thus select all the electors. (Ironically, the Federalists lost the elections, ensuring Jefferson's ultimate victory in the 1800 presidential election.)[24]

Reviewing the operation of the winner-take-all system nearly a century ago, one observer wrote appropriately: "A plurality or majority in one section may, it is true, at times be counteracted by one in another section, and thus the net result be a rude approximation to fairness, taking the country as a whole; but this theory of averages may not work constantly, and the steady suppression of minority conviction in a state is an undisputed evil."[25]

The Allocation of Electoral Votes Among States

The Constitution allocates electoral votes to each state equal to that state's representation in Congress. This system of distribution further diminishes the impact of the popular vote in electing the president. First, the number of House seats does not exactly correspond to the population of a state. The populations of some states barely exceed the threshold for an additional seat while those in other states just miss it. In 2010 Wyoming had one representative for 563,626 individuals, and Montana had one representative for 989,415 individuals.[26] As the House becomes increasingly malapportioned, the electoral college becomes further skewed in favor of the small rural states, accentuating the difference between the popular vote and the electoral college vote.[27]

We saw in Chapter 2, moreover, that the census figures used to determine the number of seats a state has in the House (and thus the electoral votes that match them) may be out of date and thus lead to the overrepresentation of some states and underrepresentation of others. The allocation of electoral votes in the election of 2000, for example, actually reflected the population distribution among the states of 1990, a decade earlier. On the basis of the 1980 census, California was allocated forty-seven electors. The Census Bureau estimate for California's population in 1988, however, would have translated into fifty-four electoral votes in the election of that year. Other high-growth states like Florida, Texas, and Arizona have also been penalized in recent elections, whereas states with slower growth or population declines have benefited from the lag in reapportionment.[28] As a result, presidential candidates who win high-growth states are penalized while those winning lower-growth states benefit.

Depending on how one views the appropriate representation of noncitizens, the higher concentration of noncitizens in some states may be another distorting factor in the allocation of electoral votes. Representation in the House is based on the decennial census, which counts all residents—whether citizens or not. Such states as California, Florida, and New York, where noncitizens compose a larger percentage of the population, receive more electoral votes than they would if electoral votes were allocated on the basis of the number of a state's citizens.

In addition, each state receives two electoral votes corresponding to the number of its U.S. senators. When states with unequal populations receive similar numbers of electoral votes, states with smaller populations gain a mathematical advantage.

Thus every voter's ballot does not carry the same weight. That is, the ratio of electoral votes to population varies from state to state, benefiting the smallest states. In the most extreme case, for example, an electoral vote in Wyoming in 2010 corresponded to only 187,875 persons, while one in California corresponded to 677,345 persons. The typical citizen of Wyoming, then, had on average more than three and a half times as much influence in determining an electoral vote for president as the typical citizen of California.[29]

The allocation of electoral votes among states overrepresents small states in the electoral college and introduces yet another deviation from voter equality into the election of the American president. Smaller states have a larger percentage of the electoral vote than of the national population.

Another way to calculate differential influence of voters on the electoral college vote is to divide the number of electoral votes for a state by all of those who voted for the winner in that state, since the votes of those voting for the loser in a state do not count for that candidate at all. As I show below, the turnout rates among states vary substantially, so the ratio of voters per electoral vote allocated to a candidate varies as well. However one chooses to measure voter influence, the fact remains that the allocation of electoral votes among the states violates political equality.

It is often said that the mathematical advantages of small states is more than compensated by the winner-take-all system of awarding electoral votes to candidates. This system is said to favor large states because the largest prizes in electoral votes are in the most populous states. Inhabitants of the large states thus benefit from candidates courting their votes.

As we saw in Chapter 1 and will analyze in more detail in Chapter 6, however, whether any large state will be courted depends on whether it is "in play" in the sense that either candidate might win the plurality of its votes. In 2000, 2004, and 2008, for example, the three largest states were not competitive on the presidential level and were largely ignored by the candidates. In 2000 neither George W. Bush nor Al Gore spent much time campaigning in New York because each concluded that a majority of New York voters would vote for Gore. After his nomination, Al Gore did not campaign in California, visiting the state only once, because he calculated that a majority of its votes were his anyway. Similarly, neither Bush nor Gore campaigned much in Texas, since Bush had the state securely sewed up.

Although the advantages of the electoral college to large states are problematic, the bias toward small states in the allocation of electoral votes is not. The theoretical advantage of citizens in large states of casting the vote that determines the pivotal bloc of electoral votes in the electoral college is an illusion. The relative probability of affecting the election outcome is outweighed by the extraordinarily low absolute probability that it will occur. The central fact remains that the typical citizen of a state with a small population has more influence in determining an electoral vote than the typical citizen of a state with a large population. Thus although the *citizenry* of large states wield much more power than the citizenry of small states, the *citizen* in a small state exercises more power in electing the president than the citizen of a large state.

Differences in Voter Turnout

There are substantial differences among states in the rate at which their citizens turn out to vote. For example, according to Michael McDonald, in 2008 only 51 percent of the voting age population of U.S. citizens in Hawaii and West Virginia, 53 percent in Arkansas, 54 percent in Utah, and 55 percent in Texas voted in the presidential election. On the other hand, 78 percent of those in Minnesota, 73 percent of those in Wisconsin, 71 percent in Maine and New Hampshire, and 70 percent of those in Iowa voted.[30] These high-turnout states had turnout rates from 27 to 53 percent greater than those states with low turnout.

In an election featuring voter equality, the number of potential voters who actually cast a vote matters, because votes are aggregated across the electorate and all votes count equally. In the electoral college, however, it does not matter whether one person or all eligible persons go to the polls. Because each state has a predetermined number of electoral votes, *the actual vote total in a state has no relevance to its electoral votes.* The state casts its electoral votes even if only one person actually votes.

As a result of differences in voter turnout, citizens who vote in states with high voter turnout have less influence on the selection of the president than citizens who vote in states with low turnout. For example, in 2008 in Minnesota, there was a ratio of about 291,000 voters per electoral vote. In Hawaii, by contrast, the ratio was only about 113,000 voters per electoral vote. Each Hawaiian who voted exercised 2.6 times as much influence on an electoral vote as each voting Minnesotan.

Size of the House

The number of electoral votes each state receives depends largely on the size of its delegation in the House of Representatives. Until early in the twentieth century, the House expanded as the nation's population and the number of states increased. Congress fixed the number of House members at 435 in 1941. Even though the population of the United States has more than doubled since then, the number of representatives has remained the same.

The election of the president depends capriciously on the choice of House size. In 2000, for example, if the size had been 490, Bush would have won. If it had been 491, the election would have ended in a tie. If the size of the House had been 492 representatives, however, Gore would have won.[31]

The larger the House, the more nearly the relative representation of a state in the electoral college matches its relative representation in the House. As the national average district size has increased, the number of states afforded only the minimum single seat also has increased. The increasing number of small states and the fixed size of House membership limit the remainder of seats available for apportioning and, thereby, limit the relative political equality of large states. For example, based on figures from the 2010 census, the population ratio of California to Wyoming is 66 to 1, but their House-seat ratio is 53 to 1.[32]

There is nothing magical about a House of 435 members. It is one more obstacle to victory in the election by the candidate who receives the most votes.

FAITHLESS ELECTORS

One other factor can affect the translation of votes into electoral votes: the fidelity of electors. Since the first presidential election, there has been controversy about the proper role of presidential electors. The main point of contention is whether they are to think and act independently or are merely to serve as agents of the people who chose them. Electors who vote for whomever they wish destroy any relationship between the popular vote in their states and their own electoral votes.

Are Electors Bound?

In 1792 the electors chosen in North Carolina met and debated the respective merits of John Adams and George Clinton and finally decided to support Clinton.[33] Debates among the Virginia electors in the same year were reported to have shifted six votes from Adams to Clinton. But even in the first elections, few electors really acted as independent evaluators. According to an editorial in the newspaper *Aurora* in 1796, "The President must not be merely the creature of a spirit of accommodation or intrigue among the electors. The electors should be faithful agents of the people in this very important business; act in their behalf as the people would act were the President and Vice President elected immediately by them . . . . Let the people then choose their electors with a view to the ultimate choice."[34]

With the passage of the Twelfth Amendment in 1804, any semblance of the electors as independent statesmen faded. In a Senate committee report in 1826, Thomas Hart Benton of Missouri said that the founders had intended electors to be men of "superior discernment, virtue and information" who would select the president "according to their own will" and without reference to the immediate wishes of the people. "That this invention has failed of its objective in every election," Benton said, "is a fact of such universal notoriety, that no one can dispute it. That it ought to have failed," he concluded, "is equally uncontestable; for such independence in the electors was wholly incompatible with the safety of the people. [It] was, in fact, a chimerical and impractical idea in any community."[35]

Even by the early nineteenth century, then, the function of the electors had become little more than ministerial. Benton said that the electors had "degenerated into mere agents." Justice Joseph P. Bradley, the famed "fifteenth man" on the Electoral Commission of 1877, characterized electors as mere instruments of party—"party puppets." Senator John J. Ingalls of Kansas commented in the same era that electors are like "the marionettes in a Punch and Judy show."[36]

Reviewing the historical failure of the electors to be free agents, as had been contemplated by the founding fathers, Supreme Court Justice Robert H. Jackson wrote in 1952: "Electors, although often personally eminent, independent and respectable, officially become voluntary party lackeys and intellectual nonentities to whose memory we might justly paraphrase a tuneful satire: 'They always voted at their party's call / And never thought of thinking for themselves at all.'" Jackson concluded that "as an institution, the electoral college suffered atrophy almost indistinguishable from rigor mortis."[37]

At the meeting of the California electoral college in Sacramento in 1960, former governor Goodwin Knight told his fellow Republican electors: "Before coming here today, many of us received messages by mail and wire urging that we cast our ballots for prominent Americans other than Richard Nixon and Henry Cabot Lodge. Among those mentioned were former Governor Allan Shivers of Texas, Senator Barry Goldwater of Arizona, and Senator Harry Byrd of Virginia. Conceding that these gentlemen have merit as statesmen," Knight said, "the fact remains it is our solemn duty, in my humble judgment, to vote for those men the people selected on November the eighth."[38]

In addition to their selection by political parties and the general expectations of their behavior, another factor constrains the independence of electors. The winner-take-all system operating in the District of Columbia and all states except Maine and Nebraska makes it impossible to run as a single unaffiliated elector. There are no legal provisions for unaffiliated electors, even in Maine and Nebraska. All electors must run as part of pledged slates.

Nevertheless, under the Constitution, once they are elected, electors remain free agents and, if they choose, can vote in any way they like. In 1826 Madison defended electoral discretion in a fashion unlikely to receive approval today:

> One advantage of Electors is, that although generally the mere mouths of
> their Constituents, they may be intentionally left sometimes to their own

judgment, guided by further information that may be acquired by them: and finally, what is of material importance, they will be able, when ascertaining, which may not be till a late hour, that the first choice of their constituents is utterly hopeless, to substitute in the electoral vote the name known to be second choice.[39]

In the same year, Benton spoke out in the Senate on the dangers of free agency:

The elector may give or sell his vote to the adverse candidate, in violation of all the pledges that have been taken of him. The crime is easily committed, for he votes by ballot; detection is difficult, because he does not sign it; prevention is impossible, for he cannot be coerced; the injury irreparable, for the vote cannot be vacated; legal punishment is unknown and would be inadequate . . . . That these mischiefs have not yet happened, is no answer to an objection that they may happen.[40]

Efforts to Bind Electors

Although there is a general expectation that presidential electors will support the candidates in whose name they are chosen, there is a lingering concern about how electors will vote. In 1944 some Texas Democratic electors indicated that they might bolt the national ticket. The party convened a special committee. One of its members, Representative Wright Patman, later explained that the committee had "tried the proposed electors for disloyalty" and "put most of them off the ticket and put loyal ones on." In 1972 an already chosen Democratic-Farmer-Labor party elector in Minnesota indicated that he would be unlikely to vote for Democratic nominee George McGovern. The state party promptly replaced him. Twenty years later, the independent presidential campaign of H. Ross Perot was plagued by doubts about the loyalty of some of its elector-nominees, as had been the independent candidacy of John B. Anderson in 1980.[41]

Most states have passed laws in an attempt to bind their electors to vote for the candidate to whom they are pledged. Some require electors to take an oath or pledge to vote for the candidates of the political party they represent, all under penalty of law, while others require a pledge or affirmation of support, without any penalty of law. Some states direct electors to support the winning ticket or to vote for the candidates of the party they represent. In addition, some state political parties require in their rules that candidates for elector affirm or pledge to support the party nominees.[42]

Efforts to bind or control electors raise serious constitutional questions. Custom may have made electors into little more than instruments of party, but the Constitution provides that they shall vote by ballot, a procedure which implies that they are free agents. In 1952 the U.S. Supreme Court ruled on the constitutionality of a requirement of the Democratic Executive Committee of Alabama that candidates for elector pledge to support the presidential and vice presidential candidates of the party's national convention as a condition to being certified as an elector candidate in the Democratic primary. The Supreme Court held in *Ray v. Blair* that such a pledge requirement does not violate the Constitution. Excluding a candidate for elector because he or she refuses to pledge support for the party's nominees, the Court said, is a legitimate method of securing party candidates who are pledged to that party's philosophy and leadership. According to the Court, such exclusion is a valid exercise of a state's right under the Constitution's provision for appointment of electors in such manner as the state legislature chooses. Even if a loyalty pledge were unenforceable, the Court said, it would not follow that a party pledge as a requisite for running in a primary was unconstitutional.[43]

However, the Court did not rule on the constitutionality of state laws that require electors to vote for their party's candidates, nor did it indicate whether elector pledges, even if given, could be enforced. No faithless elector has been prosecuted for failing to keep a pledge. The preponderance of legal opinion is that statutes binding electors, or pledges that they may give, are unenforceable. "If an elector chooses to incur party and community wrath by violating his trust and voting for some one other than his party's candidate, it is doubtful if there is any practical remedy," writes James C. Kirby Jr., an expert on electoral college law. Once the elector is appointed, Kirby points out, "he is to vote. Legal proceedings which extended beyond the date when the electors must meet and vote would be of no avail. If mandamus was issued and he disobeyed the order, no one could change his vote or cast it differently. If he were enjoined from voting for anyone else, he could still abstain and deprive the candidate of his electoral vote."[44] Similarly, Akhil Reed Amar expresses the view that "even if a legal pledge can be required, it is far from clear that any legal sanction could be imposed in the event of a subsequent violation of that pledge."[45]

Acting as Free Agents

Former president Benjamin Harrison warned in 1898 that "an elector who failed to vote for the nominee of his party would be the object of execration, and in times of high excitement might be the subject of a lynching."[46] Most electors consider themselves irrevocably bound to support the presidential candidate on whose party ticket they were elected. In the disputed Hayes-Tilden election of 1876, James Russell Lowell, who had been chosen as a Republican elector in Massachusetts, was urged to switch his vote from Hayes to Tilden—a move that would have given Tilden the election because only one vote divided the candidates in the national count. Lowell refused to take the step. "In my own judgment I have no choice, and am bound in honor to vote for Hayes, as the people who chose me expected me to do," Lowell wrote to a friend. "They did not choose me because they have confidence in my judgment but because they thought they knew what the judgment would be. If I had told them that I should vote for Tilden, they would never have nominated me. It is a plain question of trust."[47]

Nevertheless, presidential electors have broken their pledges or violated public expectations in a number of cases. The first known instance occurred in Pennsylvania in 1796, when Samuel Miles, chosen as a Federalist, voted for Thomas Jefferson. In response, an angry Pennsylvania voter wrote a letter to the *Gazette of the United States*, in which he declared, "What, do I choose Samuel Miles to determine for me whether John Adams or Thomas Jefferson shall be President? No! I choose him to act, not to think."

In 1808, six New York electors from the Democratic-Republican Party refused to support James Madison, their party's candidate for president. Instead, they voted for George Clinton, the Democratic-Republican Party's vice presidential candidate, for president. Four years later, three electors of the Federalist Party declined to cast their votes for Federalist vice presidential candidate Jared Ingersoll. All three voted instead for Elbridge Gerry, the vice presidential candidate for the Democratic-Republican Party.

In 1820 former senator William Plumer of New Hampshire cast his electoral vote for John Quincy Adams, who was not a candidate in the election, rather than James Monroe, to whom he was pledged. He also voted for Richard Rush, also a noncandidate, for vice president. Accounts vary about Plumer's motivation; he is reported to have said that only

George Washington "deserved a unanimous election," but biographers also report that he wanted to draw attention to his friend Adams as a potential president and to "protest against the wasteful extravagance of the Monroe administration."[48] Thirteen other electors voted for Federalists for vice president. In addition, single electors from Pennsylvania, Tennessee, and Mississippi did not vote.

In 1824 North Carolina's fifteen electors voted en bloc for Andrew Jackson despite a reported agreement to divide their votes according to the result of a presidential preference vote, which the voters were allowed to make by writing on the ballot the name of the man they preferred. About a third of the state's voters wrote Adams's name on the ballot, according to the historian J. B. McMaster, so that presumably Adams should have received about five electoral votes. Other authorities maintain, however, that it was understood that all of the state's votes would go to the most popular candidate.[49]

In the same election, the New York legislature picked a mixed slate of electors, including seven (from the state total of thirty-six) expected to back Henry Clay. One of the Clay electors was elected to Congress, however, and his replacement voted for Adams. By the time the New York electors actually cast their ballots, they already knew that Clay would not even qualify for the runoff in the House. Two of the remaining six Clay electors from the state then deserted him—one to vote for William H. Crawford, one to support Jackson.[50]

In 1828, seven out of the nine Democratic electors from Georgia refused to vote for vice presidential candidate John Calhoun. All seven cast their vice presidential votes for William Smith instead. Nevertheless, Calhoun won.

Four years later, all thirty Democratic electors from Pennsylvania refused to support the party's vice presidential candidate, Martin Van Buren, voting instead for William Wilkins. Van Buren won anyway. In addition, two National Republican Party electors from the state of Maryland abstained, refusing to vote for presidential candidate Henry Clay.

The Democratic Party nominated Richard M. Johnson of Kentucky as its vice presidential candidate in 1836. The twenty-three electors from Virginia refused to support Johnson because of an allegation that he had lived with an African American woman. With these twenty-three votes missing, there was no majority in the electoral college and the decision was deferred to the Senate. In the end, the Senate voted for Johnson as the vice president.

The Democratic Party nominated Horace Greeley for President in 1872. However, Greeley died after the November election but before the electoral college had voted. Sixty-three of the sixty-six Democratic electors refused to give their votes to a deceased candidate, and these electors split their votes among four other candidates. In addition, ten Democratic electors split their ballots for vice president among seven men other than Benjamin Gratz Brown, Greely's running mate.

In 1896, two parties, the Democratic Party and the People's Party, ran William Jennings Bryan as their presidential candidate. However, the two parties nominated different candidates for vice president. The Democratic Party nominated Arthur Sewall and the People's Party nominated Thomas Watson. The People's Party won thirty-one electoral votes, but four of those electors voted with the Democratic ticket, supporting Bryan as president and Sewall as vice president.

Republican President William Howard Taft and his vice president, James S. Sherman, ran for reelection in 1912. Sherman died before the election, and eight Republican electors who had pledged their votes to him voted for Nicholas Murray Butler instead.

In recent times, nine presidential electors have broken their pledges or otherwise voted differently than expected. The first of these was Preston Parks, who was nominated on two elector slates in Tennessee in 1948—the regular Democratic (pledged to Harry S. Truman) and the States' Rights (pledged to Dixiecrat candidate J. Strom Thurmond). The regular Democratic slate, including Parks, was elected, but he voted for Thurmond anyway.

In 1956 W. F. Turner of Alabama, a Democratic elector, voted for a local circuit judge, Walter E. Jones, for president instead of supporting the regular Democratic nominee, Adlai Stevenson, to whom he was pledged. Turner subsequently commented: "I have fulfilled my obligations to the people of Alabama. I'm talking about the white people."[51]

Henry D. Irwin was elected as a member of the winning Republican elector slate pledged to Richard Nixon in Oklahoma in 1960. On November 20, 1960, before the electoral college met, Irwin telegraphed all Republican electors in the country saying, "I am Oklahoma Republican elector. The Republican electors cannot deny the election to Kennedy.

Sufficient conservative Democratic electors available to deny labor Socialist nominee. Would you consider Byrd President, [Barry] Goldwater Vice President, or wire any acceptable substitute. All replies strict confidence." Irwin received approximately forty replies, some of them favorable, but most of the electors indicated that they had a moral obligation to vote for Nixon. Irwin subsequently asked the Republican national committeemen and state chairmen to free Republican electors from any obligation to vote for Nixon but received only three sympathetic replies. Republican National Committeeman Albert K. Mitchell of New Mexico wired Irwin that he had taken up the idea "with some of the leaders of the Republican National Committee level and found that while everyone was in favor of the move, they felt it should not be sponsored by the Republican organization." Mitchell encouraged Irwin, however, to take further steps "to eliminate Kennedy from the Presidency."[52]

The next July, subpoenaed to appear before a U.S. Senate Judiciary subcommittee, Irwin said he had never planned to vote for Nixon, whom he "could not stomach." Irwin revealed that he had worked in concert with R. Lea Harris, a Montgomery, Alabama, attorney, in a national movement to get the members of the electoral college to desert Nixon and Kennedy in favor of a strongly conservative candidate. An alternative was to support a plan, reportedly considered by some conservatives in the Louisiana legislature, to call a meeting of conservative southern governors in Baton Rouge, to which Kennedy would have been invited and presented with the following conditions for receiving the southern electoral votes he needed for election: "(1) Eliminate the present sizable foreign aid we presently give to the Communist economy; (2) adhere to the spirit of the Tenth Amendment [reserving powers not specified in the Constitution to the states]; and (3) appoint one of these Southern Governors Attorney General."[53]

When the electors actually cast their votes on December 19, Irwin voted for Senator Harry Byrd for president and Senator Barry Goldwater for vice president, but no other Republican elector followed his lead. Irwin, who listed his occupation as "slave labor for the federal government," explained his action on a national television program: "I was prompted to act as I did for fear of the future of our republic form of government. I feared the immediate future of our government under the control of the socialist-labor leadership. . . . I executed my constitutional right . . . as a free elector." Irwin went on to say that the founding fathers were landowners and propertied people who never intended "that the indigent, the non property owners should have a vote in such a momentous decision" as election of the president. He had performed "his constitutional duty," he proclaimed, as a "free elector."[54]

As mentioned earlier, in 1968, Dr. Lloyd W. Bailey, Republican of North Carolina, declined to abide by his pledge to support his party's nominee, Richard Nixon. A member of the ultraconservative John Birch Society, Bailey decided that he could not vote for Nixon because of his concern over alleged leftist tendencies in the early Nixon appointments of presidential advisers such as Henry Kissinger and Daniel Patrick Moynihan and Nixon's decision to ask Chief Justice Earl Warren to continue on the Supreme Court for an additional six months. When the electoral college met on December 16, Bailey therefore gave his electoral vote to George Wallace. Bailey later admitted at a Senate hearing that he would have voted for Richard Nixon if his vote would have altered the outcome of the election.[55]

In 1972 Republican elector Roger MacBride of Virginia deserted Republican nominee Richard Nixon to vote for Libertarian Party candidate John Hospers, head of the University of Southern California School of Philosophy. He also cast his vice presidential vote for Toni Nathan, the Libertarian vice presidential candidate (making Nathan the first woman to receive an electoral vote). MacBride was the cocreator of the television series *Little House on the Prairie* as well as the author of an obscure book on the electoral college. He went on to become the 1976 Libertarian presidential candidate. (The defection in 1972 made Nixon the only man in history to suffer elector defections on three separate occasions: 1960, 1968, and 1972.)

Six weeks after the November 1976 election, Washington elector Mike Padden decided that Republican nominee Gerald Ford was insufficiently forthright in opposition to abortion and thereby unsuitable to be president. Padden instead cast his vote for Ronald Reagan. As we will see in Chapter 4, if 5,559 votes in Ohio and 3,687 in Hawaii had switched from Jimmy Carter to Ford, Ford would have had 270 electoral votes to Carter's 268 and would have won the election. If Padden had withheld his support from Ford, the president's total would have been only 269 electoral votes—

one fewer than the constitutionally required majority of the 538-member electoral college—and thus neither candidate would have had an electoral college majority, throwing the election into the House of Representatives.

To the surprise of most observers, the presidential elections of 1980 and 1984 failed to produce new faithless electors. However, in 1980, Republican nominee Ronald Reagan was sufficiently concerned about this possibility to send a letter to each of his 538 elector candidates days before the election reminding them that he would expect them to fulfill their "obligation" to vote for him even if President Carter should win the national popular vote.[56]

Another faithless elector appeared in 1988. A Democratic presidential elector in West Virginia, Margaret Leach, for reasons best understood by her, cast her presidential electoral vote for Democratic vice presidential nominee Lloyd Bentsen and her vice presidential electoral vote for Democratic presidential candidate Michael S. Dukakis.

No faithless elector appeared in 1992 or 1996, but in 2000 Barbara Lett-Simmons, a District of Columbia elector for Al Gore, abstained from casting her electoral college vote to protest the lack of congressional representation for Washington, DC. However, she later signed the legal Certificate of Vote document affirming that Gore had received all three of the district's electoral votes and said in an interview that she would never have tried to jeopardize Gore's election.[57]

In 2004 one of the ten handwritten ballots cast by Minnesota's electors carried the name of vice presidential candidate John Edwards (actually spelled "Ewards" on the ballot) rather than presidential candidate John Kerry. None of the electors volunteered having voted for Edwards as a protest, nor did anyone step forward to admit an error. "It was perhaps a senior moment," suggested one of the electors.[58]

There was almost a second faithless elector in the 2004 election. The mayor of South Charleston, West Virginia, appeared on CNN and declared in September 2004 that he might vote against George W. Bush in the electoral college, even if the president carried West Virginia's popular vote. Richard Robb, long known as a maverick Republican, said that he was considering using his position as one of the state's five Republican electors to protest what he believed were Bush's misguided policies. Robb said he was considering either voting for a third candidate or withholding his vote altogether. "I know that among some in my own party, what I'm discussing would be considered treasonous," Robb said. "But I'm not going to cheerlead us down the primrose path when I know we're being led in the wrong direction."[59] In the end, however, Robb voted the party line. He then changed his registration to Democratic and declared his opposition to the war in Iraq.

Fortunately for the nation, Henry Irwin, Lloyd W. Bailey, Roger Mac-Bride, Mike Padden, and the other faithless electors were not able to change the outcome of the elections. Nevertheless, in a close election, a faithless elector or electors could determine the outcome. Senator Henry Cabot Lodge of Massachusetts asserted in 1949, "The people know the candidates for President and Vice President; rarely do they know the identity of the electors for whom they actually vote. Such 'go-betweens' are like the appendix in the human body. While it does no good and ordinarily causes no trouble, it continually exposes the body to the danger of political peritonitis."[60]

Virtually no one even attempts to justify the votes of faithless electors. Their behavior is the ultimate democratic betrayal and violation of political equality. In effect, these electors are saying that their own judgment outweighs that of thousands or even millions of their fellow citizens.

Conditionally Pledged Electors

A different face of the issue of elector fidelity is that of electors who announce before the election that in certain circumstances they may support an alternative candidate. For example, in 1912 South Dakota electors, nominally pledged to Theodore Roosevelt, let it be known before the election that if the returns from the rest of the country made it clear that Roosevelt could not be elected and the contest was between Woodrow Wilson and William Howard Taft, they would vote for Taft. The voters apparently found this assurance satisfactory, for the Roosevelt slate was victorious on election day in South Dakota. Taft had run so far behind across the country, however, that the state's electors stuck with Roosevelt anyway.

Conditionally pledged electors reappeared in the mid-twentieth century as a device by conservative, segregationist-minded southerners to force the major parties to pay more heed to southern views by denying candidates a majority of the electoral vote (see Chapter 4 for more on this issue). For purposes of our discussion here, electors of third parties have not broken their pledges and actually voted for their candidates in the electoral college.

Nevertheless, as we will see, the candidates were ready to direct their electors to support another candidate if the possibility arose that they could bargain with the eventual winner. Apparently, Ross Perot had similar thoughts in 1992. A memo from one of his strategists urged him to make loyalty the first test for his electors, with an eye to gaining leverage over policy, patronage, or personnel decisions in the case of a deadlock.[61]

DISPARITIES BETWEEN POPULAR AND ELECTORAL VOTES

One common result of the factors that distort the translation of popular votes into electoral votes is a wide disparity between the percentages of the national popular vote and of the electoral vote a candidate receives (Table 3.1).

In the election of 1860, although Stephen A. Douglas was second in popular votes, he was fourth in the electoral college. Although he won 74 percent as many popular votes as were cast for Abraham Lincoln, his electoral vote was just 7 percent of Lincoln's. Douglas's popular vote was 161 percent of John C. Breckinridge's, yet he received only 17 percent as many electoral votes as Breckinridge. And Douglas's popular vote was more than double John Bell's, but Bell had three times as many votes in the electoral college.

In 1912 William H. Taft won 85 percent as many popular votes as Theodore Roosevelt, but he carried only two small states, Vermont and Utah, with a total of eight electoral votes, or exactly one-eleventh of the Roosevelt electoral vote. Woodrow Wilson, the winner in 1912's three-way contest, saw his popular vote of 42 percent magnified by the electoral college system into 82 percent of the electoral votes. This 40-percentage point discrepancy between popular and electoral vote ties for the greatest in the history of the Republic.

In 1936 Franklin D. Roosevelt's 61 percent of the popular vote translated into 98 percent of the electoral votes. Alfred Landon received 37 percent of the total popular vote but won only 2 percent of the electoral vote. In 1972 Richard Nixon received 61 percent of the popular vote and with that won 97 percent of the electoral vote. George McGovern saw his 38 percent of the popular vote transformed into a humiliating 3 percent of the electoral vote.

Ronald Reagan benefited from two of the greatest disparities between electoral votes and popular votes in the history of American presidential

Table 3.1
Examples of Disparities Between Popular and Electoral Votes

Candidate	Popular Vote	Electoral Vote	Electoral Vote (%)	Popular Vote (%)
1860				
Lincoln	1,865,908	180	39.8	59.4
Douglas	1,380,202	12	29.5	4.0
Breckinridge	848,019	72	18.1	23.8
Bell	590,901	39	12.6	12.9
1912				
Wilson	6,293,152	435	41.8	81.9
Roosevelt	4,119,207	88	27.4	16.6
Taft	3,486,333	8	23.2	1.5
Debs	900,369	0	6.0	0
1936				
Roosevelt	27,757,636	523	60.8	98.5
Landon	16,684,231	8	36.5	1.5
Others	1,213,199	0	2.7	0
1972				
Nixon	47,169,911	520	60.7	96.7
McGovern	29,170,383	17	37.5	3.3
Others	1,378,260	1	1.8	0
1980				
Reagan	43,904,153	489	50.7	90.9
Carter	35,483,883	49	41.0	9.1
Anderson	5,720,060	0	6.6	0
Others	1,407,125	0	1.7	0
1984				
Reagan	54,455,075	525	58.8	97.6
Mondale	37,577,185	13	40.6	2.4
Others	620,582	0	0.6	0
1992				
Clinton	44,909,326	370	43.0	68.8
Bush	39,103,882	168	37.4	31.2
Perot	19,741,657	0	18.9	0
Others	670,149	0	0.7	0

Sources: Congressional Quarterly's Guide to U.S. Elections, 6th ed. (Washington, DC: CQ Press, 2010); Jerrold G. Rusk, *A Statistical History of the American Electorate* (Washington, DC: CQ Press, 2001), 132.

elections. In 1980, in a three-way division of popular votes somewhat parallel to 1912, Reagan saw his winning popular vote majority of 51 percent swell into a landslide 91 percent of all electoral votes. The difference between Reagan's popular vote and electoral vote percentages was 40 percentage points. Four years later, Reagan won reelection with an impressive 59 percent of the popular vote over Democrat Walter Mondale. That vote translated into 98 percent of the electoral vote, greatly magnifying even a landslide victory.

Noteworthy differences between popular and electoral votes also marked the three-way contest among Bill Clinton, George H. W. Bush, and Ross Perot in 1992. Winner Clinton received his solid 69 percent of the total electoral votes on the basis of a strikingly low 43 percent of the national popular vote, while Bush's 37 percent of the popular votes translated into 31 percent of the electoral votes. This diminution was minor, however, in contrast to that suffered by independent candidate Perot. He won nearly 19 percent of the national vote, more than nineteen million popular votes—the greatest number polled by any third-party candidate in the history of the Republic. Nevertheless, Perot received no electoral votes at all.

The lack of close association between the winner's percentage of the popular vote and his percentage of the electoral vote is typical. There have been forty-seven presidential elections since 1820. In only thirteen (28 percent) has the disparity between the winning candidate's popular and electoral vote been fewer than 10 percentage points. In twenty-one of these elections (45 percent), the disparities have exceeded 20 percentage points.[62]

The disparities between the popular and electoral vote are an indication of the potential for the most serious violation of political equality that the electoral college may cause, which occurs when the candidate who receives the most votes loses the election.

ELECTIONS IN WHICH THE POPULAR VOTE WINNER LOST

Since 1828 there have been eleven presidential elections in which the candidate receiving the most popular votes had a lead of fewer than 3 percentage points over his closest competitor (1844, 1876, 1880, 1884, 1888, 1916, 1960, 1968, 1976, 2000, and 2004). Of these eleven elections, the electoral college has elected the *loser* of the popular vote in four instances: 1876, 1888, 1960, and 2000 (Table 3.2), or 36 percent of the time!

Table 3.2
Electoral College Reversal of Popular Vote Winners

		Popular Votes		Electoral Votes	
Year	Candidate	N	%	N	%
1876	Tilden (D)	4,288,546	51.0	184[a]	50
	Hayes (R)	4,034,311	48.0	185	50

Tilden popular vote margin of 254,235; Hayes winner with electoral vote
  margin of 1.

1888	Cleveland (D)	5,534,488	48.6	168	42
	Harrison (R)	5,443,892	47.8	233	58

Cleveland popular vote margin of 95,096; Harrison winner with electoral vote
  margin of 65.

1960	Nixon (R)	34,108,157[b]	49.5	219	41
	Kennedy (D)	34,049,976	49.5	303	59

Nixon popular vote margin of 48,181; Kennedy winner with electoral vote
  margin of 84.

2000	Gore (D)	50,996,062	48.4	266	49
	Bush (R)	50,456,169	47.9	271	50

Gore popular vote margin of 539,893; Bush winner with electoral vote margin of 5.

Sources: Congressional Quarterly's Guide to U.S. Elections, 6th ed. (Washington, DC: CQ Press, 2010); Jerrold G. Rusk, *A Statistical History of the American Electorate* (Washington, DC: CQ Press, 2001); Clerk of the House of Representatives Jeff Trandahl, *Statistics of the Presidential and Congressional Election of November 7, 2000* (U.S. House of Representatives, 2001).

Note: The election of 1824 also resulted in a reversal of the popular vote winner, but through use of the House contingent procedure.

[a]The electoral vote results in 1876 were arrived at by a bipartisan election commission, voting along party lines, which awarded twenty disputed electoral votes to Hayes.

[b]The popular vote totals for 1960 used here are computed by crediting Kennedy with five-elevenths of Alabama's Democratic votes and the unpledged elector slate with six-elevenths.

The electoral college also caused two other violations of political equality in earlier elections. Too few states allowed popular selection of electors to make reasonable comparisons of candidates' popular vote totals in 1800. What is unequivocally clear, however, is that Thomas Jefferson benefited from the constitutional provision that counted slaves as three-fifths of a person for representation in the House and consequently in a state's votes in the electoral college. At least twelve of the electoral votes Jefferson received (he won by eight) were the result of the three-fifths rule.[63] Had there been no electoral college, which accorded slaveholders and their neighbors extra weight in selecting the president, John Adams would have won reelection in 1800.

In addition, the provision for contingent elections in the House of Representatives resulted in the candidate with the most popular votes losing the election in 1824, when the House chose John Quincy Adams over the winner of the popular vote, Andrew Jackson (this election is discussed in the next chapter).

1876

America was little more than a decade past the throes of the Civil War as it prepared to elect its nineteenth president in 1876, and the bitterness engendered by the war remained strong in both the North and the South. While the states of the old Confederacy labored to cast off the remnants of Reconstruction, Republican orators in the North waved the "bloody shirt" and warned of dire consequences if the Democratic Party, the party of the former rebels, were to return to power. The country was also enduring hard times, and many had suffered in the financial panic of 1873.

On election night, it appeared that Democrat Samuel J. Tilden, with a margin of 254,235 popular votes over Republican Rutherford B. Hayes, had won a comfortable margin of electoral college votes. The next morning, however, Republican hopes began to revive. If close tallies in South Carolina, Florida, and Louisiana could be swung to the Republican side, Hayes would become president by a single electoral vote. Republican Reconstruction state governments in each of these states eagerly cooperated in activities that found agents of both parties using illegal and corrupt tactics to achieve their ends.[64] The realization that the certification of just one Tilden electoral vote from among those under challenge would suffice to elect him intensified the conflict.

The dispute finally resulted in conflicting returns arriving from each of the three states—one certifying Hayes electors, the other Tilden electors. In addition, in Oregon, which Hayes carried easily, the Democratic governor discovered that one of the Republican electors was a postmaster and thus ineligible under the Constitution to serve in that capacity. He certified the election of a Democratic elector in the Republican's place. However, the Republican electors met, accepted the resignation of the ineligible elector, then elected the same man to the vacancy, which he now could fill because he had resigned as postmaster.[65]

It was up to Congress, then, to decide which electors to count. Democrats controlled the House and Republicans the Senate. The leaders of both parties agreed that compromise would be necessary to decide this fiercely partisan dispute. Three days before Congress was to count the electoral votes, it passed a law establishing a bipartisan election commission composed of five members of the House, five of the Senate, and five justices of the Supreme Court. The commission was to judge those cases in which more than one return from a state had been received. Its decisions would be final unless overruled by both houses of Congress.

Given the partisan makeup of each congressional chamber, it was known that the House would name three Democrats and two Republicans and the Senate just the reverse. The bill designated the names of two Democratic and two Republican justices. With seven Democrats and seven Republicans on the commission, the crucial selection, on which the entire election was to turn, was the fifth justice. The bill specified that the four justices already designated would choose him, and it was generally understood that this final member would be Justice David Davis, a Lincoln appointee who was regarded as a political independent and widely respected for both his fairness and nonpartisanship.[66] With Davis on the commission, it appeared likely that at least one of the disputed electoral votes would be awarded to Tilden, thus making the Democrat president.

In one of the greatest blunders in American political history, the Illinois Democratic Party undid all these plans and destroyed the prospects of the Democratic candidate for president. Within hours of congressional passage of the legislation establishing the election commission, news arrived in Washington that the Illinois legislature, under Democratic control, had the day before named Justice Davis to a vacancy in the U.S. Senate.[67] With Davis suddenly unable to serve, a substitute had to be found on the Court. He was Justice Joseph P. Bradley, a reputedly independent-leaning Republican. As a member of the election commission, however, Justice Bradley exhibited no independent traits. He joined with the seven other Republicans to constitute an eight-vote majority, awarding the disputed electoral votes in every instance to Hayes, the Republican.[68] In every case, the House voted to overrule these decisions while the Senate voted to uphold them. Thus, under the law, Congress sustained all the commission's decisions.[69]

A crisis was brewing in Congress as some Democrats were threatening to block resumption of the joint session that was counting the electoral votes. At the same time, negotiations were under way between associates of Hayes and a number of southern conservatives. Under the terms of the agreement, the Democrats would permit the electoral count to proceed, thus electing Hayes. In return, Hayes would agree to a number of concessions, most important the withdrawal of federal troops from the South and the end of Reconstruction. Southerners pledged to respect Negro rights. In a few months, Hayes upheld his part of the bargain by withdrawing the remaining federal troops in the Confederacy.[70]

The South doubtless would have moved to deny blacks their rights if Tilden had won. In any case, southerners did not uphold their end of the agreement. Post-Reconstruction forces in the South deprived blacks of their rights and established a regime of Jim Crow segregation. It would be almost a century until the nation began to rectify the injustices to southern blacks that stemmed from obtaining the South's acquiescence in the election commission's decisions.

Reflecting on the resolution of the election of 1876, the distinguished historian of the presidency Edward Stanwood wrote: "It is to be hoped that the patriotism of the American people and their love of peace may never again be put to so severe a test as that to which they were subjected in 1876 and 1877."[71]

1888

The election of 1888 had none of the complexities of the election of 1876. The Democratic Convention nominated President Grover Cleveland for a second term. The Republicans nominated General Benjamin Harrison of Indiana, a grandson of President William Henry Harrison. The tariff was the central issue of the campaign. With the end of Reconstruction in 1877, the Democrats had seized complete control of the South, and the question was whether the Republicans could prevent enough northern defections to overcome the solid South.

In the end, Harrison carried a number of large states, such as New York, Ohio, and Pennsylvania, by relatively small popular vote margins. For example, he won New York by 14,373 votes out of the 1,319,748 votes cast in that state. Cleveland, by contrast, carried a number of states, particularly in the South, by large margins. Harrison's slender popular vote margins were turned into solid, large blocs of electoral votes, whereas Cleveland's large popular vote margins in his states were wasted in carrying states he could have carried with far fewer votes. Although Cleveland won the popular vote by a margin of 95,096, he won fewer electoral votes than Harrison and thus lost the election (see Table 3.2).[72]

1960

The election of 1960, between Vice President Richard Nixon and Senator John F. Kennedy, was extraordinarily close. The conventional figure for Kennedy's popular vote margin is 118,574 (Table 3.3, traditional count). In fact, as we have seen, there is no official national tabulation of presidential elections, because each state certifies its own election results.

The national count in all states except Alabama was 33,902,681 for Kennedy and 33,870,176 for Nixon—a Kennedy lead of 32,505. In Alabama, state law provided that the names of the individual candidates for presidential elector appeared separately on the ballot, with the voters allowed to vote for as many or as few members of any electoral slate as they wished. Each elector slate consisted of eleven names—the number of electoral votes to which the state was entitled. All the Republican electors were pledged to vote for Nixon, and the highest Republican elector received 237,981 votes in the general election—establishing a clear Nixon popular vote total in the state.[73]

There had been stiff competition in Alabama to determine who would be placed on the ballot as Democratic electors—those pledged to support the party's national nominee or unpledged electors opposed to the party's national policies. A Democratic primary and runoff held in the spring resulted in the selection of six unpledged and five loyalist elector candidates to make up the eleven-member Democratic elector slate in the general election. Thus the question arose: For whom should the votes cast for the Democratic elector slate be counted in the national popular vote tally— for Kennedy or for the unpledged-elector movement?

On election day, the most popular unpledged elector on the Democratic slate received 324,050 votes, while the most popular loyalist or Kennedy elector received 318,303 votes. It appears that, with few exceptions, the

Table 3.3
The Election of 1960

	Popular Votes	Electoral Votes
Traditional count		
Kennedy (D)[a]	34,226,731	303
Nixon (R)	34,108,157	219
Other	503,331	15
Kennedy plurality: 118,574.		
Alternative count		
Kennedy (D)[b]	34,049,976	303
Nixon	34,108,157	219
Byrd[c]	491,527	15
Minor parties	188,559	0
Nixon plurality: 58,181.		

Sources: For traditional count, *Congressional Quarterly's Guide to U.S. Elections,* 6th ed. (Washington, DC: CQ Press, 2010); Jerrold G. Rusk, *A Statistical History of the American Electorate* (Washington, DC: CQ Press, 2001), 192; for alternative count, "1960 Vote Analysis," *Congressional Quarterly Weekly Report,* February 17, 1961, 285–288.
[a]Allocates all votes for Democratic electors to Kennedy.
[b]Divides the vote for the Alabama Democratic elector slate proportionately according to its composition.
[c]Byrd won the votes of fourteen unpledged electors from Alabama and Mississippi plus one vote from a Republican elector in Oklahoma.

same people had voted for both the unpledged and the loyalist electors. The national wire services chose to credit Kennedy with the highest vote cast for any Democratic elector in the state—the 324,050 that one of the *unpledged* members of the Democratic slate received. The wire service accounts made it appear as if no unpledged elector votes at all were cast in Alabama. The result, of course, was a gross misstatement of the actual vote in the state, an error that followed over into the wire associations' report that Kennedy won the national popular vote by some 118,574 votes.

It is implausible to award all of Alabama's votes for Democratic electors to Kennedy. First, doing so requires including some 6,000 votes that were specifically cast *against* Kennedy by Alabama Democrats who would not support loyalist electors. Second, and more important, it is not reasonable to accord Kennedy votes for electors who were unambiguously not his supporters, who won their places in a direct contest with potential electors pledged to him, and who did not vote for Kennedy in the electoral college voting.[74]

A preferable method, developed by Congressional Quarterly (see Table 3.3, alternative count), is to take the highest vote for any Democratic elector in Alabama—324,050—and divide it proportionately between Kennedy and unpledged electors. Because loyalists held five of the eleven spots on the slate, they are credited with five-elevenths of the party total—147,295 votes. The unpledged electors, holding six elector slots, are credited with six-elevenths of the Democratic vote—176,755. The state totals now read: Nixon, 237,981; Kennedy, 147,295; unpledged electors (Byrd), 176,755. When these totals are added to the popular vote results from the other forty-nine states, a significant change occurs. Kennedy no longer leads in the national popular vote. Instead, Nixon is the popular vote winner by a margin of 58,181 votes.[75]

Nixon never sought to use these figures to argue that he had been the people's choice for president in 1960. Because Kennedy was clearly the electoral college winner, Nixon may have felt that claiming a popular vote victory would have portrayed him as a poor loser. Moreover, the complex issues raised by the Alabama count were not the kind that many people would fully understand. Thus little public debate took place on the question of how Alabama's votes should be counted, and it seemed likely that the issue would not be raised again.

The problem of determining the 1960 Alabama vote reappeared in 1964, however. The Democratic National Committee, in allocating the number of delegate seats each state would have to the 1964 national convention, employed a formula that rested in part on the number of popular votes the party's nominee, Kennedy, had received in the previous presidential election. The Northern Democrats in control of the committee were anxious to minimize the weight of the southern states, especially those that had been disloyal to the national ticket in the 1960 election. So when it came to determining the number of Kennedy votes with which Alabama should be credited in determining the delegate apportionment, the national committee used exactly the same formula that Congressional Quarterly had used following the 1960 election. It took the highest vote for a Democratic elector in Alabama, divided it in eleven parts, and credited five parts to Kennedy and six to the unpledged electors. As a result, the size of the

Alabama delegation to the 1964 convention was reduced. By employing this stratagem, ironically, the committee was accepting the rationale of a counting system under which Nixon was the clear popular vote winner in 1960.

2000

It is a historical oddity that every time the son or grandson of a president has been nominated for president, he has been elected with fewer popular votes than his opponent. In 1824 the House of Representatives elected John Quincy Adams, the son of John Adams, after he finished second to Andrew Jackson in the popular vote. In 1888 Benjamin Harrison, grandson of William Henry Harrison, won the electoral vote but came in second to Grover Cleveland in the popular count. In 2000 George W. Bush was the third son or grandson of a president to be elected, again with fewer popular votes than his opponent.

The presidential election of 2000 between Democrat Al Gore and Republican George W. Bush was extremely close. Gore won the national popular vote 50,996,062 to Bush's 50,456,169, a margin of 539,893.[76] On the day following the election, Gore's electoral vote total was 267 votes while Bush's stood at 245. Neither had the majority of electoral votes necessary to win the presidency. It was not clear who had won Florida's 25 electoral votes, which were the subject of a protracted battle. As we saw in Chapter 2, the Supreme Court's decision in *Bush v. Gore* effectively ended the dispute, and Bush won Florida's electoral votes by a margin of 537 popular votes. The addition of these electoral votes pushed Bush's total to 271, one more than a majority, and he became the forty-third president.

Near Misses

Only sheer luck has saved the nation from additional instances of an electoral college victory for the popular vote loser. Statistical models show that there is a high probability that the popular vote loser will win the electoral college in close elections.[77] Many presidential elections have been so close that a small shift of votes would have changed the outcome (Table 3.4). Shifts in votes, of course, are seldom isolated in individual states but are usually part of regional or national trends. Yet shifts as small as those in Table 3.4—a fraction of 1 percent of the national vote and no more than 1 or 2 percent of the vote in critical states—could occur for many

Table 3.4

Vote Shift Required for Plurality Winner to Lose Election

Shift	Shift Needed	States
1828	12,779	Indiana, Kentucky, Louisiana, New York, Ohio
1840	8,184	Maine, New Jersey, New York, Pennsylvania
1844	2,555	New York
1848	3,229	Delaware, Georgia, Maryland
1864	37,040	Connecticut, Indiana, Maryland, New York, Pennsylvania, Oregon, Wisconsin
1868	29,697	Alabama, California, Connecticut, Indiana, Nevada, North Carolina, Pennsylvania
1876	462	Florida
1880	10,518	New York
1884	524	New York
1888	7,188	New York
1892	36,965	California, Indiana, New Jersey, New York, Wisconsin
1896	18,562	California, Delaware, Indiana, Kentucky, Oregon, West Virginia
1900	73,539	Indiana, Kansas, Maryland, Nebraska, Ohio, Utah, Wyoming
1908	75,032	Delaware, Indiana, Kansas, Maryland, Missouri, Montana, Ohio, West Virginia
1916	1,983	California
1948	29,294	California, Illinois, Ohio
1960	11,876	Hawaii, Illinois, Missouri, Nevada, New Mexico
1976	9,246	Hawaii, Ohio
2004	59,300	Ohio

Sources: Congressional Quarterly's Guide to U.S. Elections, 6th ed. (Washington, DC: CQ Press, 2010); Jerrold G. Rusk, *A Statistical History of the American Electorate* (Washington, DC: CQ Press, 2001).

reasons, independent of national trends. The point is that many elections are extraordinarily close, small shifts in voting can change the outcome, and the electoral college creates a real potential for the winner of the popular vote to lose the election.

For example, in 1884, a switch of only 524 votes in New York would have elected Republican James G. Blaine over plurality winner Grover Cleveland. In 1916 President Woodrow Wilson received 579,511 more votes than his closest challenger, Republican Charles Evans Hughes. However, a switch of just 1,983 votes in California would have made Hughes president.

In 1948 President Harry S. Truman won the national popular vote by more than 2 million popular votes and ran 114 votes ahead of Republican candidate Thomas Dewey in the electoral college. Truman's electoral vote margin was deceptive, however. A shift from Truman to Dewey of only 29,294 votes in three states (16,807 in Illinois; 8,933 in California; and 3,554 in Ohio) would have made Dewey president instead.

Even if one concludes, in the face of evidence to the contrary, that John F. Kennedy won an electoral plurality of 118,000 votes over Richard Nixon in the 1960 election, it is important to note that a shift of only 11,876 votes—out of nearly 69 million cast—dispersed across the states of Illinois, Missouri, New Mexico, Hawaii, and Nevada would have made Nixon president.

Similarly, in the election of 1976, Governor Jimmy Carter won 50 percent of the popular vote and a victory margin of nearly 1.7 million votes over President Gerald Ford. If 3,687 votes in Hawaii and 5,559 votes in Ohio—a total of only 9,246 votes—had shifted to Ford, however, he would have remained president.[78]

Most recently, a shift of 59,300 votes in Ohio in 2004 would have elected John Kerry over George W. Bush despite the fact that Bush had a margin of nearly 3 million votes nationwide.

The electoral college violates political equality. It is not a neutral counting device. Instead, it favors some citizens over others, depending solely upon the state in which voters cast their votes for president. The contemporary electoral college is not just an archaic mechanism for counting the votes. It is an institution that aggregates popular votes in an inherently unjust manner.[79]

What good reason is there to continue such a voting system in an advanced democratic nation, where the ideal of popular choice is the most deeply ingrained of governmental principles? As Chief Justice Earl Warren wrote in *Reynolds v. Sims*,

> To the extent that a citizen's right to vote is debased, he is that much less a citizen. The fact that an individual lives here or there is not a legitimate reason for overweighting or diluting the efficacy of his vote. . . . The weight of a

citizen's vote cannot be made to depend on where he lives. . . . A citizen, a qualified voter, is no more nor no less so because he lives in the city or on the farm. This is the clear and strong command of our Constitution's Equal Protection Clause. This is an essential part of the concept of a government of laws, and not men. This is at the heart of Lincoln's vision of "government of the people, by the people, [and] for the people."[80]

Chapter 4 Contingent Elections

If the presidential and vice presidential candidates fail to receive a simple majority of electoral college votes, the Twelfth Amendment provides that the House of Representatives chooses the president and the Senate chooses the vice president in a process known as "contingent" election (contingent upon the absence of a majority in the electoral college). There have been two contingent elections for president in our history, following the elections of 1800 and 1824. Very minor shifts of popular votes in the nation, however, would have sent a number of other elections to the Congress for decision.

In the House, where each state must vote as a unit, a majority of twenty-six or more votes is required to elect a president; in the Senate, a majority of fifty-one or more votes is required to elect a vice president. Although a superficial reading of these rules suggests the operation of majority rule, this process actually represents the most egregious violation of democratic principles in the American political system.

SELECTING THE PRESIDENT

The first question regarding selection of the president by the House is: Which House elects the president if a contingent election is necessary? The Constitution does not prohibit the old House from selecting the president. In both 1801 and 1825, members of the lame-duck Congress did so, because new members of Congress would not take office until March. Under the Twentieth Amendment, ratified in 1933, a new Congress—elected the same day as the presidential electors—takes office on January 3, three days before the official count of the electoral votes on January 6. The latter date is set by statute and could be changed.

The House must select the president from among the three candidates who received the most electoral votes, with each state (not including the District of Columbia) casting a single vote for president. Until the Twelfth Amendment was ratified in 1804, the Constitution stipulated that the House pick the president from the top five candidates.

The Twelfth Amendment specifies that a quorum consisting of a member or members from two-thirds of the states is necessary to proceed, and the votes of a majority of all the states are necessary to elect a presidential candidate. The amendment did not change the most important rule in contingent elections in the House: each state has one vote, regardless of its size.

There are no rules for quorums within states, so one person could cast a state's vote, even if the state had many representatives. If there were quorum rules of, say, two-thirds of the state's representatives being present, one-third plus one of the representatives (presumably in the minority of the delegation) could prevent a state's vote from being cast by not showing up.

The House rules of 1825 specify that a majority vote of those voting within a state delegation decide a state's vote. Any state whose representatives do not provide a majority vote for a candidate loses its vote altogether. If there are three candidates, none may receive a majority. Even with two candidates, a state's delegation may split evenly and thus lack a majority for any candidate.

The Constitution does not stipulate whether the House proceedings are to be open or closed. In both 1801 and 1825 the debates regarding candidates were held in secret, as were the votes cast by individual members and by states. It would be more difficult, but still legal, to conduct these actions in secret today. Although secret votes may be easier to change in later balloting as representatives move to producing a winner, the pressure to open the proceedings to public scrutiny would be intense.

The Twelfth Amendment assigns the House the task of choosing the president "immediately" if no candidate receives a majority of the electoral vote, but there is no definition of the term. In 1801 the House took thirty-six ballots to elect Thomas Jefferson. In 1825, in contrast, it needed only one ballot to select John Quincy Adams. The existing rules of the House (left over from the 1825 process) provide for continuous House balloting for president until a winner is declared. The balloting would not start until January 6, leaving only fourteen days until the constitutionally scheduled date of January 20 for the presidential inauguration. In the case of a prolonged deadlock, such that no president is chosen by January 20, the new vice president would become acting president under the specific mandate of the Twentieth Amendment.

1800: Jefferson v. Burr

The Constitution originally stipulated that each elector would cast two votes for president. If a candidate received a majority of the electoral votes, and more than any other candidate, he would be elected. Whoever received the second-most votes would become the vice president. There was no way to distinguish between a vote for president and a vote for vice president. Problems with this system emerged as early as 1796, when John Adams was elected president and the runner-up, Thomas Jefferson, was elected vice president. Adams and Jefferson were of different parties and, at that time, intense personal enemies.

By 1800 national political parties were running slates for office. That year, the Republican congressional caucus nominated Thomas Jefferson and Aaron Burr and stipulated that Jefferson was the choice for president.[1] The parties had also developed an ability to enforce party regularity and elector faithfulness. As a result, Jefferson and Burr received seventy-three electoral votes each (Table 4.1). Never a man to lose an opportunity (he has often been labeled "the man who could not wait"), vice presidential nominee Burr made no effort to step aside for his presidential running mate, and his supporters allegedly sought support from Federalist representatives to

Table 4.1

Electoral College Deadlock and Use of House Contingent Procedure

Year	Candidates	Popular Vote	% Popular Vote	Electoral Votes	House Result
1800					Jefferson winner
	Jefferson (D)	n/a		73	with 10 states to 4
	Burr (D)	n/a		73	for Burr on 36th
	Adams (F)	n/a		65	ballot
	Pinckney (F)	n/a		64	
	Jay (F)	n/a		1	
1824					Adams winner
	Adams (D)	113,122	30.9	84	with 13 states to 7
	Jackson (D)	151,271[a]	41.3	99	for Jackson and 4
	Crawford (D)	40,856	11.1	41	for Crawford on
	Clay (D)	47,531	13.0	37	1st ballot

Sources: Congressional Quarterly's Guide to U.S. Elections, 6th ed. (Washington, DC: CQ Press, 2010); Jerrold G. Rusk, *A Statistical History of the American Electorate* (Washington, DC: CQ Press, 2001).

Note: The Senate contingent procedure for selection of the vice president in case of no electoral college majority has been used only once, in 1837, after Democratic electors from Virginia refused to vote for the Democratic vice presidential nominee, Richard M. Johnson. The Senate subsequently elected him by a vote of 33 to 16.

[a]Jackson popular vote margin of 38,149.

gain the presidency. Thus in 1801 the House of Representatives was called upon to make one of the most agonizing decisions it has ever faced.

A lame-duck House session of the Sixth Congress, which was controlled by the Federalists, conducted the contingent election. Although the Democratic-Republicans had gained control of the House in the congressional elections of 1800, the new Seventh Congress did not convene until March 4, 1801. Enough Federalists voted for Burr to deny Jefferson a majority in the first round on February 11 (the vote was eight states for Jefferson, six for Burr, with two states divided).

Thirty-four more votes took place. Then, it appears—and the record is not clear—that James Bayard of Delaware made a deal with Jefferson, in which he agreed to abstain on the thirty-sixth ballot, giving Jefferson the majority of the states voting. In return, the story goes, Jefferson agreed to support the public credit, maintain the naval system, and retain bureaucrats who did not have positions in which they exercised discretion. Jefferson denied making any deals, but we do know that Jefferson acted consistently with such promises: paid the debt, did not touch the National Bank, kept the officeholders, and sought naval reductions only within the discretionary limits set by the Federalist legislation passed late in the Adams presidency.[2]

Thus Jefferson was elected on February 17, in part because of help from his ancient antagonist Alexander Hamilton, who hated only Burr more (Burr, of course, later killed Hamilton in a duel). Jefferson's final margin was ten states to Burr's four, with two remaining divided.

The election of 1800 and the subsequent House deliberations in 1801 were sufficiently painful to lead to adoption of the Twelfth Amendment, ratified in 1804. This amendment set out new rules for contingent elections and specified that electors must vote separately for a presidential and vice presidential candidate.[3]

Jefferson, having survived the first contingent election, wrote in 1823: "I have ever considered the constitutional mode of election ultimately by the legislature voting by states as the most dangerous blot on our Constitution, and one which some unlucky chance will some day hit."[4] Chance hit the very next year.

1824: Adams v. Jackson

In 1824, for the first time in U.S. history, something approximating a popular vote for president occurred, as eighteen of the twenty-four states allowed the people to vote for electors. The dominant Democratic-Republicans divided into four largely geographical factions, each with its own nominee. Among the candidates were three giants of American history: Andrew Jackson, John Quincy Adams, and Henry Clay. William Crawford, the secretary of the treasury, was also a candidate. Because the legislatures in some states, including New York, still selected their electors, we must be cautious about interpreting the vote count (see Table 4.1) as an accurate indicator of public opinion. However, Jackson finished far ahead of Adams, who obtained the second-most votes. The popular vote count was also important, because it provided Jackson's supporters an opportunity to claim that their man was the real choice of the people.

The House had to choose among the top three candidates, but the real choice was between Jackson and Adams. Henry Clay, the Speaker of the House, had finished fourth in electoral votes (although third in popular votes) and was, therefore, eliminated from House consideration.[5] Apparently, Clay intended to support Adams from the start, feeling that Jackson was not qualified to be president.[6]

Before the House vote, however, a scandal erupted when a Philadelphia newspaper printed an anonymous charge that Clay had agreed to support Adams in return for being named secretary of state and that Clay would have been willing to make the same deal with Jackson. Clay denied the charge and challenged the writer to reveal himself and fight a duel. The author did reveal himself but eluded the duel. Jackson believed the charge, and his suspicions were vindicated when Adams, after the election, actually did name Clay as secretary of state. "Was there ever witnessed such a bare faced corruption in any country before?" he exclaimed.[7] John Randolph of Virginia also was graphically critical and actually fought a duel with Clay (though neither was hurt).[8]

According to a report of the Congressional Research Service,

> Spirited debate as to the nature and requirements of contingent election preceded the actual vote. One question concerned the role of individual Representatives. Some asserted that it was the duty of the House to choose Jackson, the candidate who had won a national plurality of the popular and electoral vote. Others believed they should vote for the popular vote winner in their state or district. Another school of opinion suggested that House Members should give prominence to the popular results, but also consider themselves at liberty to weigh the comparative merits of the three candidates. Still others asserted that contingent election was a constitutionally distinct process, triggered by the failure of the people (and the electors) to arrive at a majority. Under this theory, the popular and electoral college results had no bearing or influence on the contingent election process, and Representatives were, therefore, free to consider the merits of the contending candidates without reference to the earlier contest.[9]

As the day of decision in the House approached, Adams seemed assured of the six New England states and, in large part through Clay's backing, of Maryland, Ohio, Kentucky, Illinois, Missouri, and Louisiana. Thus he had twelve of the twenty-four states and needed only one more to win election. The likeliest state to add to the Adams column was New York, since seventeen members of its thirty-four-person delegation were already reported ready to vote for him. Clay decided that the one uncommitted voter of the delegation was Stephen Van Rensselaer, an elderly, deeply religious member of one of New York's aristocratic families. The Speaker invited Van Rensselaer to his offices on the morning of the crucial vote, where he and Daniel Webster (another historical giant) urged him to vote for Adams. The entreaties of these two powerful men were reportedly unsuccessful, but the story is told that as Van Rensselaer sat at his desk in the House before the vote, he bowed his head in prayer to seek divine guidance. As he did this, his eyes fell on a slip of paper inadvertently left on the floor. The name "Adams" was written on the slip. Interpreting this as a sign from above, Van Rensselaer voted for Adams.[10]

On February 9, 1825, the lame-duck House session of the Eighteenth Congress elected John Quincy Adams as president over Andrew Jackson by a vote of thirteen states (including New York) to seven, with four states voting for William H. Crawford.

The charges and controversies resulting from Adams's victory in the House haunted him throughout his term and were a decisive issue against him. Jackson and his supporters immediately began preparing for the next election, emphasizing that Jackson had won the popular vote and was the people's choice but that the House had frustrated the popular will. In 1825, the year after the House vote, future president Martin Van Buren declared, "There is no point on which the people of the United States were more perfectly united than upon the propriety, not to say the absolute necessity, of taking the election away from the House of Representatives."[11] When the votes were counted in 1828, Jackson had won an overwhelming triumph, in both the popular and the electoral vote.

SELECTING THE VICE PRESIDENT

If, as would be likely, there is no majority in the electoral college vote for vice president, as well as for president, the Senate chooses the former. There are no procedures for electing the vice president in the standing rules of the Senate. The Senate could choose to hold all its proceedings in secret. The Twelfth Amendment requires a quorum of two-thirds of the Senate to proceed and a vote of a majority of senators to select a vice president. If opponents of the majority choice equaled more than one-third of the Senate and refused to attend, they could prevent a vote from occurring.

The Senate would probably select a vice president from the same ticket as the person the House chose as president. If there were a serious division in the Senate, however, the current rules allow the serving vice president, who is the president of the Senate, to break a tie and vote to reelect himself or herself.

If the House selects a president and the Senate fails to select a vice president by January 20, then under the Twenty-fifth Amendment, the president nominates a vice president with the approval of majority votes of both houses of Congress.

The Senate has selected the vice president only once. In 1801 the old constitutional rules applied, which specified that the person coming in second in the presidential election became the vice president. In 1824 there were four candidates for president but only one vice presidential candidate in the election, John C. Calhoun.

In 1836 Martin Van Buren won 170 of the 294 electoral votes in a split field. But his vice presidential running mate, Colonel Richard M. Johnson of Kentucky, had only 147 electoral votes—one fewer than a majority. Johnson, hailed as the man who killed the Shawnee leader Tecumseh in the Battle of the Thames during the War of 1812, was boycotted by the Virginia electors. Although they voted for Van Buren for president, they reportedly wanted to register disapproval of Johnson's social behavior (which presumably included breaches of decorum beyond the killing of Indians).[12] On February 8, 1837, the Senate elected Johnson by a vote of 33 to 16 over Francis Granger of New York, the runner-up in the electoral vote for vice president.[13]

NEAR MISSES SINCE WORLD WAR II

Although there have been only two contingent elections for president, the country has come perilously close on several other occasions. In seven other elections, the shift of a few votes in one or a few states would have deadlocked the electoral college and sent the election of the president into the House of Representatives (Table 4.2). In each case, the vote shift represented much less than 1 percent of the national vote.

Table 4.2
Vote Shift Required to Deadlock the Electoral College

Year	Vote Shift Required	% of National Vote	States
1836	14,124	0.93	New York
1856	20,625	0.51	Delaware, Illinois, Indiana
1860	25,069	0.54	New York
1860	18,707	0.39	California, Illinois, Indiana, Oregon
1948	12,487	0.02	California, Ohio
1960	9,421	0.01	Illinois, Missouri
1968	53,034	0.07	Missouri, New Hampshire, New Jersey
1976	11,942	0.01	Delaware, Ohio

Sources: Congressional Quarterly's Guide to U.S. Elections, 6th ed. (Washington, DC: CQ Press, 2010); Jerrold G. Rusk, *A Statistical History of the American Electorate* (Washington, DC: CQ Press, 2001).

Because many elections are extraordinarily close, the electoral college poses a real potential of deadlock. The following examples of near misses are from the period since World War II. Of particular interest are not only the confounding effects of third parties but also the efforts of some interests, including splinter parties, purposely to throw the election into the House, where they might be able to wield more influence on the selection of the president. In effect, House election would have given these interests greatly disproportionate say in electing the president.

1948

Almost everyone expected the Republicans to win the White House in 1948. By the summer of that year, President Harry S. Truman's popularity had plummeted to such depths that many Democrats—conservatives and liberals alike—had cast around for another nominee to head the party's ticket. In the end, however, the president was able to exert the political powers of an incumbent president and win renomination from the Democratic National Convention.

One reason for the near-universal predictions of Truman's defeat was the split-off from the Democratic party of southern segregationists on one side and left-wingers on the other. The southern defection, brewing for several months, came to a head at the Democratic National Convention when a tough civil rights plank was adopted at the instigation of Mayor Hubert H. Humphrey of Minneapolis and other party liberals. The Alabama and Mississippi delegations walked out on the spot, and rebellious southerners from thirteen states subsequently held a rump convention in Birmingham, Alabama, to nominate Governor Strom Thurmond of South Carolina as the States' Rights (Dixiecrat) Party candidate. On the other extreme of the party, former vice president Henry A. Wallace organized a new Progressive Party opposed to America's Cold War foreign policies.

Both the Dixiecrat and Progressive candidates posed serious dangers for Truman. Thurmond could deprive him of the southern electoral votes on which Democratic presidential candidates had counted ever since 1880, while Wallace could cost him enough votes to lose a number of strategic urbanized states in the North.

The biggest exception to those who expected the president's defeat was Truman himself. He launched an exhaustive, thirty-one thousand–mile barnstorming whistle-stop tour, crisscrossing the country in the face of almost unanimous predictions from pollsters, reporters, and sundry political experts that Republican nominee Thomas E. Dewey would win an overwhelming victory. On election day, Truman won the national popular vote by more than 2 million votes and ran 114 votes ahead of Dewey in the electoral college (Table 4.3). Truman's electoral vote margin was deceptive, however. A shift of only 12,487 votes in California and Ohio from Truman to Dewey would have prevented anyone from receiving a majority in the electoral college.

The Dixiecrat nominees for president and vice president, Strom Thurmond and Fielding Wright of Mississippi, won 2 percent of the popular vote and 39 electoral votes from the four states where they appeared on the ballot as the Democratic nominees: Alabama, Louisiana, Mississippi, and South Carolina. If no candidate received a majority in the electoral college, this splinter party could have determined the outcome of the election.

The Dixiecrats hoped to extract pledges from one of the major-party candidates regarding southern positions on segregation and other issues in return for the support of their electors. Although technically these would be faithless electors, they would find it easy to justify voting as their candidate directed. If that strategy failed, the election would be thrown into the House of Representatives, where the southern states and their

Table 4.3
1948 Election Results

	Popular Votes	Electoral Votes
Harry S. Truman (D)	24,179,345	303
Thomas E. Dewey (R)	21,991,291	189
Strom Thurmond (SR)	1,176,125	39
Henry A. Wallace (PR)	1,157,326	0
Minor parties	289,739	0
Truman plurality: 2,188,054.		

Sources: Congressional Quarterly's Guide to U.S. Elections, 6th ed. (Washington, DC: CQ Press, 2010); Jerrold G. Rusk, *A Statistical History of the American Electorate* (Washington, DC: CQ Press, 2001).

powerful congressional representatives might also find themselves in a crucial bargaining position.

Even with the hindsight that history affords, it is impossible to determine just what might have happened had the House been called on to pick the president in the wake of the election of 1948. The votes of twenty-five delegations (a majority of the forty-eight states) would have been required to elect a president. Loyalist Democrats would have controlled twenty-one delegations, Republicans twenty, and the Dixiecrats four. Three delegations would have been divided equally between the major parties. Assuming that House members would vote either for their own party's presidential candidate or, in the case of representatives from the four Dixiecrat states, the way the people of their states had voted in the fall elections, the outcome could have gone either way.

1960

In 1960 Vice President Richard M. Nixon faced off against Senator John F. Kennedy for the presidency. As in 1948, the Democratic candidate (Kennedy) won a substantial margin of electoral votes—303 compared to 219 for his Republican opponent. The size of Kennedy's electoral college victory belied the suspense of election night, November 8, as the nation watched the popular vote reports in what would prove to be one of the most closely contested presidential races of the century (Table 4.4; see Table 3.3 for an alternative view of the election results).

Table 4.4
1960 Election Results

	Popular Votes	Electoral Votes
Kennedy (D)[a]	34,226,731	303
Nixon (R)	34,108,157	219
Other	503,331	15
Kennedy plurality: 118,574.		

Sources: Congressional Quarterly's Guide to U.S. Elections, 6th ed. (Washington, DC: CQ Press, 2010); Jerrold G. Rusk, *A Statistical History of the American Electorate* (Washington, DC: CQ Press, 2001).
[a]Traditional count.

There was no splinter party of any consequence in the 1960 balloting, but the southern unpledged-elector movement, a successor to the Dixiecrat movement of 1948, won fourteen electoral votes in two southern states. The unpledged electors eventually cast their votes in the electoral college for Senator Harry F. Byrd of Virginia. In one major respect, however, the results were markedly different from those of 1948. Whereas Truman had amassed a popular vote plurality of more than 2 million votes, Kennedy's popular vote margin was one of the smallest in the history of presidential elections. Indeed, the fairest estimate, as we discussed in Chapter 3, is that Kennedy did not receive a plurality of the popular vote.

Although we will never know with certainty which candidate received the most popular votes in 1960, we do know that if a mere 4,430 voters in Illinois and 4,991 in Missouri had voted for Richard M. Nixon instead of John F. Kennedy, neither man would have achieved an electoral college majority and Byrd's electors would have been positioned either to dictate the outcome of the election or throw the election into the House of Representatives.

The potential of this incredibly near miss was not lost on Kennedy's opponents. There were many allegations of vote fraud, especially in Illinois. Between election day, November 8, and December 19 (when the electors met to vote), there was speculation that if Illinois's 27 electoral votes were lost to Kennedy through proof of vote fraud, thus reducing Kennedy's electoral votes to 273—only 4 more than the 269 needed for victory—southern electors might bolt and withhold votes from the Kennedy-Johnson ticket, throwing the election into the House. This immediate fear was dispelled, however, when the Illinois electoral board, consisting of four Republicans and one Democrat, certified the election of the Kennedy electors from the state on December 14.

Conservative southerners, who hoped to thwart Kennedy's election, watched the close elections in the northern states with special interest. On December 10 Alabama's six unpledged electors met in Birmingham and announced their desire to cast their presidential vote "for an outstanding Southern Democrat who sympathizes with our peculiar problems in the South." They stated, "Our position remains fluid so that we can cooperate with other unpledged electors for the preservation of racial and national integrity." The Alabamans specifically deplored the role of southerners who "ally themselves with a candidate [Kennedy] who avowedly would integrate our schools, do away with literacy tests for voting," and "otherwise undermine everything we hold dear in the South."[14]

Two days later, the six unpledged electors from Alabama and the eight who had been chosen in Mississippi held a meeting in Jackson, Mississippi. Deciding to vote for Senator Byrd of Virginia, they drafted a joint statement calling on presidential electors from other southern states to join the vote for Byrd in the hope that enough electoral votes (they needed thirty-five more) might be withheld from Kennedy to throw the election into the House of Representatives.

Mississippi's governor, Ross Barnett, one of the South's strongest segregationists, sent letters to six other states asking for support in the move to block Kennedy. In Louisiana leaders of the White Citizens' Council were at the forefront of a move to have the state's Democratic electors withhold their support from Kennedy.[15] The unpledged electors hoped that if the election reached the House, all southerners would vote for Byrd and that the Republicans, "being fundamentally opposed to the liberalism of Senator Kennedy," would follow suit.[16]

The new party lineup in the House would consist of twenty-three states controlled by northern and border state Democrats, six controlled by Deep South Democrats, and seventeen controlled by Republicans. Another four delegations were evenly split between the parties. This distribution makes it difficult to predict the outcome had the election reached the House.

As it turned out, when the electors actually cast their votes on December 19, the only vote Byrd got aside from the anticipated ones from Alabama and Mississippi came not from another Southern Democrat but from the faithless Republican elector Henry D. Irwin, whom we discussed in Chapter 3. The country was spared weeks or months of chaos following the election of 1960, but it was not thanks to the electoral college, which created the potential for harm.

Before the 1964 election, conservative southerners made substantial efforts to persuade the legislatures, or party committees if they had sufficient authority under state law, to authorize unpledged elector slates in Florida, South Carolina, Virginia, and Georgia, in addition to Alabama and Mississippi. Democrats loyal to the national party, however, were able to thwart most of these moves. In the case of Florida, President Kennedy reportedly made a personal telephone call to the state's speaker of the House to block passage of enabling legislation for independent electors.[17]

Governor George C. Wallace of Alabama announced on July 4, 1964, that he had "definite, concrete plans" to run for president in sixteen states: Alabama, Arkansas, Florida, Georgia, Illinois, Indiana, Kentucky, Louisiana, Mississippi, Missouri, New York, North Carolina, South Carolina, Tennessee, Virginia, and Wisconsin. However, he withdrew on July 19, four days after Senator Barry Goldwater of Arizona received the Republican nomination for president.[18] Goldwater's general conservatism and stand against civil rights legislation satisfied most of the segregationist southerners; of the six states he ultimately carried, four had gone Dixiecrat in 1948.

1968

In 1968 the nominees of the major parties were Vice President Hubert H. Humphrey for the Democrats and former vice president Richard M. Nixon for the Republicans. The candidate who would add the most confounding factor in the election, however, was George C. Wallace, the former governor of Alabama. His candidacy at the head of the ticket of a party of his own creation—the American Independent Party—presented the nation with the most formidable third-party campaign in decades.

In a sense, Wallace was a direct descendant of the Dixiecrats and their brand of anti–civil rights, southern politics that had propelled Strom Thurmond into the 1948 election and motivated the group of electors that eventually supported Harry F. Byrd in 1960. Wallace had a much broader appeal, however, which he had demonstrated by making strong runs in the Democratic presidential primaries in 1964. He proved it again in 1968 by galvanizing supporters to place slates of electors pledged to him on the ballots of all fifty states. Many observers had assumed it was virtually impossible for an independent candidate to qualify so broadly.

Wallace had declared in his gubernatorial inaugural address in 1963, "Segregation now—segregation tomorrow—segregation forever." Later he had stood in the schoolhouse door trying to prevent integration of the University of Alabama. Yet there was a broader attraction for his supporters than segregation. His rallies were half revival, half political meetings, with Wallace appealing to the plain folks present—steelworkers, beauticians, and cab drivers decked out in red, white, and blue—with his hot rhetoric about pseudointellectual government bureaucrats and long-haired students, bussin' and lenient judges, welfare loafers, and the fate that awaited any anarchist "scum" "who lies down in front of our car when we get to be president." (The line that always brought down the house, reflecting the quintessential violence of the Wallace appeal, was, "It'll be the last car he'll ever lie down in front of.")

Wallace's southernism worked both for him and against him. He played strongly on the region's lingering sense of inferiority, telling southerners that they were tired of being looked down upon and repeating a sure-applause line: "Folks down here in Alabama are just as refined and cultured as folks anywhere!" Yet his provinciality doubtless hurt him in the North.

When the election returns were in, Wallace won 14 percent of the popular vote and carried five states, all in the Deep South—Alabama, Mississippi, Louisiana, Georgia, and Arkansas—with 45 electoral votes.[19] It was not much different from 1948, when Thurmond had won three of those states—Alabama, Mississippi, and Louisiana—and his own South Carolina. Ironically, Strom Thurmond's all-out effort for Richard Nixon denied Wallace victory in South Carolina. Although Nixon, with a popular vote of 44 percent, led Humphrey by only 0.7 percent nationally, the vicissitudes of the electoral college resulted in Nixon receiving 302 electoral votes, or 56 percent of the total—a seemingly comfortable 32 electoral votes more than the 270 required (Table 4.5).[20]

Nevertheless, Wallace came close to being the pivotal figure in determining the outcome of the election. A shift of 53,034 votes from Nixon to Humphrey in New Jersey (30,631), Missouri (10,245), and New Hampshire (12,158) would have reduced Nixon's electoral vote by 33 votes to a total of 269, one less than the majority required for election, with Humphrey then

Table 4.5
1968 Election Results

	Popular Votes	Electoral Votes
Richard M. Nixon (R)	31,785,480	301
Hubert H. Humphrey (D)	31,275,166	191
George C. Wallace (AIP)	9,906,473	46
Minor parties	244,756	0
Nixon plurality: 510,314.		

Sources: Congressional Quarterly's Guide to U.S. Elections, 6th ed. (Washington, DC: CQ Press, 2010); Jerrold G. Rusk, *A Statistical History of the American Electorate* (Washington, DC: CQ Press, 2001).

receiving 224 and Wallace 45. A shift of 111,674 popular votes in California alone—1.5 percent of the vote cast in that state—would have had the same result.

If we take into account that Nixon elector Lloyd W. Bailey voted for Wallace, and if we assume that his vote would have been the same in our scenario, only 32 rather than 33 electoral votes would have had to shift to prevent Nixon from receiving a majority of the electoral vote. In this case, a shift of 41,971 votes from Nixon to Humphrey in New Jersey (30,631), Missouri (10,245), and Alaska (1,095) would have deadlocked the election.

Asked how he would have handled the situation, Wallace first made it clear to journalist Neal Peirce that he would have instructed his electors how they should vote in the electoral college. His electors, Wallace said, "were pledged to go along with me in the matter, and they would have gone with me."[21] In fact, he had demanded that his electors sign a pledge to vote either for him or for someone he designated.[22]

How would he have instructed his electors? "The chances are the votes probably would have gone to Mr. Nixon, because we were violently opposed to Mr. Humphrey's philosophy and ideology." Would he have demanded concessions, in advance, from Nixon? "We would probably have asked Mr. Nixon to reiterate some of his campaign statements he'd already made . . . just to restate what he had already said in substance: 'I want to work for world peace, I want tax reduction, tax reform. I want the neighborhood school concept protected. I'm in substance for freedom of choice in the public school system and against busing.' "[23]

Wallace on other occasions talked of a "solemn covenant" to stop foreign aid to Communist nations and left-leaning neutrals, of revamping the U.S. Supreme Court, and of a halt to federal civil rights enforcement. Wallace might well have forced on Nixon the same kind of a "hands-off" attitude toward the South that Rutherford B. Hayes had agreed to in 1877 in exchange for the electoral votes he needed to be elected. The South's price then had been termination of the first Reconstruction, a decision that would be followed by three-quarters of a century of violation of African Americans' rights in the South. The results of Wallace's demands might have put a halt to the civil rights advances of the 1960s.

If the electoral college meetings on December 16 had resulted in a deadlock, with no candidate receiving 270 electoral votes, the action would have shifted to the newly elected House of Representatives, meeting in the afternoon of January 6, 1969, only fourteen days before the constitutionally scheduled inauguration of the new president.[24] The candidates had positioned themselves for such an event during the campaign. Humphrey stressed the need to follow the prescribed constitutional contingent procedure (election by the House), while Nixon stated his belief that "whoever wins the popular vote should be the next President of the United States."[25]

In 1968 it was widely assumed that the House would have elected Humphrey. Democrats controlled twenty-six state delegations, Republicans had majorities in nineteen delegations, and the representatives from five states were evenly divided and consequently would cast no vote if each member voted for the candidate of his or her party. The assumption of a Humphrey victory, however, was based on the premise that each representative would have voted along party lines. A closer analysis shows that such a premise may have been faulty.

One important complicating factor was the issue of how the House delegations from the five Deep South states carried by Wallace, with percentages up to 66 percent, would vote. Although at least nominally Democratic and thus counted in the twenty-six-state Democratic total, the representatives from these states would probably have felt pressure to support Wallace in the House voting. However, if they broke party ranks and failed to support the Democratic nominee at this critical moment, they would have been subject to strong retribution, including loss of patronage, party seniority, and committee chairmanships.

Adding further complications to this dilemma was that fact that at least thirty candidates for the House—mainly Southern Democrats in Wallace- or Nixon-leaning districts—made campaign pledges that if elected, and if the election came to the House, they would not automatically vote for Humphrey but would vote however their district had voted.[26] Among these candidates were the six men who were elected to the House from South Carolina. All were Democrats, but three of their districts went for Nixon, two for Wallace, and one for Humphrey. If these representatives had honored their pledges, South Carolina's vote would have gone to Nixon, despite its solid Democratic representation.

The Virginia delegation was evenly divided between Republicans and Democrats. However, two Democratic representatives, David E. Satter- field III and John O. Marsh Jr., had made the pledge and Nixon had carried their districts. A third Virginia Democrat, W. C. Daniel, also had made the pledge, and his district had voted for Wallace. Virginia's vote might thus have gone to Nixon. Finally, Nevada's lone congressman, Wal- ter S. Baring, a Democrat, publicly pledged to cast his state's vote for Nixon, who won the state.[27]

The results of these publicly recorded pledges alone would be—assum- ing uniform party loyalty otherwise and no Wallace defections—a House vote not of twenty-six to nineteen and five states split but twenty-four to twenty-two and four states split. In this scenario, there would have been no majority of twenty-six states.

The pressures on House members in this situation would have been intense, and it is not clear how they would have resolved their dilemma. It is entirely possible that the idiosyncratic behavior of a few members would have determined the election of the president.

1976

The election of 1976 went down in the history books as another in which the electoral college barely did its work, although the results were not nearly as complicated as in 1960 and 1968. Governor Jimmy Carter of Georgia beat President Gerald Ford by a popular vote margin of 1,682,790 votes. The final electoral vote was 297 for Carter and 241 for Ford (Table 4.6). Ford's total was later reduced to 240 because of one faithless Ford elector in Washington State.

Table 4.6
1976 Election Results

	Popular Votes	Electoral Votes
Jimmy Carter (D)	40,830,763	297
Gerald R. Ford (R)	39,147,793	240
Eugene J. McCarthy (Ind.)	756,691	0
Roger MacBride (Libert.)	173,011	0
Others	647,631	1
Carter plurality: 1,682,970.		

Sources: Congressional Quarterly's Guide to U.S. Elections, 6th ed. (Washington, DC: CQ Press, 2010); Jerrold G. Rusk, *A Statistical History of the American Electorate* (Washington, DC: CQ Press, 2001).

Had an exceedingly small number of votes shifted from Carter to Ford—5,559 in Ohio and 3,687 in Hawaii—Ford would have had 270 electoral votes to Carter's 268 and won the election. However, if the same faithless elector had then withheld his support from Ford, the president's total would have been only 269—one fewer than the constitutionally required majority of the 538-member electoral college—and thus neither candidate would have had an electoral college majority. Similarly, if only 11,952 popular votes in Delaware (6,383) and Ohio (5,559) had shifted from Carter to Ford, Ford would have carried these two states. The result would then have been an exact tie in electoral votes—269–269. In either case, the election of the president would not have been decided on election night but rather through deals or switches at the electoral college meetings on December 13 or through the later uncertainties of the House of Representatives.

If only 5,559 voters has switched from Carter to Ford in Ohio, Carter would have lost that state and had only 272 electoral votes, 2 more than the 270 needed for election. In that case, two or three Democratic electors seeking personal recognition or attention to a pet cause could have bargained with the presidential candidates in exchange for their votes and thus have exercised disproportionate power. Or they could have withheld their electoral votes and sent the selection of the president to the House, with an uncertain outcome.

Such a scenario was not implausible. Senator Robert Dole, the Republican vice presidential nominee in 1976, testified that during the election count,

> We were looking around on the theory that maybe Ohio might turn around because they had an automatic recount.
>
> We were shopping—not shopping, excuse me. Looking around for electors. Some took a look at Missouri, some were looking at Louisiana, some in Mississippi, because their laws are a little bit different. And we might have picked up one or two in Louisiana. There were allegations of fraud maybe in Mississippi, and something else in Missouri.
>
> We needed to pick up three or four after Ohio. So that may happen in any event.
>
> But it just seems to me that the temptation is there for that elector in a very tight race to really negotiate quite a bunch.[28]

In other words, the electoral college created an incentive for candidates to encourage electors to be unfaithful to those who elected them— the American public. On reflection, Dole favored abolishing the electoral college.

THE IMPLICATIONS OF CONTINGENT ELECTIONS

Few Americans have found much commendable in the system of contingent election of the president in the House and the vice president in the Senate. According to Lucius Wilmerding, George Mason and others made it a ground of objection to ratifying the Constitution.[29] James Madison called for a constitutional amendment to alter it: "The present rule of voting for President by the House of Representatives is so great a departure from the Republican principle of numerical equality, and even from the federal rule which qualifies the numerical by a State equality, and is so pregnant also with a mischievous tendency in practice, that an amendment of the Constitution on this point is justly called for by all its considerate and best friends."[30] Madison was correct. The process is fatally flawed.

Violation of Political Equality

In a Senate speech in 1873, Senator Oliver P. Morton of Indiana declared: "The objections to this constitutional provision for the election of a

President need only to be stated, not argued. First, its manifest injustice. In such an election, each state is to have but one vote. Nevada, with its 42,000 population, has an equal vote with New York, having 104 times as great a population. It is a mockery to call such an election just, fair or republican."[31] Morton showed that under the apportionment then in effect, 45 members of the House, drawn from nineteen states, could control an election in a House then consisting of 292 members representing thirty-seven states. The nineteen states with an aggregate population in 1870 of some 8 million people would be able to outvote eighteen states with an aggregate population of 30 million. Morton declared, "the rotten borough system was a mild and very small bagatelle" in comparison.[32]

The potential for distortion of the popular will in the case of an election of a president by the House continues unabated in the twenty-first century. As a result of the 2010 census, for example, which determines the House apportionment through 2020, seven states have only one congressional representative. These 7 House members, representing a total of 5,306,118 citizens, in casting their state's one vote for president, would be able to outvote 179 members of the House from the six largest states with a total population of 126,111,940—twenty-four times as great. In the case of a contingent election in the House, the vote of the single representative from Wyoming, representing only 563,626 people, would count the same as the votes of all 53 representatives from California, representing more than 37 million people!

It is difficult to find anyone who even attempts to justify such gross violations of democratic principles. If the House selects the president, we have an election that begins with the principle of popular voting and ends with a principle that accords some people's votes much more weight than others.

Disenfranchisement of the District of Columbia

Although the Twenty-third Amendment, ratified in 1961, granted the District of Columbia three votes in the electoral college, the District sends neither senators nor representatives to Congress and thus has no votes in contingent elections. Thus the more than a half-million residents of the District of Columbia are disenfranchised in the election of the president of all the American people in a contingent election.

Misrepresentation

In addition to the blatant violation of political equality, contingent elections of the president and vice president are objectionable on other grounds. Representatives and senators are elected for many reasons, but rarely with an eye to their preference for president or vice president. Many districts and states elect congresspersons and senators of one party and vote for the presidential candidate of another. For example, in the election of 2000, Texas elected a majority of Democrats to its House delegation. Yet 59 percent of Texans also voted for George W. Bush for president in that election.[33] Is it sensible to argue that this House delegation accurately represented Texans' views about who should be president? In the same election, pluralities of voters in 86 (20 percent) of the 435 districts voted for a representative of one party and a presidential candidate of the other.[34] Bush won five states (including Texas) that also sent a Democratic majority delegation to the House, while Al Gore won four states with majority Republican House delegations and three states in which the delegation was evenly split.

Executive Independence

One of the framers' principal goals in creating the electoral college was to avoid legislative selection of the president. They feared that if the legislature chose the president, it would undermine the Constitution's carefully crafted separation of powers and make the president too dependent on Congress. In addition, they were concerned about the intrigues that might attend legislative selection of the chief executive. As we have seen in the case of 1825, they had reason to be concerned.

The Power of a Few

In contingent elections, a few individuals can wield extraordinary power in selecting the president. We have seen how a single person, such as Stephen Van Rensselaer, may determine the vote of a crucial state. More important, in the seven states represented by only one member of the House, these representatives can provide 27 percent of the votes needed to elect the president. Other individuals may determine outcomes by not participating and thus preventing a quorum from forming within the House or the Senate.

President and Vice President from Different Parties

Because the Senate can consider only the two vice presidential candidates receiving the most electoral votes, and because each senator has a single vote, it should be easier to select a vice president than a president—unless there is an exact tie! If the House is deadlocked in selecting a president, the Senate might feel that it needed to choose a vice president so that someone would be in office on Inauguration Day. The House might not choose a president of the same party.

In addition, it is possible that the House would select the presidential candidate who finished third in the electoral college balloting as a compromise between the two major contenders. Under this circumstance, the Senate, which is restricted to the top two candidates for vice president, would have no choice but to select a vice president from another party.

A Tie for Third

The Constitution does not explain the procedure if a tie for third place should occur in the electoral balloting for president. Would the House consider just the top two or in reality the top four candidates?

After conducting extensive research on the electoral college, one political scientist noted wryly, "A certain amount of perseverance is needed in order to discover something good to say about the possibility of an election of the President in the House of Representatives."[35] Even as ardent a supporter of the electoral college as Judith Best agrees, writing that it is "hard to find anyone who approves of the current contingency procedure."[36]

The electoral college's provisions for contingent elections of the president and vice president blatantly violate political equality, directly disenfranchise hundreds of thousands of Americans, have the potential to grossly misrepresent the wishes of the public, make the president dependent upon Congress, give a very few individuals extraordinary power to select the president, have the potential to select a president and vice president from different parties, and fail to deal with a tie for third in the electoral college. In addition, any resolution of a congressional choice of the president is likely to be tainted with charges of unsavory transactions.

It is no wonder that even the most stalwart defenders of the electoral college choose to ignore contingent elections in their justifications of the system of electing the president. Yet this is the system, and we have come very close to having to rely on it to resolve a number of elections in recent decades.

Chapter 5 The Origins of the Electoral College

The Constitution's framers chose a unique and complex method of selecting the president, one that clearly violates fundamental tenets of political equality and majority rule. How did they arrive at this decision? Was it an effort to restrain the democratic mob? Was their decision based on a coherent political theory that made subtle trade-offs between political equality and other important values? Can their intentions justify violating majority rule in the twenty-first century?

Arriving at the electoral college was no easy matter. As James Wilson declared near the end of the Constitutional Convention on September 4, "This subject . . . is in truth the most difficult of all on which we have had to decide."[1] Similarly, on December 11, he told the Pennsylvania state ratifying convention that the convention was "perplexed with no part of this plan so much as with the mode of choosing the President of the United States."[2]

How the delegates to the Constitutional Convention resolved the issue is a complex story. They deliberated on the method of selecting the president on twenty-two days and subjected the topic to thirty votes (Table 5.1).[3]

The delegates were obviously perplexed about how to select the president, and their confusion is reflected in their voting. On July 17, for example, the delegates voted for selection of the president by the national legislature. Two days later, they voted for selection by electors chosen by state legislatures. Five days after that, they again voted for selection by the national legislature, a position they rejected the next day and then adopted again the day after that. Then, just when it appeared that the delegates had reached a consensus, they again turned the question over to a committee. This committee changed the convention's course once more and recommended selection of the president by electors chosen by state legislatures, a position the delegates adopted.

Because the electoral college is a peculiar method of selecting a public official, one never employed to select any other federal official, it is quite natural to seek to understand *why* the founders created this mechanism. The explanation is not as straightforward as one might expect, however, at least partly because the electoral college was the subject of little discussion during the ratification debates following the convention.[4] Indeed, the lack of attention to the electoral college led Alexander Hamilton to observe that "the mode of appointment of the chief magistrate of the United States is almost the only part of the system, of any consequence, which has escaped without severe censure."[5]

What considerations drove the framers to create the electoral college? Are these concerns still relevant? If they are, is the electoral college necessary to realize them?

LEGISLATIVE INTRIGUE

Perhaps the most prominent criterion the delegates applied to evaluating schemes for selecting the president was a desire to limit the potential for cabal, intrigue, faction, and corruption in the selection of the chief executive. Although the Constitutional Convention tentatively approved legislative election of the president on four occasions during the summer, there was strong opposition to this plan on the grounds that cabals were more easily organized in the national legislature.[6] Eventually, the framers insisted

Table 5.1
Consideration of Presidential Selection in the Constitutional Convention

Date	Issue or Action
May 29	Virginia Plan includes selection by national legislature.
June 2	Delegates vote 2–7–1 (or 2–8) against electors.
	Delegates vote 8–2 for selection by national legislature.
June 8	Delegates vote 9–2 to reconsider selection by national legislature.
June 9	Delegates vote 0–10–1 (or 0–9–1) against selection by governors.
June 15	New Jersey Plan calls for selection by national legislature.
June 25	Delegates vote 9–2 for selection by state legislatures.
July 17	Delegates vote 1–9 against direct election of president.
	Delegates vote 10–0 for selection of president by national legislature.
July 19	Delegates vote 6–3–1 for selection of president by electors.
	Delegates vote 8–2 for selection of electors by state legislators.
July 23	Delegates vote 7–3 to reconsider selection by electors.
July 24	Delegates vote 7–4 for selection by national legislature.
July 25	Delegates vote 4–7 against selection by national legislature.
July 26	Delegates vote 7–3–0 for selection by national legislature.
August 6	Committee on Detail reports in favor of selection by national legislature.
August 24	Delegates reject 2–9 attempt to change from selection by national legislature to popular vote.
	Delegates vote 4–4–2 on abstract question of selection by electors.
August 31	Delegates cannot decide on choosing the president; assign problem to new Committee of Eleven.
September 4	Committee of Eleven recommends selection by electors chosen by decision of state legislatures.
September 6	Delegates vote 9–2 for selection by electors.
	Delegates change venue of contingent election from Senate to House.
	Delegates vote 8–3 for one vote per state in House contingent elections.
September 7	Delegates approve electoral college plan for selecting president.

Source: Max Farrand, ed., *The Records of the Federal Convention of 1787,* rev. ed., vols. 1, 2 (New Haven: Yale University Press, 1966).

that the electors vote in their own states, further limiting the potential for cabals.[7] According to Hamilton in *Federalist 68,* no corruption could be possible because of the "transient existence" and "detached situation" of the electors.

PRESIDENTIAL INDEPENDENCE

The delegates originally favored Congress selecting the president, and some even wanted the president to be an agent of the legislature.[8] Nevertheless, many delegates worried that a president selected by the legislature would be too dependent on it to exercise independent judgment.[9] (Hamilton feared the reverse—that the president would corrupt the legislature to stay in office.)[10] In the end, the framers were committed to the separation of powers and could not reconcile this principle with legislative selection of the president.

VOTER PAROCHIALISM

The most obvious alternative to selection of the president by the new Congress was election by the nation's citizens. This option faced stern opposition, however.[11] Many delegates held important concerns about a direct election, especially that voters would not be able to make a reasoned and informed choice. They worried that the large distances and lack of communication within the new country made it likely that the typical citizen would not know the leading characters of the country well enough[12] and thus would support only candidates from their states[13] or be misled by a few designing men.[14] If the people voted only for candidates from their states, the big states would have a decided advantage.

Not everyone agreed with this view of voter incapacity and parochialism. Direct election by the people had strong support from some of the leaders at the convention, including James Madison of Virginia and Gouverneur Morris and James Wilson, both of Pennsylvania.[15] John Dickinson, Rufus King, Daniel Carroll, and Abraham Baldwin also supported popular election.[16] Still other delegates argued that the people would know the leading candidates well enough[17] and that the people could not be misled easily by a few men in a large country.[18]

Equally important, the framers did not avoid direct election of the president out of fear of the democratic mob. Slonim argues that "only a few delegates—most notably Mason, Gerry, and Butler—were opposed in principle to direct election of the executive. . . . Antimajoritarianism was by no means the primary motivation behind the creation of the electoral college."[19] Lucius Wilmerding, citing a number of statements by the framers when they were explaining and defending the Constitution after the convention, also argued that their intent was for presidential selection to be based on the wishes of the citizenry. "It is clear," he argues, "that the framers wanted and expected the popular principle to operate in the election of the President."[20]

There is some support for this argument. When Wilson could not convince the delegates to support direct election in June, he proposed that the voters choose electors in districts within the states, and that the electors would then select the president. This, he felt, was the next best thing to direct election.[21] In September the delegates were still considering congressional election of the president. After John Dickinson criticized the idea, James Madison sat down and sketched out the idea of an electoral college.[22]

Madison was foremost in claiming the essentially democratic character of the election procedure. The president, he told the Virginia ratifying convention, "will be the choice of the people at large." It was only because of the difficulties of direct vote in as large a land as America, he indicated, that the indirect system was proposed, but the people would choose the electors.[23] In *Federalist 39*, Madison declared: "The president is indirectly derived from the choice of the people." Wilson told his fellow Pennsylvanians: "The choice of this officer is brought as nearly home to the people as practicable. With the approbation of the state legislatures, the people may elect with only one remove.[24] And Hamilton wrote in *Federalist 68* that the president should be dependent on his continuation in office on none "but the people themselves."

THE NECESSITY OF INTERMEDIARIES

Yet there was a contradiction in the way Madison, Hamilton, and others explained the electoral college system. Although they suggested that the president would be a man of the people and spring almost directly from them, they also suggested either that electors would make independent decisions regarding presidential selection or that the real power would lie in the hands of the state legislatures.

Unfortunately, there seems to have been no debate in the Constitutional Convention on what role electors should play or how state legislatures should select electors. Nevertheless, it appears that most delegates supported the electoral college because they believed that the electors would exercise discretion in selecting the president. Hamilton made the case for the electoral college in *Federalist 68,* where he argued that the mode of selecting the president was at the very least "excellent." A primary reason was that although the people had a role in choosing the president, they would actually exercise influence only indirectly, through a body of "men" chosen for this purpose. These men would "possess the information and discernment" for such an important decision and would be those "most capable of analyzing the qualities" required in a chief executive.

Meeting in the various states, there would be less potential for mischief and less exposure to "heats and ferments"—in other words, *pressure*—from the people, than if they all convened together. The electors would provide protection against "tumult and disorder" by serving as a buffer between the many (the people) and the one (the president). Dispersion would also reduce the potential for "cabal, intrigue, and corruption," including that by foreign powers. Because electors formed a temporary group, it would be more difficult to tamper with them beforehand. In addition, the Constitution excludes government officials, who might be too close to a sitting president, from service as electors. All of these provisions were designed to make the electors "free from any sinister bias."

Hamilton ended his defense of the electoral college and electors' discretion with a sweeping prediction of its primary consequence: "The process of election affords a moral certainty, that the office of President will never fall to the lot of any man who is not in an eminent degree endowed with the requisite qualifications. . . . It will not be too strong to say, that there will be a constant probability of seeing the station filled by characters preeminent for ability and virtue."

John Jay, in *Federalist 64,* echoed Hamilton's views: "As the select assemblies for choosing the President . . . will in general be composed of the most enlightened and respectable citizens, there is reason to presume that their attention and their votes will be directed to those men only who have become the most distinguished by their abilities and virtue."

Hamilton and Jay were great men, but history has not been kind to their prophecies.

Although Wilmerding asserts that the electoral college was equivalent to election by people and that electors were not meant to exercise discretion, there is a great deal of additional evidence that the founders intended the electors to make independent decisions in selecting the president.[25] For example, Constitutional Convention delegate Rufus King observed in 1816 that electors had become rubber stamps, contrary to what the framers had contemplated. A Senate committee report in 1826 concluded that electors had not met their obligations of acting independently as "they were intended to."[26] In his famous *Commentaries on the Constitution* in 1833, Joseph Story reported that the framers intended that electors "would be most likely to possess the information, and discernment, and independence, essential for the proper discharge of the duty."[27]

The Supreme Court has also weighed in on the question of the framers' intentions regarding the role of electors. In *McPherson v. Blacker* (1892), the Court said the framers expected that electors would exercise discretion in their selection of the president.[28] Justice Robert Jackson, in *Ray v. Blair* (1952), wrote that the original electoral college plan was for electors to be free agents and exercise independent judgment in the selection of the president.[29] In *Williams v. Rhodes* (1968), Justice John Harlan wrote that the motivation behind the electoral college was to permit the most knowledgeable people to choose the chief executive because the founders were concerned that citizens would not be informed enough to make the choice themselves.[30]

Some delegates felt that the state legislatures would actually select the president, because they could chose the electors. Madison wrote in *Federalist 45,* "Without the intervention of the state legislatures, the President of the United States cannot be elected at all. They must in all cases have a great share in his appointment, and will perhaps in most cases of themselves determine it." Another future president, James Monroe, opposed ratification of the Constitution, telling the Virginia ratifying convention: "I believe that he [the president] will owe his election, in fact, to the state governments, and not the people at large."[31]

Thus the founders never provided a clear definition of the role of the popular will in the selection of the president, and the best evidence is that the Constitution's framers expected intermediaries, principally electors, but also state legislatures, to play a critical role in selecting the president.

PRESIDENTIAL POWER

Another undertone at the convention among some of the delegates was a fear of executive power. Although the framers sought to make the president independent from the legislature, they were also concerned with balanced government. The overall effort to create a system of separation of powers and checks and balances was motivated by a fear of concentrated power. Leaders of a revolution against a king were not going to create another in the guise of the president. Electing the chief executive of a nation was unknown at the time, so they had little experience to guide them. As a result, some, and perhaps many, delegates feared that direct election of the president would consolidate too much power and influence in one person.[32]

POPULATION DIFFERENCES AMONG STATES

The states' different sizes posed an especially difficult problem for the framers. Some delegates feared that voters in states with larger populations would overwhelm voters in smaller states and by themselves determine the outcome of the election if the president was selected by direct election.[33] Some also feared the power of organized groups like the Cincinnati.[34]

On September 4 the Committee of Eleven reported to the convention the details of its intermediate elector plan, which carried over the Connecticut Compromise, which gave each state two U.S. senators regardless of population, into the presidential election and gave the small states some relative advantage because of the two extra electoral votes each received. According to Madison, the ratio of population of the largest state, Virginia, to the smallest in population, Delaware, was about ten to one. With the electoral college vote distribution, the ratio would be only four to one.[35]

One of the most common statements about the creation of the electoral college is that the apportionment of electors was the result of a compromise between large and small states. The founders did not conceive the electoral college to be a bulwark of small states' rights. If anything, they saw it as favoring large states—or at least the principle of population.[36] On August 24, for example, the small states helped to defeat a proposal to elect the president by a joint ballot in Congress, a proposal that would have given the small states exactly the same relative power they achieved in the electoral college.[37]

The delegates did *not* consider the extra electoral votes for small states significant. The apportionment of votes in the electoral college did reflect the Connecticut Compromise about congressional representation. However, this feature of the electoral college was due more to expediency than to philosophy. At no time after the Committee of Eleven reported was any mention made on the convention floor of the supposed advantage to small states of the senatorial "counterpart" votes. Nor was this apparent concession mentioned in the subsequent ratifying conventions.

What the delegates *did* consider a major concession to the small states was the provision of the presidential selection plan that stipulated that in the event there was no majority in the electoral college, the Senate, where each state would have equal voting power, would choose the president. Although the convention subsequently voted to shift the responsibility for contingent elections to the House of Representatives, it preserved the provision for equality of state voting power.[38]

The key to acceptance of this two-stage plan for presidential selection lay in the different character of electoral college and contingent House voting. The electoral college reflected in a rough way the population of states. When the contingent House procedure went into effect—as the delegates expected it most often would—the voting would be one vote per state delegation, thus representing equally weighed individual states regardless of population. This mechanism was a compromise between the principle of population and that of equal state interest.[39]

The small states also expected to benefit from the provision that the Senate (or later the House), when called on to choose the president, would be required to choose from among the *five* persons who received the largest number of electoral votes. There was a good chance that one or more of the five would be candidates from small states. Similarly, the requirement that electors vote for two candidates, one of whom must be from a different state than the elector, increased the probability of a candidate from a small state being included in the pool of five.

The framers expected that the electors would, in effect, nominate a number of prominent individuals. The delegates believed that many of the presidential electors would vote for men from their own state and region and that diverse state and regional interests would usually prevent any one man from receiving a majority of electoral votes. At times, a George Washington might be the unanimous electoral choice, but, as George Mason of Virginia argued in Philadelphia, nineteen times out of twenty, the electoral college itself would not make the final choice of president. Instead, the House of Representatives, voting by states with one vote per state, would select the president from the top contenders.[40] In *Federalist 66,* Hamilton argues approvingly that it "cannot be doubted" that the House of Representatives "will sometimes, if not frequently" select the president, choosing from "among the most illustrious citizens of the Union."

This conception of the electoral arrangements envisioned a mechanism for the selection of the president somewhat similar to today's national nominating conventions and general election procedure, except in this view the electoral college would serve the nominating function and the House the electing function. This assumption about how the electoral college would work in practice—an assumption that was not to be borne out by events—was implicit in the agreement on the electoral college system.[41] As James Madison later described the electoral college, it was "the result of compromise between the larger and smaller states, giving to the latter the advantage of selecting a President from the candidates, in consideration of the former in selecting the candidates from the people."[42]

At the same time, Madison recognized the challenge House election presented to democratic principles. On September 7, the last day the delegates considered selection of the president, he complained to the convention that House election "was liable to a further weighty objection that the representatives of a *Minority* of the people, might reverse the choice of a *majority* of the *States* and of the *people*" and asked for some cure for this problem.[43]

Later, opposition to the electoral college arose in the Virginia ratifying convention, where it was pointed out that if the election were thrown into the House, the majority could consist of fifteen representatives constituting a majority of the delegations of seven states—outvoting fifty other representatives from the other six states. George Mason contended that the elector system "was a mere deception—a mere *ignis fatuus* on the American people—and thrown out to make them believe they were to choose" the president. "They will, in reality, have no hand in the election," Mason said.[44]

SLAVERY

Madison felt that the "great division of interests in the U.S. . . . did not lie between the large & small States: it lay between the Northern & Southern." The critical interest dividing the North and South, of course, was slavery: "States were divided into different interests not by their difference in size, but by other circumstances; the most material of which resulted partly from climate, but principally from [the effects of] their having or not having slaves."[45]

An earlier compromise allowed states to count three-fifths of the slaves living within them in calculating the basis for their representation in the House of Representatives. However, the slave population would not count with direct election of the president by the people because slaves could not vote. Thus some delegates were concerned that direct election of the president would cause a reduction in the relative influence of the South because of its large nonvoting slave population.[46] As Madison put it, "The people at large was in his opinion the fittest," for choosing the president, but "there was one difficulty, however, of a serious nature attending an immediate choice by the people. The right of suffrage was much more diffusive in the Northern than the Southern States; and the latter could have no influence in the election on the score of the Negroes. The Substitution of electors obviated this difficulty."[47]

The electoral college, then, protected the interests of slaveholders in two ways. First, a state received electoral votes based in part on the number of slaves within it, although the slaves, of course, had no role in the selection of electors. As we saw in Chapter 3, the three-fifths compromise directly influenced the election of the president in 1800. In addition, the expected final selection of the president by the House, with each state receiving one vote, provided the ultimate protection for slaveholders.[48]

SHORT-TERM POLITICS

The Constitutional Convention of 1787 thus created out of disagreement a system with broad, if somewhat artificial, support. "What really moved the delegates to accept the electoral system, with little enthusiasm and no unanimity of conviction, were certain practical considerations, dictated not by political ideals but by the social realities of the time—realities that no longer exist."[49] Among these realities were (1) the pressure on the delegates at the Constitutional Convention to avoid additional conflict, (2) the delegates' fatigue and impatience to leave Philadelphia, and (3) their lack of immediate concern about the operation of the electoral college.

Pressure to Avoid Conflict

The Constitutional Convention, which met in Philadelphia from May 25 to September 17, 1787, was beset with massive tensions and rivalries as it sought to draft a new constitution. With profound differences of opinion existing on such questions as the degree of centralized power for the new federal government, the type of special recognition to accord small states, the division of powers among the different branches of government, and the extent to which sectional interests would be protected, the delegates to the convention found themselves engaged in the most difficult of political negotiations in their attempts to achieve consensus—a task so demanding of their political astuteness as to cause John Dickinson of Delaware to cry out, "Experience must be our guide. Reason may mislead us."[50]

During the summer of 1787, successive crises threatened to destroy the work of the convention as delegates fell to bitter quarreling over regional and large-state–small-state differences. The most profound and dangerous of these conflicts was between large-state and small-state plans for representation in the new congress: proponents of the Virginia Plan, which provided for congressional representation to be based on population, were locked in battle with supporters of the New Jersey Plan, which established equal congressional representation for each state. This deadlock was finally broken on July 16 through acceptance of the Connecticut Plan—the "Great Compromise"—which provided for one house of Congress to be based on population and the other on equality of states.

As the Constitutional Convention moved, in late August, to determine finally the means for selecting the president, there was little wish to see the conflicts and tensions that had plagued the preceding months of the convention renewed. When plans were advanced concerning the selection of the president that seemed likely to renew conflict, the delegates sought alternatives. On August 31 the delegates commissioned a Committee of

Eleven to study various possible methods for the election of the president and to work out a plan on which the delegates could agree. As we have seen, their task was formidable.

As early as June 2 James Wilson had suggested, as a possible compromise, an *intermediate election* plan involving an electoral college, and during the summer this alternative developed as "the second choice of many delegates though it was the first choice of few."[51] When the Committee of Eleven met in the first few days of September, it turned to this compromise in order to avoid further deadlock and conflict.

Fatigue and Impatience

By the time the delegates made their decision regarding the selection of the president, they had been cloistered together in secrecy for nine weeks during a steaming Philadelphia summer. They were hot, tired, and eager to leave Philadelphia. Madison recalled that as the decision on the electoral college "took place in the latter stage of the Session, it was not exempt from a degree of the hurrying influence produced by fatigue and impatience in all such Bodies."[52] As James McHenry put it in his notes on the debates of September 5, "The greatest part of the day spent in desultory conversation on that part of the report respecting the mode of chusing the President—adjourned without coming to a conclusion."[53]

The Washington Factor

As practical men, the delegates sought to put off until a later time what could be postponed and reconsidered later. Thus another reason why the electoral college plan quickly gained support was the belief of most delegates that any problems that might arise in this method of electing the president would not be immediate: everyone knew that George Washington was going to be chosen president no matter what the electoral system. Felix Morley suggests that "without this assured initial unanimity, it is probable that the electoral system would have been more closely scrutinized, with better anticipation of the troubles that lay ahead."[54]

CONTEMPORARY RELEVANCE OF THE FOUNDERS' INTENTIONS

Can the intentions of the framers justify the violation of majority rule in the twenty-first century? Most of the motivations behind the creation of the electoral college are simply irrelevant today and can be easily dismissed. Legislative election is not an option, there is little danger that the president will be too powerful if directly elected, voters have extraordinary access to information on the candidates, there is no justification at all for either electors or state legislatures to exercise discretion in selecting the president, defending the interests of slavery is unthinkable, and the short-term pressures have long dissipated. Those delegates who wanted electors to exercise independent judgment or be selected by state legislatures would soon be disappointed, as we saw in Chapter 2. There is no support—and no justification—today for either option.

Whether it is necessary to employ the electoral college to protect the interests of small states is our next focus. Clearly, however, it is virtually impossible to find anyone who will defend the selection of the president by the House of Representatives, with each state having one vote. Even the most ardent supporters of the electoral college ignore this most blatant violation of democratic principles. It is important to understand that the founders did not expect the states to remain with such unequal populations. Madison, for example, felt that the problem of different percentages of qualified voters in northern and southern states would decrease under the "Republican laws" in the southern states and the more rapid increase in their population.[55] Recent research by Bartholomew Sparrow shows that the Louisiana Purchase and its promotion of yet further continental expansion soon altered the framers' expectations. They did not foresee the combination of a large number of new states and the low populations of many of those states.[56]

The electoral college was *not* the result of a coherent design based on clear political principles but, rather, a complex compromise that reflected the interests of different states and the search for consensus. There was certainly no theory articulated to justify political inequality. Although there was concern about protecting interests within states, especially slavery, the framers were not concerned with designing a system that protected states as states. As Madison forthrightly declared, "The President is to act for the *people* not for *States*."[57] No one rose to disagree. Moreover, the framers wanted to design a strong national government and quickly and overwhelmingly rejected proposals for state governors to select the president.[58] As Martin Diamond put it, "The Electoral College . . . in its genesis and inspiration was not an anti-democratic but an anti-states-rights device, a way of keeping the election from the state politicians and giving it to the people."[59]

When the Committee of Eleven reported the intermediate elector plan to the convention on September 4, Gouverneur Morris, who served on the committee, cited six grounds for the proposal. They were all essentially negative, centering on the dangers of legislative election. The only real advantage Morris could cite for the electoral college was that "the great evil of cabal" could be avoided since the electors would vote at the same time throughout the United States and at a great distance from each other.[60] The framers could not agree on—much less articulate—a view of the appropriate role of the people in selecting the president.

Ultimately, the electoral college was the end result of a process of elimination. As the distinguished historian Jack Rakove put it, "The Electoral College was cobbled together nearly at the last minute and adopted not because the framers believed it would work, but because it was less objectionable than two more obvious alternatives: election of the president by the people or by Congress. . . . It had no positive advantages of its own."[61]

The most basic reason that the founders invented the electoral college was that the Convention was deadlocked on simpler schemes like direct election and choice by Congress, and thus invented a system that could be "sold" in the immediate context of 1787. The chief virtue of the electoral college was that it replicated other compromises the Constitutional Convention had already made: large states were allocated the most electors; the South was allowed to count three-fifths of the slaves toward its electors; and small states received a disproportionate number of electors (replicating the Senate). What did not replicate the rest of the Constitution was the decision on September 6 to accord the smaller states greatly disproportionate power when the House selected the president. In addition, states' rights advocates won the right for the state legislatures to choose electors as they saw fit and proponents of legislative supremacy were perhaps assuaged with the electors as intermediary between the people and the president.

One distinguished commentator on this period, John Roche, puts it pointedly: the electoral college "was merely a jerry-rigged improvisation which has subsequently been endowed with a high theoretical content." "The future," Roche writes, "was left to cope with the problem of what to do with this Rube Goldberg mechanism."[62] Robert Dahl, America's leading student of democracy, seems to have it right when he concludes that the deliberations on selecting the president in the Constitutional Convention suggest a "group of baffled and confused men who finally settle on a solution more out of desperation than confidence."[63]

The defense of the electoral college system's violation of political equality, then, must rest on arguments about how its current operation provides other fundamental benefits, such as protecting federalism or the two-party system. Or the argument can be made that any alternative proposed to the electoral college will have serious defects that outweigh the claimed advantages of change. It is to such questions that we now turn.

Chapter 6 Protecting Interests

One of the core justifications for the electoral college, and for its violations of political equality, is that it is necessary to protect important interests that would be overlooked or harmed under a system of direct election of the president. Advocates argue that allocation of electoral votes by states that then cast their votes as units ensures that presidential candidates will be attentive to and protective of state-based interests, especially the interests of states with small populations. One proponent went so far as to claim that presidential candidates "tour the nation, campaigning in all states and seeking to build a national coalition."[1] Some supporters of the electoral college go further and argue that the electoral college forces candidates to pay greater attention to the interests of racial minorities.

On their face, such claims seem far-fetched. It is no secret, for example, that candidates allocate proportionately more campaign stops and advertisements to competitive and large states (see, for example, Table 1.1).[2] Because these justifications for the electoral

college are so common, however, we must investigate them more systematically. (It is illuminating—and frustrating—that advocates of the electoral college virtually never offer systematic evidence to support their
claims.) How much additional protection do states—especially small states
—require? Do presidential candidates appeal directly to state interests and
give disproportionate attention to small states in their campaigns? Does
the electoral college give minorities special influence in the selection of
the president?

DO STATE INTERESTS REQUIRE PROTECTION?

The argument that one of the major advantages of the electoral college is
that it forces candidates to be more attentive to and protective of state-
based interests, especially the interests of states with small populations, is
based on the premises that (1) states have interests as states; (2) these
interests require protection; (3) interests in states with smaller populations
both require and deserve special protection from federal laws; and (4) candidates focus on state interests, especially those of smaller states.[3]

State Interests

The view that the electoral college protects state interests is based, first, on
the assumption that states embody coherent, unified interests and communities. However, they do not. Even the smallest state has substantial diversity within it. There is not just one point of view within a state. That is why
Alaska may have a Republican governor and a Democratic senator, why
"conservative" states like Montana and North and South Dakota can vote
for Republican presidential candidates and then send liberal Democrats to
the U.S. Senate. California, New York, and Massachusetts, among the
bluest of states, often elect Republican governors.

As the historian Jack Rakove put it, "States have no interest, as states, in
the election of the president; only citizens do." He adds, "The winner-
take-all rule might make sense if states really embodied coherent, unified
interests and communities, but of course they do not. What does Chicago
share with Galena, except that they both are in Illinois; Palo Alto with
Lodi in California; Northern Virginia with Madison's home in Orange
County; or Hamilton, N.Y., with Alexander Hamilton's old haunts in

lower Manhattan?"[4] As an illustration of this point, Table 6.1 shows the substantial ideological differences between pairs of senators of different parties representing the same state in 2005.

Madison, recognizing the diversity within states, was opposed to aggregating the presidential vote by state (as in the unit rule) and hoped that, at the least, votes could be counted by districts within states. Disaggregating the vote and allowing districts within different states to support the same candidate would help encourage cohesiveness within the country and counter the centrifugal tendencies of regionalism.[5] Moreover, Madison did not want candidates to make appeals to special interests. As he proclaimed at the Constitutional Convention, "local considerations must give way to the general interest [even on slavery]. As an individual from the S.[outhern] States, he was willing to make the sacrifice."[6]

Judith Best, perhaps the most diligent defender of the electoral college, recognizes the heterogeneity within states but nevertheless argues that citizens within states share a common interest—managing the resources of a community—that includes roads, parks, schools, local taxes, and the like. True enough. She also argues that these interests are as or more important than the characteristics they share with people in other states like race, gender, religion, and ethnicity.[7] Many women, blacks, Hispanics, farmers, and members of other groups will be surprised to hear that the local roads and parks are more important to their lives than their fundamental position in the economic and social structure of the country.

Equally important, Best makes a series of either logically or empirically incorrect statements about the relation between community interests and the election of the president. First, she confuses local communities with states. Her examples are largely local, not state, issues, and there is a wide variance in the policies of local governments within states.

Second, she argues that the president must be responsive to state interests to win and that candidates must "build the broadest possible coalitions of local interests" to win.[8] No evidence exists to support such assertions, and Best provides none whatsoever. We have already seen that "state interest" is a dubious concept. Best does not offer a single example of such an interest.

Do presidents focus on local interests in building their electoral coalitions? They do not. As we will see, candidates ignore most of the country in their campaigns, and they do not focus on local interests where they do

Table 6.1

Ideological Differences Between Senators Representing the Same State

| State | *National Journal* Ideology Scores, 2005 | | Difference |
	Liberal Score	Conservative Score	
Iowa			64
Charles Grassley, R	25	75	
Tom Harkin, D	89	11	
Nevada			60
Harry Reid, D	78	22	
John Ensign, R	18	82	
Colorado			51
Wayne Allard, R	9	91	
Ken Salazar, D	60	40	
Minnesota			49
Mark Dayton, D	84	17	
Norm Coleman, R	34	66	
Florida			45
Bill Nelson, D	66	34	
Mel Martinez, R	21	79	
South Dakota			45
Tim Johnson, D	74	26	
John Thune, R	29	71	
New Mexico			36
Pete Domenici, R	30	70	
Jeff Bingaman, D	66	34	
Rhode Island			36
Jack Reed, D	95	5	
Lincoln Chafee, R	59	41	
Montana			34
Max Baucus, D	61	39	
Conrad Burns, R	27	73	
Oregon			31
Ron Wyden, D	81	19	
Gordon Smith, R	50	50	
Louisiana			28
Mary Landrieu, D	58	42	
David Vitter, R	31	70	
Indiana			24
Richard Lugar, R	47	53	
Evan Bayh, D	71	29	
Nebraska			19
Chuck Hagel, R	31	69	
Ben Nelson, D	50	50	

campaign. Similarly, nowhere in the vast literature on voting in presidential elections has anyone found that voters choose candidates on the basis of their stands on state and local issues. Indeed, candidates avoid such issues, because they do not want to be seen in the rest of the country as pandering to special interests. In addition, once elected the president has little to do with the issues that Best raises as examples of the shared interests of members of communities. There is no reason, and certainly no imperative, to campaign on these issues.

The Need for Protection

As every student of American politics knows, the Constitution places many constraints on the acts a simple majority can make. Minorities have fundamental rights to organize, communicate, and participate in the political process. The Senate greatly overrepresents small states, and, within that chamber, the extraconstitutional filibuster is a powerful tool for thwarting majorities in the upper chamber. Moreover, simple majorities cannot overcome minority opposition by changing the Constitution.

With these powerful checks on simple majorities already in place, do some minority rights or interests require additional protection from national majorities? If so, are these minorities concentrated in certain geographic areas? (Because it allocates electoral votes on the basis of geography, the electoral college protects only geographically concentrated interests.) Does anything justify awarding interests in certain geographical locations —namely small states—additional protections in the form of extra representation in the electoral system that citizens in other states do not enjoy?[9]

Two of the most important authors of the Constitution, James Wilson and James Madison, understood well the diversity of state interests and the protections of minorities embodied in the Constitution. They saw little need to confer additional power to small states through the electoral college. "Can we forget for whom we are forming a government?" Wilson asked. "Is it for *men,* or for the imaginary beings called *States?*" Madison was equally dubious, proclaiming that experience had shown no danger of state interests being harmed and that "the President is to act for the *people* not for *States.*"[10]

The framers designed Congress, whose members are elected by districts and states, to be responsive to constituency interests. The president, as Madison points out, is to take a broader view. When advocates of the electoral college express concern that direct election of the president would suppress local interests in favor of the broader national interest,[11] or declare approvingly that the electoral college would force George W. Bush to placate the interests of states he carried narrowly in 2000,[12] they are endorsing a presidency responsive to parochial interests in a system that is already prone to gridlock and which offers minority interests extraordinary access to policymakers and opportunities to thwart policies they oppose.

Supporters of the electoral college virtually never specify what geographically concentrated rights or interests require special protection through the electoral system. The primary exception in recent years has been the development of Yucca Mountain in Nevada as a nuclear waste storage site. This is a rare example of a highly concentrated and salient state interest. Nevadans have opposed the project, following the familiar NIMBY (not in my backyard) approach to environmental protection. Supporters of the electoral college argue that it forces candidates to be responsive to local interests. However, George W. Bush, who narrowly carried the state in both 2000 and 2004, *supported* the use of Yucca Mountain as a nuclear waste storage site—exactly the opposite of what electoral college advocates predict. John McCain also supported the project in 2008. The sole exception among major party candidates was Barack Obama. The future president did not adopt his policy for the general election, however. Instead, Senate Majority Leader Harry M. Reid of Nevada, a staunch opponent of the Yucca Mountain site and someone the founders would expect to be defending state interests, helped extract campaign promises from both Obama and then-Senator Hillary Rodham Clinton during the closely contested 2008 Democratic presidential primary in Nevada.[13]

Thus supporters of the electoral college cannot identify geographically concentrated rights or interests that require special protection through the electoral system or that receive it from the electoral college. They also certainly have not developed a general principle to justify additional protections for some interests rather than others. Nevertheless, we can do our own analysis of the distribution of interests in the United States.

The Interests of Small States

Do states with small populations, those that receive special consideration in the electoral college, have common interests to protect? In the Constitutional Convention, Madison pointed out that it was not necessary to protect small states from large ones, because the large ones—Virginia, Massachusetts, and Pennsylvania—were divided by economic interests, religion, and other circumstances. Their size was not a common interest. Indeed, rivalry was more likely than coalition.[14] States were thus divided into different interests not by their size but by other circumstances. Madison was prescient. The great political battles of American history—in Congress or in presidential elections—have been fought by opposing ideological and economic interests, not by small states versus large states.

A brief look at the seventeen states that have the fewest electoral votes (three, four, or five), plus the District of Columbia, which has three electoral votes, shows that this group is quite diverse. Maine, Vermont, New Hampshire, and Rhode Island are in New England; Delaware, the District of Columbia, and West Virginia are in the Middle Atlantic region; North and South Dakota, Montana, and Nebraska are in the Great Plains; New Mexico is in the Southwest; and Nevada, Wyoming, Utah, and Idaho are in the Rocky Mountain region. Alaska and Hawaii are regions unto themselves.

Some of these states have high average levels of income and education, while others have considerably lower levels. Some of the states are quite liberal while others are very conservative, and their policies and levels of taxation reflect these differences. Several of these states are primarily urban, while many others are rural. They represent a great diversity of core economic interests, including agriculture, mining, gambling, chemicals, tourism, and energy. Even the agricultural interests are quite diverse, ranging from grain and dairy products to hogs and sheep. In sum, small states do not share common interests. It is not surprising that their representatives do not vote as a bloc in Congress or that their citizens do not vote as a bloc for president.

Even if small states share little in common, are there some interests that occur only in states with small populations? The first interest that may come to mind is agriculture, with visions of rural farmers in small states. But most farmers live in states with large populations, such as California, Texas, Florida, and Illinois. Low-population states on the Great Plains may have a larger percentage of its population working in agriculture, but there are actually more farmers in states with large populations. The market value of the agricultural production of California, Texas, Florida, and Illinois exceeds that of all seventeen of the smallest states combined.[15]

Moreover, agriculture is a widespread enterprise in the United States and does not lack for powerful champions, especially in Congress, which has taken the lead in providing benefits, principally in the form of subsidies, for agriculture. Rather than competing to give farmers more benefits, presidents of both parties have attempted to restrain congressional spending on agriculture. The electoral college has not turned presidents into champions of rural America.

In addition, the idealized vision of rural America as a series of small, remote towns and family farms is no longer accurate. Over the past half-century, the geographic and social distinctions between urban and rural life have greatly blurred. Today, farms are home to only 3 million people—about 1 percent of the national population and 5 percent of the rural population. Farming employs less than 6 percent of nonmetropolitan workers. Among the households that still live on farms, at least 80 percent of their income comes from activities other than farming. Manufacturing employs a larger proportion of the rural labor force than the urban labor force.[16]

It is difficult to identify interests that are centered in a few small states. Even if we could, however, the question remains whether these few interests, out of the literally thousands of economic interests in the United States, deserve special protection. What principle would support such a view? Why should those who produce wheat and hogs have more say in electing the president than those who produce vegetables, citrus, and beef? Is not the disproportionate representation of states in which wheat and hogs are produced in the Senate enough to protect these interests? There is simply no evidence that interests like these deserve or require additional protection from the electoral system.

ATTENTION TO STATE INTERESTS

As we have seen, a core justification for the electoral college and its violations of political equality is that allocating electoral votes by states forces candidates to pay attention to state-based interests in general and to the interests of small states in particular. In their enthusiasm for the electoral college, some advocates go further and claim that under the electoral college "all states are 'battlegrounds' " in the presidential election and that candidates "rarely" write off regions in the presidential campaign.[17]

Although defenders of the electoral college almost never specify just what interests the electoral college is protecting, they nevertheless argue that candidates would ignore these interests if the president were elected in a direct popular election. They base this argument on the premise, among others, that candidates do appeal directly to state interests and give disproportionate attention to small states.

Do presidential candidates in fact focus on state-level interests in their campaigns? Do they devote a larger percentage of their campaign efforts to small states than they would if there were direct election of the president? To answer these questions, we need to see what candidates actually do and whether there is evidence that the electoral college forces candidates to be more attentive to small states. If candidates are not more oriented to small states and the interests within them than we would expect in a system of direct election, then we have reason to reject one of the principal justifications for the electoral college's violation of political equality.

Candidate Speeches

A prominent means by which a candidate can attend to the interests in a state is by addressing them in speeches to that state's voters. What do candidates actually say when they campaign in the various states? The presidential election of 2000 provides an excellent test of the hypothesis that the electoral college forces candidates to focus on state-based interests. Because the outcome in every single state was crucial to an electoral college victory in this extraordinarily close election, each candidate had the maximum incentive to appeal to state interests.

A team of researchers led by Shanto Iyengar at the Political Communication Lab at Stanford University compiled, read, and classified by broad topics public speeches delivered by George W. Bush and Al Gore from June 1 until October 7, 2000. This period covers the bulk of the 2000 presidential election. In some instances, the Stanford researchers coded two or three topics for the same speech.[18]

The candidates provided the speeches to Iyengar and his colleagues. The speeches do not necessarily represent a statistical sample, but they represent a much larger percentage of the total speeches than would a sample. Most important, they give us the best view of what candidates actually say on the stump.

My research assistants and I then coded the speeches by such issue areas as the economy, crime, and the environment to allow for finer delineations of the subject matter. We further coded each speech as focused on interests

Table 6.2
Focus of Candidate Speeches, 2000

	Candidate Speeches			
	Al Gore		George W. Bush	
Focus	# of Speeches	% of Speeches	# of Speeches	% of Speeches
Small state	1	2	0	0
Large state	1	2	7	18
National	49	96	33	82

Source: In Their Own Words: Sourcebook for the 2000 Presidential Election, © 2000 by The Board of Trustees of Leland Stanford Junior University and http: //pcl.stanford.edu/campaigns/ 2000/sourcebook/index.html.

concentrated in an individual state or on a national constituency. For example, we coded a speech on salmon conservation as aimed at a local rather than a national constituency. Because we wanted to bias our results *against* a national focus, we were generous in our attributions of focus on state interests. Thus when the candidates spoke about Social Security or Medicare prescription drug benefits in Florida, we coded the speech as aimed at an interest concentrated in a state—even though there is clearly a national constituency for Social Security, health care, and related issues of special interests to seniors.

The results are instructive (Table 6.2). Only two of the fifty-one speeches by Al Gore focused on interests concentrated in a state. One was in Tallahassee, Florida, and discussed a prescription drug plan for senior citizens. The other speech, and the only one in a small state (Iowa), discussed reform of the estate tax. Gore also gave a speech in Tennessee that focused on his upbringing there. He did not discuss issues, however, and made no appeal to interests concentrated in that state. Similarly, in a speech in Arkansas he focused on the importance of that state to the election outcome but did not address Arkansas-specific issues.

George W. Bush delivered no speeches that focused on the special interests of small states during this period. The closest he came was a speech in Monroe, Washington, on salmon recovery and environmental protection on September 13. Washington had eleven electoral votes in 2000; only fourteen states had more.

The other six state-oriented speeches Bush delivered were in Florida and focused on Social Security, health care for seniors, and cooperation and trade with Latin America. Florida is the fourth-largest state, hardly one requiring special protection by the electoral college. In addition, it is highly likely that a candidate would address Social Security and health care for seniors under any mechanism for electing the president. These issues are simply too important to ignore, especially given the graying of the entire nation's population. Florida simply provided a symbolically useful venue for Bush's speeches.

Was the presidential election of 2000 unique in the focus of the candidates' speeches? Apparently not. The Annenberg School for Communication and the Annenberg Public Policy Center of the University of Pennsylvania collected transcripts of 102 speeches given by Bill Clinton and 71 speeches given by Robert Dole during the period of September 1 until election day in 1996.[19] Only two of Clinton's speeches and none of Dole's focused on issues that could be viewed as being of primarily local interest. On October 14, Clinton made a 600-word speech on firefighting to firefighters in New Mexico, emphasizing the importance of the issue to the West. This was in effect a brief bill-signing ceremony. The next day he made a 445-word speech to Native Americans in the same state that was almost completely symbolic. These two speeches together probably lasted about five minutes.

Whether or not advocates of the electoral college choose to recognize it, there are actually few interests concentrated within particular states. In addition, whatever state interests there may be, the candidates do not focus on them. They certainly do not devote attention to interests concentrated in small states. In other words, the fundamental justification of the electoral college—that it forces candidates to be attentive to particular state interests, especially those concentrated in small states—is based on a faulty premise.

Contributing to the lack of candidate pandering to state interests is that they largely ignore many of the states.

Candidate Campaign Appearances

The most straightforward means of appealing to voters is for candidates to visit their states and address them directly. Modern transportation has made it relatively easy for candidates to crisscross the nation in search of votes. Proponents of the electoral college argue that one of its principal advantages is that it forces candidates to pay attention to small states that would otherwise be lost in a national electorate and to build a broad national coalition by appealing to voters in every region.

What do candidates actually do? The election of 2000 was one of the most competitive in history, providing strong incentives to leave no stone unturned during the campaign. Every single electoral vote counted. If candidates did not campaign broadly across the country in such an election, it is unlikely they would do so in any election.

Daron Shaw tabulated the campaign appearances of presidential and vice presidential candidates in each state during the presidential general election of 2000, covering the period of August 24 to November 6, 2000 (Table 6.3).

None of the seven states with only three electoral votes received a visit from a presidential candidate in this election. There were also no campaign appearances in Washington, DC. Six states had four electoral votes each, and they received a total of seven appearances by presidential candidates of both parties—including vacation visits of George W. Bush to Maine. Four more states had five electoral votes each, and two of them had no visits from presidential candidates. New Mexico and West Virginia, highly competitive states, were the exceptions. In sum, presidential candidates did not visit thirteen of the seventeen smallest states at all. One candidate only paid a visit to one other state.

Among the eleven states with six, seven, or eight electoral votes, Arkansas, Iowa, Oregon, and Kentucky were highly competitive, and presidential candidates made multiple appearances in them. The presidential candidates visited only one of the other seven states with six, seven, or eight electoral votes, however—a single visit to Arizona. Thus, nineteen of the twenty-eight smallest states had no visits from presidential candidates. Two others had a single appearance from the candidate of only one party.

Vice presidential candidate visits tell a similar story. Dick Cheney and Joe Lieberman made twenty-seven campaign appearances in the seventeen smallest states and only two in the seven smallest. They did not appear at all in eleven of these states or Washington, DC. No presidential or vice presidential candidate of either party made a campaign appearance in eleven of the seventeen smallest states or Washington, DC.

In addition to its failure to encourage candidate visits to small states, the

Table 6.3
Candidate Campaign Appearances in States, 2000 Election

State	Electoral Votes (2000)	Candidate Campaign Appearances		
		Presidential Candidates	Vice Presidential Candidates	Total
Wyoming	3	0	0	0
Alaska	3	0	0	0
Vermont	3	0	0	0
District of Columbia	3	0	0	0
North Dakota	3	0	0	0
Delaware	3	0	2	2
South Dakota	3	0	0	0
Montana	3	0	0	0
Rhode Island	4	0	0	0
Idaho	4	0	0	0
Hawaii	4	0	0	0
New Hampshire	4	3	4	7
Nevada	4	1	5	6
Maine	4	3	6	9
New Mexico	5	6	8	14
Nebraska	5	0	0	0
Utah	5	0	0	0
West Virginia	5	3	2	5
Arkansas	6	4	7	11
Kansas	6	0	0	0
Mississippi	7	0	0	0
Iowa	7	17	7	24
Oregon	7	7	9	16
Oklahoma	8	0	0	0
Connecticut	8	0	0	0
Colorado	8	0	1	1
South Carolina	8	0	0	0
Arizona	8	1	0	1
Kentucky	8	3	7	10
Alabama	9	0	0	0
Louisiana	9	5	3	8
Minnesota	10	1	4	5

Table 6.3

Continued

| | | Candidate Campaign Appearances | | |
State	Electoral Votes (2000)	Presidential Candidates	Vice Presidential Candidates	Total
Maryland	10	0	0	0
Washington	11	9	9	18
Tennessee	11	11	7	18
Wisconsin	11	16	15	31
Missouri	11	18	12	30
Indiana	12	0	0	0
Massachusetts	12	0	0	0
Virginia	13	0	0	0
Georgia	13	2	1	3
North Carolina	14	3	1	4
New Jersey	15	2	4	6
Michigan	18	26	13	39
Ohio	21	12	15	27
Illinois	22	17	12	29
Pennsylvania	23	20	16	36
Florida	25	23	24	47
Texas	32	0	0	0
New York	33	0	0	0
California	54	20	14	34

Source: Daron R. Shaw, *The Race to 270* (Chicago: University of Chicago Press, 2006), 86–87.

electoral college also provides incentives to ignore many larger states. For example, presidential candidates made only eight campaign appearances in the nine medium-sized states of Alabama, Minnesota, Maryland, Indiana, Massachusetts, Virginia, Georgia, North Carolina, and New Jersey—counting for 108 electoral votes. In 2000 candidates even completely ignored very large states like New York and Texas.

As usually happens, the electoral college distorted the political process by providing an incentive to visit *competitive* states, especially large competitive states. In addition, presidential candidates made twenty-three campaign appearances in New Mexico and Iowa, with a total of twelve electoral votes. This was only one fewer appearance than they made in the other twenty-six of the twenty-eight smallest states combined. The candidates also made more visits in New Mexico and Iowa than in Texas, New York, and Ohio combined.

Moreover, the candidates did not take their campaigns to voters of every region of the country. After carefully studying candidate visits in the 2000 presidential election, Michael Hagen, Richard Johnston, and Kathleen Hall Jamieson concluded that "the candidates made little effort to appear before the residents of the Great Plains, the Rockies, the Southwest (with the exception of New Mexico), and the Deep South." The candidates ignored even the big cities in these regions, among them Atlanta, Phoenix, Denver, Charlotte, Salt Lake City, and Birmingham.[20]

In the presidential election of 2000, one of the most competitive elections in history, the electoral college distorted the political system by providing incentives for candidates to campaign actively in only fifteen "battleground" states and largely to ignore the other thirty-five states and Washington, DC. No presidential candidate made a campaign appearance in half the states and Washington, DC. Three other states experienced only a single appearance, while candidates made a total of two or three appearances in seven other states. With few exceptions, small states were not included among the battleground states. Indeed, the *National Journal* reported there were no presidential candidate visits at all to fourteen states, all with eight or fewer electoral votes, over the more than seven months from April 1 through November 7, 2000.[21]

Was 2000 a deviant election? The most competitive election preceding 2000 was that of 1976, when President Gerald Ford faced Democratic challenger Jimmy Carter.[22] The number of candidate campaign stops for each state and the number of electoral votes those states had in that election appear in Table 6.4. It is important to note that these data are for campaign "stops" rather than state visits, so two or more campaign stops can be made in the visit to one state on one day. It is also important to note that the dates for each candidate's campaign stops do not completely overlap. Nevertheless, these data do provide a reasonably accurate picture of the attention candidates devoted to different states.

The results are much like those for the 2000 election. The candidates ignored many states, especially small states. President Gerald Ford, locked in an extremely tight race with Jimmy Carter, visited only four of the twenty-five smallest states between September 15 and October 31. He visited none of the nineteen smallest states during that period. Competitive states received the lion's share of candidate visits. All four candidates made a combined total of only twenty-five campaign stops in the fifteen smallest states (those with 3 or 4 electoral votes). They made more campaign stops in *each* of the large states of Ohio (38), Illinois (37), Pennsylvania (27), New York (42), and California (43) than in the smallest fifteen states combined. The candidates made another thirty-five campaign stops in Florida and Texas. Small and midsize states that were exceptions to the general trend of campaign stops were either the homes of one of the candidates (Kansas, Minnesota, and Georgia) or highly competitive, such as New Mexico, Oregon, Iowa, and Missouri.[23]

Candidates' emphasis on campaigning in competitive states is not unusual. Stanley Kelley found that in 1960 John Kennedy and Richard Nixon spent 74 percent of their campaign time in twenty-four competitive states.[24] Daron Shaw identified similar patterns to 1976 and 2000 in the elections of 1988, 1992, and 1996.[25] Examining the Annenberg collection of presidential speeches discussed earlier reveals that in 1996 Bill Clinton visited only five of the seventeen smallest states. In all, he did not visit nineteen of the fifty states. Bob Dole visited only three of the seventeen smallest states—and also ignored those with six or seven electoral votes. In all, he visited only twenty-one of the fifty states.[26]

What about more recent elections? In the 2004 general election, no presidential candidate visited any of the seven states with only three electoral votes, and the only visit from a vice presidential candidate came when Dick Cheney went to his home state of Wyoming. Presidential candidates did not visit twelve of the seventeen smallest states, nor did vice presidential candidates visit ten of them.[27]

Candidates also ignored the three states with 6 electoral votes in 2004, except for a single vice presidential candidate visit to Arkansas. Indeed, presidential candidates appeared at campaign events in only nine of the twenty-nine smallest states during the entire general election campaign. In two of these nine states, only one candidate visited, making a single visit in each case. The presidential candidates also avoided eight of the thirteen states with 10–15 electoral votes.

On the other hand, the candidates lavished attention on the thirteen competitive states: New Hampshire, West Virginia, New Mexico, Nevada,

Table 6.4
Campaign Stops by Candidates in States, 1976 Election

| State | Electoral Votes (1976) | Candidate Campaign Appearances | | Total |
		Presidential Candidates[a]	Vice Presidential Candidates[b]	
Alaska	3	0	0	0
Wyoming	3	0	0	0
Vermont	3	0	1	1
Nevada	3	0	2	2
Delaware	3	0	1	1
North Dakota	3	1	1	2
South Dakota	4	1	1	2
Montana	4	1	2	3
Idaho	4	0	0	0
New Hampshire	4	0	2	2
Hawaii	4	0	0	0
Rhode Island	4	0	2	2
Maine	4	1	3	4
New Mexico	4	1	3	4
Utah	4	1	1	2
Nebraska	5	0	5	5
West Virginia	6	0	1	1
Arizona	6	1	0	1
Arkansas	6	0	1	1
Oregon	6	2	4	6
Colorado	7	1	4	5
Mississippi	7	5	1	6
Kansas	7	0	9[c]	9
Oklahoma	8	3	2	5
South Carolina	8	3	4	7
Iowa	8	3	9	12
Connecticut	8	2	4	6
Kentucky	9	0	1	1
Washington	9	1	4	5
Alabama	9	2	1	3
Louisiana	10	6	6	12
Minnesota	10	2	5[d]	7

Table 6.4

Continued

State	Electoral Votes (1976)	Candidate Campaign Appearances		
		Presidential Candidates[a]	Vice Presidential Candidates[b]	Total
Maryland	10	1	3	4
Tennessee	10	1	2	3
Wisconsin	11	4	11	15
Georgia	12	11[e]	3	14
Virginia	12	5	5	10
Missouri	12	5	14	19
North Carolina	13	2	5	7
Indiana	13	5	8	13
Massachusetts	14	1	1	2
Florida	17	6	10	16
New Jersey	15	4	7	11
Michigan	21	5	8	13
Ohio	25	11	27	38
Illinois	26	18	19	37
Texas	26	9	10	19
Pennsylvania	27	12	15	27
New York	41	21	21	42
California	45	22	21	43

Source: U.S. Senate, *The Electoral College and Direct Election: Hearings Before the Subcommittee on the Constitution of the Committee on the Judiciary, Suppl.,* 95th Cong., 1st sess., July 20, 22, 28, August 2, 1977, exhibit no. 9, *Candidate Stops Along Campaign Trail—1976,* 29.
[a]September 15–October 31 for Gerald Ford, September 1–November 2 for Jimmy Carter.
[b]August 20–November 2 for Robert Dole, August 15–November 2 for Walter Mondale.
[c]Eight of the nine visits are for Robert Dole, who lived in Kansas.
[d]Four of the visits are for Walter Mondale, who lived in Minnesota.
[e]All of the visits are for Jimmy Carter, who lived in Georgia.

Iowa, Colorado, Minnesota, Wisconsin, Missouri, Michigan, Ohio, Pennsylvania, and Florida.

The total number of campaign visits to the highly populated states of California, Texas, New York, and Illinois for both parties' presidential and vice presidential candidates was two. One of these visits was a home-state rally for George W. Bush in Texas on the last night of the campaign. New Mexico and Iowa, with a total of only 12 electoral votes, received as many visits as the other thirty of the smallest thirty-two states combined. They also received more visits than California, Texas, New York, Illinois, Michigan, and New Jersey combined.

We saw in Chapter 1 that campaigning during the 2008 general election followed the same pattern. Both presidential candidates personally campaigned in only five of the twenty-nine smallest states. In all, Barack Obama campaigned in only fourteen states and John McCain went to only nineteen states.

It is clear that, contrary to the arguments of its proponents, the electoral college does *not* provide an incentive for candidates to be attentive to small states and take their cases directly to their citizens. It also does not force candidates to build coalitions across the country. Indeed, it is difficult to imagine how presidential candidates could be less attentive to small states. Candidates are not fools. They go where the electoral college makes them go, and it provides strong incentives to focus on competitive states, especially large competitive states. They ignore most small states; in fact, they ignore most of the country.

In a 1979 Senate speech, Republican Senator Henry Bellmon of Oklahoma described how his views on the electoral college had changed as a result of serving as national campaign director for Richard Nixon and as a member of the American Bar Association's commission studying electoral reform. "While the consideration of the electoral college began—and I am a little embarrassed to admit this—I was convinced, as are many residents of smaller States, that the present system is a considerable advantage to less populous States such as Oklahoma. . . . As the deliberations of the American Bar Association Commission proceeded and as more facts became known, I came to the realization that the present electoral system does not give an advantage to the voters from the less populous States. Rather, it works to the disadvantage of small State voters who are largely ignored in the general election for President."[28]

Candidate Advertising

Candidates most typically reach voters through television advertising. Technology makes it easy to place advertisements in any media market in the nation at short notice. Do candidates operating under the electoral college system compensate for their lack of visits by advertising in small or noncompetitive states?

In the hotly contested presidential election of 2000, advertising expenditures in each state closely resembled the number of candidate appearances in that state. Some voters were bombarded with television advertising; others saw none at all. Hagen, Johnston, and Jamieson found that Americans living west of Kansas City and east of Las Vegas, with the exception of those living in New Mexico, saw virtually no presidential campaign advertising, and Americans from Natchez to Richmond saw very little. The states receiving the most advertising were the large, competitive states of Florida, Pennsylvania, Michigan, and Ohio.[29]

Table 6.5 shows the large media markets and states in which the two major-party campaigns ran no or only a few ads during the general election period (beginning on August 17, 2000, the day after the Democratic National Convention).[30] The candidates and their parties ran no ads at all in twenty-five of the seventy-five largest media markets in the country. In another ten, their advertising campaigns were purely symbolic, sometimes numbering in single digits. (An ad counts as one if it is run one time. To provide perspective on the small number of ads in these ten states, it is useful to note that the candidates ran 28,635 ads in Florida, 28,099 in Ohio, 24,282 in Michigan, 16,740 in Wisconsin, and 14,838 in West Virginia.)

The candidates thus ignored thirty-five—almost half—of the seventy-five largest media markets in the nation in their advertising in a hotly contested campaign. In doing so, they bypassed such major American cities as Phoenix, Denver, Indianapolis, Washington, Baltimore, New York, Charlotte, Houston, and Dallas–Fort Worth. The Gore campaign also bypassed Los Angeles, San Francisco, and San Diego. Apparently, neither the candidates nor their respective parties or allied interest groups spent any money whatsoever advertising on television in Texas or New York.[31]

The candidates advertised in only four of the thirteen smallest states (Delaware, New Hampshire, Nevada, and Maine) and also ignored Washington, DC. Of the next fifteen smallest states, both candidates advertised in only five and only Al Gore advertised in Kentucky. Thus the candidates presented no advertisements on their behalf to the citizens of two-thirds of the twenty-eight smallest states and Washington, DC.

Table 6.5

Distribution of Ads in States and Large Media Markets During the Presidential General Election of 2000

State	Major Media Market with Few or No Ads	States with Few or No Ads in Any Media Market[a]	Campaign Not Running Ads
Alabama	Birmingham–Anniston–Tuscaloosa		Bush and Gore
Alaska		entire state	Bush and Gore
Arizona	Phoenix	entire state	Bush and Gore
Arkansas			Gore
California			
	Fresno–Visalia[b]		
	Los Angeles		Gore
	Sacramento–Stockton–Modesto		Gore
	San Diego		Gore
	San Francisco–Oakland–San Jose		Gore
Colorado	Denver[c]	entire state	Bush and Gore
Connecticut	Hartford–New Haven[d]	entire state	Bush and Gore
Delaware			
District of Columbia		entire District	Bush and Gore
Florida			
Georgia	Atlanta[e]	entire state	Bush and Gore
Hawaii		entire state	Bush and Gore
Idaho		entire state	Bush and Gore

State	Media market	Scope	Candidates
Illinois			
Indiana	Indianapolis	entire state	Bush and Gore
Iowa			
Kansas	Wichita–Hutchinson	entire state	Bush and Gore
Kentucky	Lexington		Gore
Louisiana			
Maine			
Maryland	Baltimore		Bush and Gore
Massachusetts			
Michigan			
Minnesota			
Mississippi		entire state	Bush and Gore
Missouri			
Montana		entire state	Bush and Gore
Nebraska	Omaha^f	entire state	Bush and Gore
Nevada			
New Hampshire			
New Jersey		entire state	Bush and Gore
New Mexico			
New York	New York City	entire state	Bush and Gore
	Rochester		Bush and Gore
	Albany–Schenectady–Troy		Bush and Gore
	Buffalo		Bush and Gore
	Syracuse		Bush and Gore

(continued)

Table 6.5
Continued

State	Major Media Market with Few or No Ads	States with Few or No Ads in Any Media Market[a]	Campaign Not Running Ads
North Carolina	Charlotte[g]	entire state	Bush and Gore
	Greensboro–High Point–Winston Salem[h]		Bush and Gore
			Bush and Gore
	Raleigh–Durham[i]		Bush and Gore
North Dakota		entire state	
Ohio			Bush and Gore
Oklahoma	Oklahoma City[j]	entire state	Bush and Gore
	Tulsa		Bush and Gore
Oregon			
Pennsylvania			
Rhode Island	Providence–New Bedford[k]	entire state	Bush and Gore
South Carolina	Greenville–Spartanburg–Asheville–Anderson	entire state	Bush and Gore
South Dakota		entire state	Bush and Gore
Tennessee			
Texas	Austin	entire state	Bush and Gore
	Dallas–Fort Worth		Bush and Gore
	Houston		Bush and Gore
	San Antonio		Bush and Gore
Utah	Salt Lake City	entire state	Bush and Gore

State	Market		
Vermont		entire state[l]	Bush and Gore
Virginia	Norfolk–Portsmouth–Newport News	entire state	Bush and Gore
	Richmond–Petersburg		Bush and Gore
	Roanoke–Lynchburg		Bush and Gore
Washington			
West Virginia			
Wisconsin			
Wyoming		entire state	Bush and Gore

Sources: Michael Hagen, Richard Johnston, and Kathleen Hall Jamieson, "Effects of the 2000 Presidential Campaign," paper delivered at the Annual Meeting of the American Political Science Association, August 29–September 1, 2002; Daron Shaw, *The Race to 270* (Chicago: University of Chicago Press, 2007), chapter 4; Kenneth Goldstein, Michael Franz, and Travis Ridout, *Political Advertising in 2000* (Combined File [dataset], Department of Political Science, University of Wisconsin–Madison and Brennan Center for Justice at New York University, 2002).

[a]Market centered in that state.

[b]1 Gore ad.

[c]8 Gore ads.

[d]230 Bush ads and 82 Gore ads.

[e]217 Bush ads.

[f]218 Bush ads and 148 Gore ads.

[g]131 Bush ads.

[h]196 Bush ads.

[i]191 Bush ads.

[j]5 Bush ads.

[k]23 Gore ads.

[l]A very few ads were run, aimed at New Hampshire.

In some states, the campaigns ran few or no ads (see Table 6.5, third column). In most instances, we can interpret these in a straightforward manner. However, some media markets cross state boundaries, and ads placed in a market centered in one state may spill over into the living rooms of citizens of another state. Iowa ads, for example, spilled over to Nebraska, South Dakota, and Illinois; Missouri ads spilled over into Kansas, Oklahoma, Illinois, Kentucky, and Tennessee.

Usually the spillover reached only a small percentage of the population. But there are some examples of citizens of a state having access to ads even though none were placed in a media market in that state. In New Jersey, which is sandwiched between two large media markets, New York and Philadelphia, most residents saw no ads at all. However, about 25 percent of the population was saturated with them as a result of ads placed in the Philadelphia media market aimed at winning competitive Pennsylvania.

In contrast, some media markets are credited with ads actually aimed at the citizens of another state. Some media markets centered outside competitive states provided the avenues into competitive states. Ads had to be run in the Boston and Vermont markets to reach New Hampshire—even though the candidates were not actively campaigning in those states. Candidates reached the Florida panhandle through Mobile, Alabama.[32]

We must interpret the data on little or no media advertising with care. Even so, the story of advertising in the 2000 presidential election is clear. People in a large percentage of the country saw little or no advertising on behalf of the presidential candidates, since the candidates essentially ignored twenty-six states and the District of Columbia. Thus, just as in the case of candidate visits, we find that the premises that the electoral college forces candidates to take their cases to small states and to build coalitions from all regions of the country are erroneous. To win candidates' attention, states must be "in play" and have a significant number of electoral votes. As a result, the electoral college encourages campaigns largely to ignore most people in the nation.

Focusing advertising on competitive states is nothing new. Hubert Humphrey, the 1968 Democratic presidential candidate, told the Senate Judiciary Committee in 1977 that campaigns are directed disproportionately at large states: "We had to ignore large sections of the country." Douglas Bailey, who headed the advertising firm that handled Gerald Ford's 1976 campaign, added that "those areas that you are sure to win or lose, you ignore."[33] Daron Shaw shows similar patterns for 1988–2004.[34]

In 2004, in the period between September 26 and November 2, the heart of the campaign, 73 percent of all the spending on advertising occurred in five states: Florida, Ohio, Pennsylvania, Wisconsin, and Iowa. Indeed, more money was spent in Florida than in the other forty-five states and Washington, DC, combined.[35] There was a similar pattern in 2008. More than 98 percent of the advertising spending between September 24 and election day occurred in fifteen states, representing about a third of the nation's population. Fifty-five percent of the advertising budget focused on only four states (Florida, Pennsylvania, Ohio, and Virginia).[36]

In sum, the electoral college not only discourages candidates from paying attention to small states, it also distorts the presidential campaign, causing candidates to ignore most of the country. In theory, candidates make their cases to the people, and citizens then choose for whom to vote. In reality, candidates under the electoral college do *not* take their cases to the people.

PRESIDENTIAL PRIMARIES

Candidates campaign in many states during the presidential primaries and caucuses. Are these efforts dependent on the electoral college? Does the electoral college cause states to hold primaries and thus attract candidate attention? Clearly not. The current primary system is unrelated to the electoral college. Under it, we have had a range of systems for nominating presidential candidates, including no primaries at all, a few primaries, and our current system, which is heavily dependent on primaries. Not only is the primary system unrelated to the electoral college, but direct election of the president would be compatible with exactly the primary system we have now and would not diminish whatever benefits it offers.

Has the increase in presidential primaries caused candidates to avoid most states in the general election, knowing they had campaigned in them during the primary season? Again, the answer is no. Party nominees ignored most states in the presidential election before the current period of numerous primaries. In addition, campaigning in primaries, often nearly a year before the general election, is no substitute for campaigning during the general election period. In primaries, the focus is on differentiating *within* parties, while the focus in the general election is on the more important differences between parties.

The fundamental justification of the electoral college—that it forces candidates to be attentive to particular state interests, especially those concentrated in small states—is based on a faulty premise. In reality, the electoral college discourages candidates from paying attention to small states and to much of the rest of the country, as well. In 2004 neither George W. Bush nor John Kerry ran a single national television advertisement. In 2008, when the advertising budgets, especially for Barack Obama, were larger, far less than 1 percent of the candidates' ads were national.[37] When winning an increment of votes in most states does not matter, candidates do not waste money reaching the public in them.

THE INTERESTS OF AFRICAN AMERICANS AND OTHER MINORITIES

An argument on behalf of the electoral college that arose in the 1960s, and is still articulated today, is that it gives an advantage to African Americans.[38] The reasoning is that minorities are concentrated in large, politically competitive states and thus could determine which candidate won that state and thus perhaps the election. As a result of their power, minorities could force candidates to bargain for their votes by promising to advance their interests.

This argument is actually built on a tower of faulty premises. First, African Americans and other minorities are not concentrated in large states. The greatest concentration of blacks, for example, is in the Deep South states of Louisiana, Mississippi, Alabama, Georgia, South Carolina, North Carolina, and Virginia, where they make up from 20 to 37 percent of the population. (They also make up 30 percent of the population of Maryland.) In contrast, African Americans make up only 7 percent of Californians, 12 percent of Texans, 17 percent of New Yorkers, 16 percent of those living in Florida, 15 percent in Illinois, and 11 percent of Pennsylvanians.[39] (It is also the case that African Americans are not concentrated in small states that benefit from the allocation of a minimum of three votes for each state.)[40]

Second, the large states are not necessarily competitive ones. In the elections of 2000, 2004, and 2008, for example, four of the five largest states—California, Texas, New York, and Illinois—were not competitive in the presidential election, and, as we have seen, the candidates largely ignored them. There was not much chance for bargaining for policies favorable to minorities.

The electoral college provides no more advantage for African Americans in the southern states, where they account for substantial percentages of the population. Almost all African Americans in these states vote for Democratic presidential candidates, but in a competitive election nationally, these states are likely to go Republican. The electoral college thus prevents the votes of African Americans in these states from contributing to the national totals of the Democratic candidate.

Third, African Americans are not "swing" voters. They are the most loyal component of the Democratic electoral coalition. How would any leader persuade African Americans (or any other group) to break radically from their traditional political loyalties and shift their votes rapidly to another candidate? It is not a sensible proposition.

Few politicians miss the point, and few Republican presidential candidates under the electoral college have been willing to compete aggressively for African Americans' votes. For example, what did Nixon, Ford, or Reagan offer? Republicans often attempt to inject race into presidential politics, but not to appeal for African American votes.[41] From opposition to the Civil Rights Act in 1964 to the Willie Horton ads in 1992, some campaigns have employed code words and careful manipulation of racial imagery to appeal to racially conservative white voters. The shift of southern conservative whites from the Republican to the Democratic Party is partially the result of such appeals and also encourages their persistence.

African Americans are not in a position to swing either large states or medium-sized states to the candidate that offers them the most favorable policies. It is difficult to bargain when only one side is making offers. It is equally difficult to receive credit from winning candidates for being the decisive element in a successful coalition. Not only have African Americans been in few winning coalitions for president in the past four decades (there have been only four Democratic victories since 1964), but it is also difficult to determine the "decisive" element in any election. (Of course, African American votes, as those of any other group, can be critical to the success of a candidate in a close election in a state.)

In reality, neither party invests much time in appealing directly for black votes.[42] Among the speeches of the presidential candidates in the 2000 election that we examined earlier, the only ones that focused on black interests were the addresses of both George W. Bush and Al Gore to the annual convention of the National Association for the Advancement of Colored People in July. Democratic candidates have to walk a fine line between preserving the bloc of African American votes and alienating white voters. In 1992 Bill Clinton made a point of publicly criticizing Sister Souljah, an African American rap singer, at a meeting of Jesse Jackson's Rainbow Coalition shortly before the Democratic National Convention.

The electoral college thus *discourages* attention to the interests of African Americans because they are unlikely to shift the outcome in a state as a whole.[43] The winner-take-all system ensures that African Americans have little or no voice in presidential elections in the South.[44] This lack of attention to African American interests as a result of the electoral college is nothing new. Research has found a positive and significant relationship between a state's competitiveness and voting rights enforcement activity in the late nineteenth century.[45] The noncompetitive Solid South provided little incentive to enforce the franchise for African American voters.

Under direct election of the president in which all votes are valuable, African American voters in the South and in the urban Northeast, for example, could coalesce their votes and become an effective national bloc. The votes of southern African Americans, in particular, might for the first time be important in determining the election outcome. One reason that Judith Best, perhaps the best-known advocate of the electoral college, supports the status quo is precisely because it inhibits what she calls "private minorities" from uniting votes across state lines.[46]

The evidence clearly shows, then, that the argument that the electoral college aids African Americans is based on false premises. Although it may be possible to construct a principled argument that members of a disadvantaged race deserve more say in the election of the president than members of other races, such an argument is unlikely to win many adherents in the twenty-first century. It is difficult in a democracy to give people electoral weight based on the rightness of their cause.

Hispanics are now the largest minority group in the United States. They also have endured discrimination, represent something of an economic underclass, and have a particular interest in immigration policy. Hispanics are concentrated in a few states, comprising 37 percent of the population of Texas and California, 17 percent of New Yorkers, 22 percent of Floridians, and 15 percent of the population of Illinois. They also make up large percentages of smaller states like Arizona, New Mexico, Nevada, and Colorado.[47] Does the electoral college provide them special protections that they would lose in a system of direct election of the president?

Because Hispanics represent 16 percent of the population of the whole country, because they are a rapidly growing segment of the public, and because they less uniformly support one party than African Americans do, it is difficult to imagine a political party ignoring them. Certainly, Republicans such as George W. Bush and Karl Rove have made great efforts to appeal to them in recent years. There seems little need to jury-rig an electoral system to accord special protection to the interests of Hispanics.

Moreover, California, Texas, New York, Illinois, and Arizona are not reliably swing states, so there is no leverage from residing there under the electoral college. Florida certainly has been a swing state, but only a particular subgroup of Hispanics—Cubans—has benefited, extracting promises from some presidential candidates of a stiff embargo on Cuba and loose interpretations of immigration rules for those escaping the island.

The electoral college provides the potential for *any* cohesive special interest concentrated in a large, competitive state to exercise disproportionate power. Wall Street workers in New York, movie industry employees in California, citrus growers in Florida, autoworkers in Michigan, and those earning a living in the energy business in Texas could, in theory, swing their states to one candidate or the other. Tara Ross, who favors amplifying the voices of concentrated minorities in states, provides what in her view is a positive example: supporters of Strom Thurmond in 1948![48] Do we really want a system of electing the president that provides such potential to special interests? Should Cuban Americans set our foreign policy toward Cuba? Disproportionate power to any group is difficult to reconcile with political equality. As James Madison proclaimed at the Constitutional Convention, "local considerations must give way to the general interest."[49]

A core justification for the electoral college, and its violations of political equality, is that it is necessary to protect important interests that would be overlooked or harmed under a system of direct election of the president.

Yet such claims are based on faulty premises. States—including states with small populations—do not embody coherent, unified interests and communities, and they have little need for protection. Even if they did, the electoral college does not provide it. Contrary to the claims of its supporters, candidates do not pay attention to small states. The electoral college actually distorts the campaign so that candidates ignore many large and most small states and devote the bulk of their attention to competitive states.

Similarly, African Americans and other minority groups do not benefit from the electoral college because they are not well positioned to determine the outcomes in states. As a result, the electoral college system actually discourages attention to minority interests.

In sum, the electoral college does not protect anyone's interests. In the following two chapters, I analyze other justifications advocates make on its behalf.

Chapter 7 Maintaining Cohesion

Advocates of the electoral college offer a second set of justifications for selecting the president by electoral votes. These arguments center on maintaining the harmony and cohesion of the Republic. The focus here is different from the rationales we examined in Chapter 6. Instead of emphasizing what the electoral college does for the country, advocates call attention to alleged harm that alternative methods of presidential selection, especially direct election, would cause the nation.

To begin, defenders of the electoral college charge that direct election of the president would encourage electoral fraud and vote recounts, sow national disharmony, and deny the president a mandate for governing. Most supporters of the electoral college also maintain that it is an essential bulwark of federalism and that electing the president directly would undermine the entire federal system. In this chapter I examine these charges and, equally important, explore whether the electoral college actually has the benefits its advocates claim for it.

FRAUD AND RECOUNTS

Supporters of the electoral college often argue that direct election of the president would lead to increased voter fraud and endless recounts and challenges. Judith Best argues that direct election would remove "the quarantine on fraud and recounts."[1] Supporters reason that the electoral college localizes fraud to a few states. Because the electoral votes of these states would not change the outcome of an election, they argue, candidates do not seek recounts. If there were a close election under direct election of the president, they surmise, fraud would be an increased problem as the accumulation of a few votes in each political unit across the country could change the outcome of the election. Thus challenges and contests would not be limited to one or a few states,[2] but "a recount of every ballot box in the country could be necessary."[3]

Does the electoral college contain fraud and discourage recounts? Would direct election encourage fraud and recounts, or is this another faulty premise on which support for the electoral college is based?

Electoral Fraud

First, let us focus on fraud. In reality, the electoral college does *not* contain the results of fraud and accidental circumstances within states. Instead, it magnifies their consequences for the outcome nationally. Under the unit rule, a few votes can change the outcome of an entire state, which may affect the national election result, as we learned in Chapter 3. Thus the electoral college creates incentives for fraud because there may be a large payoff from stealing a few votes.

The election of 1960 illustrates these incentives. In the days and weeks following the election, the nation's attention focused on the question of fraud. Two days after the election, Republican national chairman Thurston B. Morton sent telegrams to party leaders in eleven states asking them to look into allegations of voting irregularities. A Republican spokesman reported receiving many complaints alleging fraud, payment of money, and other irregularities, most of them from Illinois, Texas, North and South Carolina, Michigan, and New Jersey. Republicans were especially bitter over the outcome in Illinois, which Kennedy had won by 8,858 votes out of 4,757,409 cast amid allegations of irregularities in the count in heavily Democratic Cook County (Chicago). The Cook County Republican chairman alleged that 100,000 fraudulent votes had swung Illinois to Kennedy through "systematic" looting of votes in twelve city wards and parts of two others.[4] Republicans laid stress on one precinct, virtually deserted because of highway demolitions, where the vote reported was 79 for Kennedy and 3 for Nixon, although there were fewer than 50 registered voters on election day.[5] They alleged widespread "tombstone" voting and tampering with voting machines. The Democrats replied angrily that the Republicans had no proof of substantial irregularities and that they were darkening the name of the city before the nation.

The recounts in Chicago soon bogged down in legal maneuvering, and the Republicans were never able to produce hard evidence to show that fraud had been a big enough factor to give the state to Kennedy. (In 1962, however, three Democratic precinct workers in Chicago did plead guilty to "altering, changing, defacing, injuring or destroying ballots" in the election.)[6] Republicans were even less hopeful of a reversal in Texas, where the Kennedy-Johnson ticket led by 46,233 votes, although Republicans charged that Democratic-controlled election boards had consistently invalidated Republican ballots with slight defects while counting Democratic ballots with identical deficiencies.

These suspicious circumstances occurred under the electoral college system. Conversely, under direct election of the president, a large change in votes would typically be necessary to alter the national outcome—even if the electoral vote would have been very close. Florida in 2000 is a case in point. Anyone wishing to employ fraudulent means to alter the outcome in the state, and thus the nation, would have had to "steal" only 538 votes. To alter the outcome of the vote under direct election would have required fraudulently adding or subtracting approximately 540,000 votes! The vote in individual states is usually closer than the vote in the entire nation.

Thus under direct election, fraud and accidental circumstances can affect only the relatively few votes directly involved. Direct election would create a *disincentive* for fraud, because altering an election outcome through fraud would require an organized effort of proportions never witnessed in the United States. And because no one in any state could know that his or her efforts at fraud would make a difference in the election, there would be little reason to risk trying. Moreover, direct election would also promote party competition, which would encourage better policing at the polls and more incentive to do so, since each vote would count toward a national total.

In addition, it is not clear why advocates of the electoral college expect previously honest states to become corrupt under direct election. In reality, organized election fraud in federal elections is a nonissue. Nearly a decade after the Bush administration began a crackdown on voter fraud, the Justice Department has turned up no evidence of widespread, organized fraud in federal elections. Instead, the department has found isolated, small-scale activities that often have not reflected criminal intent. Many of the few who have been charged appear to have mistakenly filled out registration forms or misunderstood eligibility rules. A handful of convictions involved people who voted twice. A few others were linked to small vote-buying schemes in which candidates, generally in local sheriff's or judge's races, paid voters for their support.[7] Similarly, the U.S. Election Assistance Commission found that the greatest number of cases reported on fraud and intimidation seemed to have shifted from past patterns of stealing votes to current problems with the voting of individual voters.[8]

In sum, the argument that direct election of the president would encourage fraud is based on faulty premises.

Recounts

What about elections that, for whatever reason, are simply extraordinarily close? Some argue, for example, that without the electoral college, the recount in Florida in 2000 would have occurred in many more states, paralyzing the country for weeks as states tallied absentee ballots, and candidates disputed ballot designs and challenged votes cast and decisions not to allow others to vote at all. Instead, the argument goes, the electoral college protected us from an even worse nightmare by centering the post-election battles in Florida. According to Senator Mitchell McConnell, "Without it [the electoral college] I fully expect we would have seen vote recounts and court battles in nearly every state of the Union."[9]

Jack Nagel and a colleague studied the outcomes in presidential elections under different definitions of disputability. They found that disputable elections in states that could have changed the outcome of the election were about two to six times more frequent than the disputable elections if the nation had been one electoral district for president. They also employed an a priori formal model and found a compatible intermediate ratio of 4:1. In other words, the disputability of an election (wherein the outcome is close enough to challenge in the hope that a recount will turn up enough errors to reverse the result) is significantly less for a single nationwide vote pool than for the electoral college system in which each state's votes are counted separately.[10]

Thus under a system of direct popular election of the president, recounts would be *less* likely. In order to undertake a recount, there has to be the reasonable possibility that enough corrections can be found to change the outcome of the election. The fewer total votes in an electoral unit, the more likely it is that a close contest may result in a small number of votes deciding the election. As we have seen, under the electoral college a few votes in one state may be able to make the difference in swinging a large block of electoral votes and possibly decide the election. This is what happened in Florida in 2000; the election was so close that adding or subtracting a few hundred votes might have changed the election outcome. A recount thus had a plausible possibility of altering the outcome. If the election had been by popular vote, George W. Bush would have had to find about a thousand times as many additional votes to win the election—a daunting task.

It is also unclear why advocates of the electoral college fear recounts. The laws in twenty states *require* them when the votes are close for elections, and they occur without incident or undue delay.[11] It is better to obtain an accurate count of Americans' preferences than a rapid denouement that elects the candidate who is not the public's choice. There would be little purpose to holding an election if our primary goal were to produce a winner independent of how citizens cast their votes.

It is somewhat amusing that advocates of the electoral college often argue that one of its advantages is that it produces a swift and sure decision.[12] In the wake of the election of 2000, such assertions seem naive. It is also noteworthy that throughout the protracted battle over Florida's electoral votes, most Americans never believed that permanent harm was being inflicted on the country as a result of the challenge to the Florida vote.[13]

NATIONAL HARMONY

Another important issue related to the means of selecting the president is the promotion of national harmony. According to supporters of the electoral college, a primary virtue of the system is that winning candidates must obtain *concurrent majorities* from around the country to win. In other words, these advocates argue, by guaranteeing a specific number of electoral votes to each state, the electoral college forces the winner to pay attention to all regions of the country and build broad coalitions by winning a wide geographic distribution of states that helps his coalition mirror the nation.[14] For this reason, Best declares that the right winner is not necessarily the candidate with the most votes but the one whose votes are "properly distributed."[15] A "proper" distribution seems to mean that the candidate won a majority of the electoral college, implying that such a victory would be based on winning states from all regions of the country.

If states did not employ the unit rule, allocating all their electoral votes as a bloc, the argument goes, candidates might appeal to clusters of voters whose votes could be aggregated across states and regions. This could potentially be divisive and lead to discord because the coalition behind a candidate might represent only one stratum of society, such as metropolitan areas. To avoid such appeals, Best would even amend the Constitution to impose the unit rule on all states. In addition, she argues, voting by state makes it necessary for candidates to compromise within the state level with a variety of interests to form majorities. The unit rule, she concludes, promotes national harmony.[16]

John C. Calhoun developed the concept of concurrent majorities to justify the actions of states in nullifying the acts of the federal government.[17] Advocates of the electoral college continue to view it as a useful constraint on majority rule. They point out that there are other nonmajoritarian provisions in the Constitution, including the rules for amending it and the requirement of a two-thirds vote in the Senate to ratify treaties. Moreover, providing some groups more votes than their numbers would warrant in a direct election, they feel, can be a consensus-building device and help to legitimize the election results.[18]

Yet again, advocates build their case for the virtues of the electoral college on faulty premises. It is important that we explore assertions about the appeals and electoral coalitions of candidates, compromises within states, the role of supermajority provisions in the Constitution and the electoral college in restraining majority rule, the need to provide extra influence to certain groups, and the effectiveness of presidents' electoral coalitions for governing.

Candidate Appeals

Do candidates try to build broad national coalitions by appealing to voters throughout the nation? Except in a superficial fashion, they do not. We saw in Chapter 6 that candidates of both parties virtually ignore large sections of the country in their campaigns. We have also seen that candidates typically do *not* make special appeals to local interests.

WINNING SUPPORT ACROSS REGIONS

Do candidates actually win support across all regions of the country? Anyone examining the red and blue states on an election-night map knows that candidates tend to win with regional support. Candidates under the electoral college do *not* obtain concurrent majorities from all areas of the country. In an electoral sweep, the distribution of states won (and the electoral college) is irrelevant, as one candidate wins almost all of them. In a more competitive race, however, it is unusual for candidates to win significant support across all regions.

Defenders of the electoral college suffer from myopia here. For example, Tara Ross argues that George W. Bush pieced together a broad national coalition in 2000. Gore, she claims, had "virtually no support" in two large sections of the country and the bulk of his support was "isolated on the east and west coasts."[19] Aside from the obvious facts that most Americans live on the east and west coasts and that Gore won 22 million votes in states he lost, she also ignores that Gore won Iowa, Wisconsin, Minnesota, Michigan, and Illinois in the Midwest and that Bush won no state on the West Coast. Instead, he won the South, the Rocky Mountain states, and the rural Midwest.

A map of the election a century earlier also shows a clear regional pattern of candidate support. In 1900 President William McKinley won the Northeast, Midwest, and West Coast, while William Jennings Bryan won every state in the South, including Texas, and some of the Rocky Mountain states.

The election results in 2004 were very similar to those in 2000. We saw in Chapter 1 that Barack Obama lost twenty-two states in 2008. Moreover, many of these states voted decisively against him.

WINNING SUPPORT ACROSS SOCIAL STRATA

Do winning candidates receive majority support across social strata? In 2000 George W. Bush did *not* win a larger percentage than Al Gore of the votes of women; blacks, Hispanics, and Asian Americans; voters aged 18–29 or those aged 60 or older; the poor; members of labor unions; those with less than $50,000 in household income; those with a high school education or less and those with postgraduate education; Catholics, Jews, and Muslims; liberals and moderates; urbanites; or those living in the East and West.[20]

It strains credulity to claim that Bush's vote represents concurrent majorities across the major strata of American society. What actually happened in 2000 was that the electoral college imposed a candidate supported by white male Protestants—the dominant social group in the country—over the objections not only of a plurality of all voters but also of most "minority" interests in the country. This antidemocratic outcome is precisely the opposite of what defenders of the electoral college claim for the system.

One-State Dominance

Is there a chance that a candidate under direct election could win a plurality of the vote by carrying one big state by a large margin but win no other states?[21] Could a candidate enjoy extraordinary support in a state as diverse as, say, California, and lack substantial support in other areas of the country? Such a scenario is far-fetched. Nothing in American history would lead one to believe that such an outcome is a realistic possibility.

Moreover, a candidate could win the plurality vote in such a scenario only by essentially tying the vote in the other forty-nine states, with each one decided in the opposition party candidate's favor. It is mathematically possible that forty-nine consecutive coin tosses would all come up heads. But no one has ever seen it happen.

Even if such a highly unlikely scenario did occur, there is not a problem. We have seen that states do not have interests as states in presidential elections. It makes perfectly good sense that the fiftieth state should, in effect, break the tie created by the other forty-nine.

Encouraging Moderation

Some defenders of the electoral college argue that the necessity of winning individual states forces candidates to moderate their stances and compromise with interests within states, producing moderate presidents.[22] There is no evidence that the electoral college is more likely to encourage moderation than would direct election of the president. Ultimately, candidates under the electoral college or direct election must obtain the votes of large numbers of voters if they are to win the presidency.[23]

I will show in the next chapter that parties would not become more polarized under direct election of the president and that they have actually become highly polarized under the electoral college. The electoral college did not prevent blatant class appeals by candidates on the left such as Franklin D. Roosevelt in 1936 or Harry Truman in 1948. Nor did it prevent the election of ideologues on the right such as Ronald Reagan in 1980 and 1984 and George W. Bush in 2000 and 2004. These and others were polarizing elections in which differences of opinion among the coalitions supporting the candidates were considerable.

Another way to approach the question is to ask whether direct election has led to extremism in the states, where it is almost the exclusive means of electing statewide officials. Governors and U.S. senators represent a range of points on the political spectrum. Many are elected from states with considerable diversity. Yet it is not plausible to characterize either group of officials as extremists—even though they win election by receiving a plurality of the vote in their states, not by winning a majority of the counties.

Does the unit rule force candidates to compromise within a state to win a majority in it? Advocates of the electoral college do not provide any evidence of such compromises. It is not even clear what such a compromise would look like or with whom such a compromise could be made. It is also not true that winning candidates win majorities in states. George W. Bush won a majority of the vote in only twenty-five states in 2000, most of them states with small populations. He won majorities in only seven states with more than nine electoral votes.

Constitutional Consistency

Some defenders of the electoral college argue that its violations of majority rule are just an example of constitutional provisions that require supermajorities to take action.[24] Is the role of the supermajority provisions in the Constitution comparable to the role of the electoral college in restraining majority rule and, in theory at least, promoting harmony? No, it is not. There is a crucial difference between such rules and the electoral college system for selecting the president. Requirements for supermajorities make taking positive action more difficult. In other words, it requires a large coalition, two-thirds of those voting, to send a constitutional amendment to the states or ratify a treaty. Such rules may force proponents of action to compromise with opponents to obtain their votes.

The framers designed all such supermajoritarian provisions to allow minorities to *prevent* an action. These provisions do not, however, allow a minority to take positive action. The electoral college is fundamentally different. It does not make it more difficult to select a president. Instead, it simply allows for a minority to take positive action to choose the president against the wishes of the majority or a plurality of voters. It is the only device of its kind in the Constitution.

In addition, the broad thrust of constitutional revision over the past two centuries has been in the direction of democratization and majority rule. The Fifteenth Amendment (1870) prohibited discrimination on the basis of race in determining voter eligibility. The Nineteenth Amendment (1920) ensured women the right to vote. The Twenty-third Amendment (1961) accorded the residents of Washington, DC, the right to vote in presidential elections. Three years later, the Twenty-fourth Amendment prohibited poll taxes (which discriminated against the poor). Finally, the Twenty-sixth Amendment (1971) lowered the voter eligibility age to eighteen.

Extra Influence for Some Interests

Do some groups need or deserve extra influence in the selection of the president in order to preserve national harmony? The discussion in Chapter 6 showed that there is no justification for awarding a state power disproportionate to its population in presidential elections. In addition, we have seen that those, such as African Americans, to whom some would like to give an extra increment of influence do not actually benefit from the electoral college.

Providing an Effective Governing Coalition

Last, does the electoral college provide the president with an effective governing coalition? There is no reason to think so. We have already seen that the electoral college does not ensure that the winning candidate will have formed a broad coalition in the country.

As a result, the electoral college does nothing to overcome the central feature of the U.S. constitutional system—the horizontal fragmentation of power encapsulated by the phrases "separation of powers" and "checks and balances." Because the power to pass legislation is much more likely to be shared than separated, it is the checks and balances that are most relevant to building coalitions. The White House must build coalitions in Congress because the president generally cannot act without Congress's consent. Under the U.S. constitutional system, Congress must pass legislation and can override vetoes. The Senate must ratify treaties and confirm presidential nominations to the cabinet, the federal courts, regulatory commissions, and other high offices.

A useful indicator of the president's ability to build coalitions is the White House's success in obtaining passage of its potentially most significant legislative proposals. A study of 287 presidential initiatives of potentially significant legislation over the period 1953–1996 found that 41 percent became law. Opposition in Congress may delay or dilute other presidential initiatives. In short, presidents fail most of the time under the electoral college.[25]

Most winning coalitions in Congress have one of the parties at their core. The president is the leader of his party and depends heavily on it to pass his initiatives and stop legislation which he opposes. How much support does the president typically receive from his party? On contested votes on which the president has taken a stand, the president obtains the support of approximately three-fourths or more of his co-partisans, three or four times the level he receives from members of the opposition party (Table 7.1).

On one hand, the president can depend on the support of most members of his party most of the time. On the other hand, there is plenty of slippage in party support, and the opposition party opposes him most of the time. If the opposition party is in the majority, which it frequently is, the odds are against the president's ability to build a winning coalition.

Most of the time the president finds it difficult to move legislation through Congress. Assertions that the electoral college provides the president with an effective governing coalition are hyperbolic at best. Some advocates of the electoral college have such a lack of understanding of presidential power that they express concern that direct election might give

Table 7.1
Partisan Support for Presidents, 1953–2009

President (party)	House of Representatives			Senate		
	% Support[a]			% Support[a]		
	President's Party	Opposition Party	Difference in Support[b]	President's Party	Opposition Party	Difference in Support[b]
Eisenhower (R)	63	42	21	69	36	33
Kennedy (D)	73	26	47	65	33	32
Johnson (D)	71	27	44	56	44	12
Nixon/Ford (R)	64	39	25	63	33	30
Carter (D)	63	31	32	63	37	26
Reagan (R)	70	29	41	74	31	43
G. H. W. Bush (R)	73	27	46	75	29	46
Clinton (D)	75	24	51	83	22	61
G. W. Bush (R)	84	20	64	86	18	68
Obama[c] (D)	92	16	76	95	25	70

Source: George C. Edwards III, *At the Margins: Presidential Leadership of Congress* (New Haven: Yale University Press, 1989), table 3.3; updated by author.

[a]On roll-call votes on which the winning side was supported by fewer than 80 percent of those voting.
[b]Differences expressed as percentage points.
[c]2009.

the president *too much* power because it would magnify the plebiscitary foundations of the presidency.[26] Presidents of all political stripes must find such assertions bewildering.

A Proper Distribution?

The argument that the electoral college provides winning candidates the "proper" distribution of the vote cannot bear scrutiny. A simple example nicely summarizes the point. If Al Gore had received 538 more votes in Florida in 2000, he would have been elected president. If Ralph Nader had not been on the ballot in New Hampshire (or Florida) in 2000, Gore would have won. Advocates of the electoral college are in the position of having to argue that Bush was the proper winner because of the distribution of his vote but that if either of these very modest changes had occurred, Gore would have been the proper winner (proper because the electoral college elected him)—even though Bush's coalition may not have changed by a single vote. Such an argument is simply nonsense.

PRESIDENTIAL MANDATE

Another concern among some opponents of direct election of the president is that if we chose the president through direct election and there were more than two candidates, a new president might have received the support of only a minority of the electorate and thus lack a mandate for governing.[27]

It is interesting that those harboring such worries seem to hold the incongruous beliefs that counting votes across state lines is not useful for selecting the president but is important for producing a mandate for the president.[28] In addition, three implicit premises underlie this criticism of direct election. The first is that the electoral college, in contrast with direct election, produces presidents who win with a majority of the vote. The second premise is that winning a majority of the vote accords presidents important advantages in governing. The final premise is that presidents receive a mandate to govern when they win a majority of the vote. In investigating these assertions, we once again find faulty premises at the base of arguments on behalf of the electoral college.

Majority Election?

Do presidents win a majority of the vote under the electoral college? In fact, presidents quite often do *not* receive a majority of the popular vote under the electoral college system. Since World War II, for example, no candidate received a majority of the vote in 1948, 1960, 1968, 1992, 1996, and 2000. And from 1824 until World War II, the winner did not receive a majority of the vote in twelve presidential elections (Table 7.2). In all, since 1824, the president has not received a majority of the vote nearly 40 percent of the time.

Advantages of Majority Election?

Did winning plurality elections hinder these presidents? Would they have been more successful if they had won a majority of the vote and received a stronger "mandate"?

Presidents who won election without a majority of the vote could not

Table 7.2
Presidents Elected Without a Majority of Popular Votes

Year	Winning Candidate	% Popular Vote
1824	Adams	30.9
1844	Polk	49.5
1848	Taylor	47.3
1856	Buchanan	45.3
1860	Lincoln	39.8
1876	Hayes	48.0
1880	Garfield	48.3
1884	Cleveland	48.9[a]
1888	Harrison	47.8
1892	Cleveland	46.0
1912	Wilson	41.8
1916	Wilson	49.2
1948	Truman	49.6[b]
1960	Kennedy	49.7
1968	Nixon	43.4
1992	Clinton	43.0
1996	Clinton	49.2
2000	G. W. Bush	47.9

Sources: Congressional Quarterly's Guide to U.S. Elections, 6th ed. (Washington, DC: CQ Press, 2010); Jerrold G. Rusk, *A Statistical History of the American Electorate* (Washington, DC: CQ Press, 2001).

[a]Includes votes for the Fusion Democratic–Greenback slate in Michigan.

[b]Includes votes in thirty-five Texas counties not included in the official Texas return.

credibly claim a mandate, but plurality election did not hinder them. From Lincoln through Wilson, from Truman to George W. Bush, such presidents have acted vigorously in pursuit of their policy goals, in both domestic and foreign policy. In addition, Lincoln, Wilson, Nixon, Clinton, and Bush were reelected (Wilson and Clinton won with less than 50 percent of the vote twice, as did Cleveland, who lost a reelection bid, then was elected a second time). All recent presidents elected without a majority of the popular vote have begun their terms with approval ratings of 57 percent or higher in the Gallup Poll, hardly evidence of a crippled presidency.[29]

A striking feature of a listing of the presidents who won without a majority of the electorate's vote is that it includes several presidents whom political scientists and historians view as among the strongest and most successful of their eras, including James Polk, Abraham Lincoln, Grover Cleveland, and Woodrow Wilson. The only notably strong presidents during the period of 1824 until Franklin D. Roosevelt was elected in 1932 who *received* a majority of the vote are Andrew Jackson and Theodore Roosevelt. Reviewing more recent decades, it would be difficult to term Harry Truman, John Kennedy, Richard Nixon, Bill Clinton, or George W. Bush "weak" presidents.

When we control for the size of a president's party's delegation in Congress, there is little relation between popular electoral majorities in presidential elections and the president's subsequent success in Congress.[30] There is certainly nothing magical about a majority. Was Jimmy Carter in a better position to move Congress with his 51 percent of the vote in 1976 than Bill Clinton was with his 43 percent in 1992? Was the first President Bush better off in 1988 with his 53 percent of the vote than Richard Nixon was with his 43 percent in 1968? There is no reason to think so, and advocates of the electoral college have never shown an advantage to presidents winning majority vote victories.

This is not to argue that presidents would not benefit from the perception that they had received a mandate, that the people had clearly spoken on behalf of their policies.[31] Mandates can be powerful symbols in American politics. They accord added legitimacy and credibility to the newly elected president's proposals. Concerns for representation and political survival encourage members of Congress to support the president if they feel the people have spoken. And members of Congress are susceptible to such beliefs. According to David Mayhew, "Nothing is more important in Capitol Hill politics than the shared conviction that election returns have proven a point."[32] Members of Congress also need to believe that voters have not merely rejected the losers in elections but have positively selected the victors and what they stand for.

More important, mandates change the premises of decisions. Following Franklin D. Roosevelt's decisive win in the 1932 election, the essential question became *how* government should act to fight the Depression rather than *whether* it should act. Similarly, following Lyndon Johnson's overwhelming win in the 1964 election, the dominant question in Congress was not whether to pass new social programs but how many social programs to pass and how much to increase spending. In 1981 the tables were turned: Ronald Reagan's victory placed a stigma on big government and exalted the unregulated marketplace and large defense efforts. Reagan had won a major victory even before the first congressional vote.

Majorities into Mandates?

Such mandates are rare, however. Merely winning an election does not provide a president with a mandate. Every election produces a winner, but mandates are much less common. When asked about his mandate in 1960, John F. Kennedy reportedly replied, "Mandate, schmandate. The mandate is that I am here and you're not."[33]

POPULAR VOTE MARGIN

There is more to perceptions of mandates than a straightforward summing of the election results. Presidents elected by large margins often find that perceptions of support for their proposals do not accompany their victories. In the presidential elections held between 1952 and 2008, most of the impressive electoral victories (Richard Nixon's 61 percent in 1972, Ronald Reagan's 59 percent in 1984, and Dwight Eisenhower's 57 percent in 1956) did not elicit perceptions of mandates (Lyndon Johnson's 61 percent in 1964 is the exception). Equally important, winning a relatively small percentage of the vote does not necessarily preclude perceptions of a mandate. For example, Ronald Reagan was perceived as having won a mandate with only 51 percent of the vote in 1980.[34]

In the absence of a perception of a mandate, does the size of a popular vote victory influence a president's success with Congress? The elections of 1980 and 1984 offer a striking paradox: in 1980, Ronald Reagan received only 51 percent of the vote. His first approval rating in the Gallup Poll after his inauguration was lower than that of any postwar president, again only 51 percent.[35] Yet there is general agreement that in the areas of defense, taxes, and domestic programs, he and his supporters significantly altered American public policy.

By contrast, in 1984 Reagan won a great electoral victory with 59 percent of the vote. Public opinion polls at the time of the election showed that the voters viewed him in a very positive light as a strong, effective leader and strongly supported his performance on the economy and national security policy.[36] Moreover, the first Gallup poll after the inauguration found that

Reagan enjoyed an approval rating of 62 percent.[37] Yet the president immediately faced strong opposition in Congress to his proposals on domestic and foreign policy. As an example, in the Congress of 1985–1986 the president won no real increase in his cherished defense budget. Much of the time, he was on the defensive, as in his embarrassing defeat on sanctions against South Africa.

Some commentators claim that the electoral college's magnification of the size of a popular vote victory, which we discussed in Chapter 3, benefits the president. The argument seems to be that at least some people will ignore the actual popular vote and focus on the electoral vote instead. This orientation, in turn, will give the president more credibility in claiming a mandate and more success in persuading Congress to support his programs.

Such an assertion fails on three grounds. The first is ethical and the second and third are empirical. To begin, what possible justification can there be for a presidential selection process that may fool people as to the actual outcome? It is difficult to imagine a response.

Second, there is no evidence that anyone ignores the popular vote in favor of the electoral vote. Electoral vote totals—except in 2000—are forgotten the day after the election. Journalists, scholars, and members of Congress know the popular vote, and they reflect it in their commentaries. Members of Congress, moreover, are attuned to how the president ran in their constituencies.

There is no evidence that electoral college margins encourage perceptions of mandates. In nine of the thirteen presidential elections in the latter half of the twentieth century, the disparity between the popular vote and the electoral vote exceeded 20 percentage points. Yet only the elections of 1964 and 1980 produced perceptions of a popular mandate.[38]

The presidents who won by a large margin in the popular vote also won by a large margin in the electoral college, and most of them won without a perception of a mandate. Their large electoral vote totals made no difference. George Bush won a large electoral vote victory in 1988, but it did little to turn his 53 percent in the popular vote into a mandate. After election night, few pay serious attention to the electoral college totals, and commentators quite sensibly focus on the popular vote.

Similarly, Franklin D. Roosevelt and Lyndon Johnson, who benefited from perceptions of mandates, received large popular vote victories and required no help from the electoral college. The electoral college contributed nothing to these mandates, and abolishing it would not detract from mandates in the future. Reagan's election in 1980 may seem to be an exception, since he won just 51 percent of the popular vote but a large electoral vote majority and enjoyed the perception of a mandate. There are several more plausible explanations for this perception, however, as I will show.

THE MEANING OF ELECTIONS

Why do election victories not automatically translate into perceptions of mandates for the newly elected president? The most straightforward explanation of perceptions of a mandate is that a clear majority of the populace has shown through its votes that it supports certain policies proposed by the winning candidate. Yet elections, by their very nature, rarely provide clear indications of the public's thinking on individual proposals.

If presidential elections are to provide majority support for specific policies, the following conditions must be met: (1) voters must have opinions on policies; (2) voters must know candidates' stands on the issues; (3) candidates must offer voters the alternatives the voters desire; (4) there must be a large turnout of voters; (5) voters must vote on the basis of issues; and (6) voter support must be able to be correlated with voters' policy views. These conditions are rarely, if ever, met.[39] For this reason, it is difficult to discern the relation between voters' policy preferences and a president's victory at the polls.

Even landslide elections are difficult to interpret. For example, Stanley Kelley found that in Lyndon Johnson's victory in 1964, issues gave the president his base of support, and concerns over the relative competence of the candidates won the swing vote for him. In 1972, however, the question of competence dominated the election. Although traditional domestic issues associated with the New Deal were salient, they actually favored George McGovern, not the landslide winner, Richard Nixon.[40] Similarly, voters were closer to the views of Walter Mondale on most major issues in 1984 than to those of landslide winner Ronald Reagan.[41]

There are two additional complicating factors. First, there may be no majority opinion on an issue, even among those who have an opinion. Public opinion polls often force respondents to choose one of a restricted number of possible answers. But opinion on any issue is probably quite fragmented, providing no majority opinion to identify. For example, in

September 2007, the Gallup Poll asked whether respondents favored the plan of General David Petraeus and President George W. Bush to withdraw about forty thousand troops from Iraq by the summer of 2008 but not to make a commitment to further withdrawals until that time. Gallup also asked whether respondents supported a plan introduced by Democratic senators that called for the withdrawal of most U.S. troops within nine months. The muddled results revealed that similar and large percentages of Americans favored each plan—and 45 percent of the public favored both plans.[42]

Second, voters may be concerned with several issues in an election, but they have only one vote with which to express their views. Citizens may support one candidate's position on some issues yet vote for another candidate because of concern for other issues or general evaluations of performance. In 1984 voters preferred Walter Mondale to Ronald Reagan on the issues of defense spending, aid to the Contras, environmental protection, protection of civil rights, and helping the poor and disadvantaged, but most voted for Reagan for president.[43] When they cast their ballots, voters signal only their choice of candidate, not their choice of the candidates' policies. One should be cautious in inferring support for specific policies from the results of this process, for the vote is a rather blunt instrument for expressing one's views.

Coattails

The switch of a large number of new seats to the president's party in Congress is an indicator used by commentators, and certainly by members of Congress, in evaluating the significance of a president's electoral victory. If observers attribute long coattails to the president, they are likely to see the election as especially meaningful, because the people appear to be sending strong signals of support for the chief executive.

The absence of notable gains for the president's party in Congress detracts from the euphoria of victory and inserts an unsettling element into analyses that follow the election. If the president's party loses seats, as Republicans did in both houses of Congress in 1956 and in the Senate in 1972 and 1984—in the face of sweeping Republican victories for the White House—it makes it easy to conclude that the voters were sending mixed signals on election day and that the basis of the president's victory was more personal than political. The results of such congressional elections may also demonstrate to members of Congress that their electoral fortunes are not connected with the president's.

ORIENTATION OF THE CAMPAIGN

The winning candidate's inclination to present policy alternatives during the campaign may also affect perceptions of a mandate. Often, in the interests of building broad electoral coalitions, candidates avoid specifics to such a degree that they undercut future claims of policy mandates. In American politics, the electoral and governing processes are often quite separate.

Since 1952, all four elections in which the winner obtained more than 55 percent of the vote (1956, 1964, 1972, and 1984) were races in which an incumbent won reelection (Table 7.3). With the exception of Lyndon Johnson, who had been in office only a year, the presidents used their campaigns to appeal as broadly as possible and run up the score. Yet in producing impressive personal victories, they undermined their ability to govern after the election. Eisenhower, Nixon, and Reagan all experienced considerable difficulties with Congress in the two years immediately following their landslide victories.

The election of 1984 illustrates how winning candidates can compromise their ability to govern after the election. Ronald Reagan's rhetorical style, marked by the repetition of uplifting generalities, was well suited to a medium that places a premium on straightforward communication of broad, simple ideas. He appealed to shared, basic values and invoked themes of leadership and opportunity that stirred the emotions of his audience. In addition, the dazzling technical competence of his campaign staff in lighting, sound, and the creation of backdrops painted to complement his skin tones created outstanding visual images. The repetition, simplicity, and consistency of the president's message served him well in obtaining support, but it did little to encourage interpretations of a mandate.

The Reagan campaign asked voters to make retrospective rather than prospective choices. By steadfastly refusing to deal with specific questions of policy and relying on broad generalities, Reagan undercut later claims for a mandate. His failure to present a blueprint for a second term wasted political capital that would have been necessary for generating a major change in policy. His landslide appeared as more a personal victory than one based on policy.

Table 7.3
Presidential Election Results, 1952–2008

Year	Winning Candidate	Popular Vote %	Electoral Votes
1952	Eisenhower	55.1[a]	442
1956	Eisenhower	57.4	457
1960	Kennedy	49.7	303
1964	Johnson	61.1	486
1968	Nixon	43.4	301
1972	Nixon	60.7	520
1976	Carter	50.1	297
1980	Reagan	50.7	489
1984	Reagan	58.8	525
1988	G. H. W. Bush	53.4	426
1992	Clinton	43.0	370
1996	Clinton	49.2	379
2000	G. W. Bush	47.9	271
2004	G. W. Bush	50.7	286
2008	Obama	52.9	365

Sources: Congressional Quarterly's Guide to U.S. Elections, 6th ed. (Washington, DC: CQ Press, 2010); Jerrold G. Rusk, *A Statistical History of the American Electorate* (Washington, DC: CQ Press, 2001).
[a]Includes both slates pledged to Eisenhower in South Carolina.

One might assume that the policies of incumbent presidents seeking reelection would be clear to the public. Yet their current policies are not always clear to voters or, if clear, not necessarily accurate guides to the future. Incumbent presidents are usually vaguer than their challengers on issues, and they rarely present detailed plans for future policy on the campaign trail, as was made clear in the campaign of 1984. In addition, incumbents usually have to defend their records. In some instances, such as in 1972, 1976, and 1980, incumbent presidents simply employ the "Rose Garden strategy" and do not campaign actively.[44]

The election of 1964 was unusual. President Johnson had a reasonably clear platform of proposals, most of which had been on the agenda for several years. Furthermore, he had not served in office long enough to see many of his programs become law, despite his success with Congress in 1964. Thus observers were aware of Johnson's proposals and could tie them directly to the election. The Eighty-ninth Congress was very responsive to the president's legislative requests.

CONTINUITY AND CHANGE

Related to the orientation of the campaign is the relative impact of continuity and change on perceptions of the election's outcome. Again, the contrast between the elections of 1980 and 1984 illustrates the point nicely. The results of the election of 1984 were less explosive than those of 1980, despite their far more impressive proportions, because the outcome represented continuity rather than change. In 1984 the incumbent was reelected; in 1980 the incumbent was thrown out of office, which had not happened to an elected president since Herbert Hoover.

As a candidate in 1980, Reagan advocated major changes in public policy. Although he did not always specify the details of these changes, few observers were unaware of the thrust of his commitments. Four years later, however, President Ronald Reagan asked for continuity. He wanted voters to reward him for a successful term. Members of Congress not surprisingly interpreted the two elections differently. It is easier for members of Congress to oppose programs without appearing to oppose a popular president if the incumbent frames the campaign as a referendum on his qualities as a leader and does not associate himself with new policies.

In addition, the results in 1984 were easy to anticipate and surprised virtually no one. They also reinforced the status quo. Continuity has considerably less psychological impact than change, especially if the change appears to be substantial. The proportions of a victory may thus be less important than its predictability and emotional impact.

TIDES OF OPINION

All presidents must work within the confines of public opinion. Although they may influence its texture, they rarely if ever can shape its basic contours. If perceptions of a mandate are to take hold, the president's policy proposals must match the national mood. Things often do not work out that way. Some presidents, such as Harry Truman, may fight the grain of opinion, whereas others, such as John Kennedy, may be waiting for it to mature. Conversely, a president such as Franklin Roosevelt arrives at the crest of a wave of opinion and can ride it freely. Sometime a president, like

Jimmy Carter, may move with the grain of history but against the domi- nant perspective of his own party. As Carter reflected more than a quarter- century after leaving the White House, "The Democratic Party was never mine. . . . I was never able to consolidate support in the Democratic Party, particularly after [Edward] Kennedy decided to run for president."[45]

The electoral college often does not produce popular vote majority win- ners, and there is no evidence that the size of the president's majority (as opposed to the size of his party's bloc in Congress) influences his ability to govern. Moreover, presidents elected under the electoral college rarely ben- efit from the perception of a mandate, and when they do, the electoral college is irrelevant to that perception. There are many reasons why elec- tion victories, even landslide victories, do not translate into perceptions of mandates. But the bottom line is that there is no distinction in the ability of majority and plurality winners to govern.

PRESERVING FEDERALISM

One of the most serious assertions in opposition to abolishing the electoral college and instituting direct popular election of the president is that doing so would undermine the federal nature of our government. Judith Best maintains that direct popular election would "deform our Constitution" and would constitute a serious "implicit attack on the federal principle."[46] William C. Kimberling argues that national popular election "would strike at the very heart of the federal structure laid out in our Constitution and would lead to the nationalization of our central government—to the detri- ment of the States."[47]

These defenders of the electoral college base their assertions on the premise that the electoral college is a key underpinning of the federal system.[48] Actually, it is unclear what federalism has to do with the presi- dency, the one elective part of the government that is designed to represent the nation as a whole rather than as an amalgam of states and districts. Federalism is certainly an important component of the constitutional sys- tem, but is the electoral college system an example of the federative princi- ple or essential to maintaining the federal system? Would direct election of the president have other deleterious effects on federalism?

A Federal Principle?

To begin, the founders did *not* design the electoral college on the federal principle. The electoral college does not enhance the power or sovereignty of the states. Moreover, the founders, as we have seen in Chapter 5, expected electors to exercise their discretion and cast individual votes (as they actually did in the early district system). They did not expect electors to vote as state blocks of electoral votes. There is no reference in the Constitutional Convention to the electoral college as being an element of the federal system or important to the overall structure of the Constitution.

Similarly, the founders did not see the electoral college serving as a means of implementing the Connecticut Compromise. They did not allocate on a federative principle the two extra votes they gave to each state. Instead, the extra votes were to serve as a corrective for large-state power. The federative principle would have required that these extra electors be organized like the Senate as a separate body with a veto on popular representation.

The framers did not design the electoral college to protect state interests. If they had, they would have insisted that state legislatures choose electors, who would be agents of state officials. As we saw in Chapter 5, they did not do so. Madison, for example, opposed selection by state legislatures, fearing that it would make the president a mere power broker among interests of the states rather than the symbol of a unified nation.[49] According to Martin Diamond, the electoral college was "an anti-states-rights device," designed to keep the election of the president away from state politicians.[50]

Essential for Federalism?

Even if the electoral college is not an aspect of federalism itself, is it essential for preserving federalism? It is telling that no other federal system has adopted anything close to an electoral college for choosing its chief executive. An electoral college clearly is not necessary for maintaining a federal system.

We have already seen that the electoral college does not force presidential candidates to devote attention to states as states in general or to small states in particular. Neither the existence nor the powers and responsibilities of state governments depend in any way on the existence of the electoral college. If it were abolished, states would have the same rights and duties that they have now. Federalism is deeply embodied in congressional elections, in which two senators represent each state just because it is a state and in which members of the House are elected from districts within states. Direct election of the president would not alter these aspects of the constitutional structure.

Would direct election of the president endanger federalism? Federalism is well protected by members of the House and Senate as well as by the legislatures and governors of the states. It is simply unthinkable that a constitutional amendment altering the federal structure could pass with the support of two-thirds of both houses of Congress and three-fourths of the states. There is virtually no aspect of the constitutional system more secure against fundamental change than federalism.

Representation in Congress and the constitutionally guaranteed rights of states are the core protections of federalism, not the system of electing the president. These prominent features of the political system make it difficult to imagine how direct election of the president would undermine federalism. A leading expert on federalism, Neal Peirce, has said it best: "The vitality of federalism rests chiefly on the constitutionally mandated system of congressional representation and the will and capacity of state and local governments to address compelling problems, not on the hocus-pocus of an eighteenth-century vote count system."[51]

A Diminished Role for State Parties and Politicians?

Martin Diamond and others have raised a related issue, expressing concern that under a system of direct election of the president, state and local politicians would become less important in the election because winning a city or state per se would be less important than under the electoral college. Candidates, he feared, would rely more on direct mail, media experts, and personal coteries in their campaigns. These new features of campaigning would in turn disengage the presidential campaign both from the party machinery and from the state parties and isolate the presidency from their moderating effect.[52]

Diamond and others base their apprehensions on the premise that presidential campaigns are now decentralized efforts, relying heavily on state and local politicians to deliver votes. It is highly questionable how many current state and local leaders can "deliver" votes. There certainly is no systematic evidence to support such an assertion. Moreover, even if a few leaders could deliver votes, why would we wish to encourage such a system?

In addition, it is clear that exactly what Diamond feared has occurred— *under the electoral college.* Presidential candidates run national campaigns managed from the center. They rely on direct mail and media experts, and they take control of the party machinery by placing their personal representatives in charge. Campaigns develop and coordinate advertising from a central point. The campaigns do this now, and there would be no difference under direct election of the president. More generally, the national organizations of parties have become stronger in relation to state parties. They are more effective in raising funds. They have made strides in nationalizing party programs, such as the Republicans' "Contract with America" in the 1990s.

It is not at all evident, however, that either the party machinery or state parties have moderating effects. Equally important, successful candidates, such as Bill Clinton, running as a "new Democrat," and George W. Bush, running as a "compassionate conservative," knew that they could win only by taking moderate stances. It is the voters, not state parties, who enforce moderation.

There are many reasons for state party organizations to exist, such as electing thousands of state-level officials and all members of Congress. Filling these offices provides more than sufficient incentive for the maintenance of vigorous state parties. In addition, although presidential campaigns are candidate- rather than party-centered, state party organizations can provide invaluable aid. Interviews with national party professionals found that they foresaw the role of state parties becoming *stronger* under direct election of the president because of the vital function these organizations would play in maximizing voter registration and turnout.[53]

Other advocates of the electoral college express concern that direct election of the president would change the system of nominating the president, leading to a national primary and the elimination of the nominating convention.[54] Yet these fears seem misplaced and, again, are based on faulty premises. Political parties, not states, determine the number of delegates a state receives and the acceptable means of selecting them. States choose whether to hold primaries or caucuses, and when to have them, to advantage themselves. It is not clear that the nation benefits from the disproportionate say of Iowa and New Hampshire in culling presidential candidates, but direct election of the president would not change their ability to schedule delegate selection at their discretion.

In addition, there is no imperative of the electoral college that encourages a particular form or date of nominating delegates. For most of U.S. history under the Constitution, states held few presidential primaries. Now, under the electoral college system, almost all states hold primaries, and they have moved toward "Super Tuesday"–style primaries in which states across the country hold primaries on the same day. The front-loading of delegate selection has moved states toward a version of a regional or national primary—*under the electoral college.* There is no reason to think that direct election of the president would accelerate such a trend.

The widespread use of state presidential primaries and the practice of holding them in the winter or early spring of presidential election years has led to the emergence of a nominee long before the nominating conventions occur. Decisions about presidential nominees are not made in the conventions. National conventions do have other functions, however, such as rallying the faithful and providing an opportunity for a party to make its case to the public. These functions would be valuable under any system of electing the president and are certainly not dependent on the electoral college.

Greater National Control of the Electoral Process?

Occasionally, a defender of the electoral college laments that fact that direct election of the president would probably bring greater national control of the electoral process. Actually, however, this change has already occurred. The Fifteenth, Eighteenth, Nineteenth, Twenty-third, Twenty-fourth, and Twenty-sixth Amendments to the Constitution expanded the electorate. Federal law effectively determines voter eligibility, and in the wake of the debacle in counting votes in Florida in the presidential election of 2000, federal law provides rules for voter registration, voter access to the polls, counting votes, correcting voters' errors on their ballots, resolving challenges to a citizen's right to vote, and ensuring that voting systems have minimal rates of error. The federal government also provides aid to states to improve their voting machinery and registration lists.

Federal standards are here to stay—*under the electoral college.* Moreover, Americans and their elected representatives overwhelmingly support such legislation. The enormous disparity in ballot designs across the states and the large number of individual state ballot designs that are inconsistent and needlessly complex make a strong case for greater uniformity.[55] The Caltech / MIT Voting Technology Project concluded that between four million and six million votes were lost in the 2000 election as a result of problems with ballots, voting equipment, and registration databases.[56] As President George W. Bush said when he signed the Help America Vote Act of 2002, "The administration of elections is primarily a state and local responsibility. The fairness of all elections, however, is a national priority."[57]

Many of the justifications for the electoral college focus on maintaining the harmony and cohesion of the Republic. Defenders of the electoral college argue that direct election of the president would encourage electoral fraud and vote recounts, sow national disharmony, and deny the president a mandate for governing. Upon closer scrutiny, however, we find that the electoral college does not contain the results of fraud and accidental circumstances within states. Instead, it magnifies their consequences for the outcome nationally. Direct election, by contrast, would create disincentives for fraud and recounts.

Similarly, the notion that the electoral college produces concurrent majorities around the country and forces winning candidates to moderate their stances to appeal successfully to all segments of society and all geographic locations is pure fantasy. Nothing like that actually occurs. Equally problematic is the view that victory in the electoral college ensures presidents effective coalitions for governing. Moreover, the electoral college does not produce compromise within states, and it is fundamentally different from constitutional provisions that require supermajorities to take positive action.

Presidents often win election under the electoral college without a majority, and winning a majority of the vote in and of itself does not make a president more effective in dealing with Congress. Although widespread perceptions of a mandate are an advantage for a president, election results under the electoral college seldom translate into them. When they do, the electoral college is irrelevant to that perception.

The electoral college is also not a bastion of federalism. It is not based on federative principles and is not essential for the continuance of a healthy federal system. Direct election of the president would not diminish the role of state and local parties and officials or the nominating conventions, and national standards for elections are already in place and not to be feared. As former Senate majority leader and Republican presidential nominee Robert Dole put it, direct election is "commonsense federalism."[58]

Once again, we find that defenders of the electoral college base their arguments on faulty premises. Direct election of the president cannot diminish benefits that do not exist.

Chapter 8 Preserving the Party System

Perhaps the most significant charge leveled against direct election is that it would fragment and polarize the party system and lead to corrupt deals among political leaders. Defenders of the electoral college argue that it is one of the key bulwarks of the two-party system in the United States.

It is important to note at this point that most critics of direct election of the president assume that it will require a runoff if no candidate receives, say, 40 percent of the vote in the first round of voting. I will show later that a runoff is not necessary, rendering irrelevant claims of fragmenting the party system. Nevertheless, it is useful to examine the claims of critics. In addition, some defenders of the electoral college seem to think that even a single round of direct election would fragment the party system.[1]

It is the presence of the runoff that is at the heart of the matter. Opponents of direct election charge that under direct election of the president, third parties could accumulate votes across states. As a result, they would have an incentive to run candidates for president in the hope that they would be able to attract enough votes, along with other splinter parties, to prevent either of the two major-party candidates from winning 40 percent of the vote and thus force a runoff. In a runoff, the argument goes, the third parties would be in a position to extract concessions in return for their support.[2]

As Judith Best puts it, "It is the very existence of a popular vote runoff, a second chance provision, that tempts more candidates to enter and voters to cast what they would otherwise consider to be a protest vote." She even goes so far as to predict that if the 40 percent runoff had been in effect in 1992, Ross Perot would not have temporarily withdrawn from the race and could have offered his support in a runoff to one of the candidates in exchange for policy concessions.[3]

Similarly, Arthur Schlesinger Jr. has argued that a runoff would provide "potent incentives for radical zealots (Ralph Nader, for example), freelance media adventurers (Pat Buchanan), eccentric billionaires (Ross Perot), and flamboyant characters (Jesse Ventura) to jump into presidential contests; incentives, too, to 'green' parties, senior-citizen parties, nativist parties, right-to-life parties, pro-choice parties, anti-gun-control parties, homo-sexual parties, prohibition parties, and so on down the single-issue line."[4]

Opponents of direct election of the president also fear that parties would become more homogeneous and that more extreme groups would form their own parties.[5] The runoff system, they say, would provide little incentive for parties to moderate their stands until after the first vote.[6] Candidates would try to obtain the most votes for their "pure" stands and then use these votes for bargaining in the runoff if they did not finish first or second. As parties became more internally homogeneous, politics would become more ideologically charged, and citizens might be less willing to accept the result when more appeared to be at stake.[7]

These assertions raise four important issues. First, is maintaining the electoral college necessary to preserve the two-party system? Second, would a runoff under direct election of the president encourage third parties? Third, would a runoff polarize the party system? Finally, would a runoff lead to corrupt deals among presidential candidates? It is also critical to evaluate the necessity of a runoff under direct election of the president.

CAUSES OF TWO-PARTY SYSTEMS

At least five broad theories offer explanations for the existence of two-party systems. The first is the structure of the electoral system. Are officials elected in single-member districts in plurality elections or in multimember districts by proportional election? A second theory emphasizes social diversity and cleavages. Into how many interests and groups is a society divided, and are these divisions reinforcing?[8] The third explanation stresses an underlying duality of interests in a society. A fourth theory is a cultural explanation that focuses on the political maturity of the citizenry and the development of a political culture that recognizes the need for compromise, the wisdom of pragmatism, and the need to avoid dogmatism. Last, there is the social consensus theory, which traces the two parties to a broad acceptance of social, economic, and political institutions.[9]

Only the first explanation, the structure of the electoral system, is open to change in the short run, and it is this structure that has attracted the attention of opponents of direct election of the president. A half-century ago, Maurice Duverger concluded that plurality election single-ballot procedures are likely to produce two-party systems whereas proportional representation and runoff designs encourage multipartyism.[10] Since then, many other scholars have studied the impact of electoral systems on party division and found that electoral systems influence the number of parties much as Duverger said and that, despite the importance of social structure, electoral structure has an independent impact on the number of parties.[11]

Single-member districts with plurality elections (elections with no runoffs) are winner-take-all methods of selecting officials. The impact of such an electoral system on the number of parties is commonly explained as operating through two complementary influences. The *mechanical* effect is that in a plurality-rule, single-ballot system all but the two strongest parties are underrepresented because votes for third parties do not translate into pluralities in many districts. The *psychological* factor reinforces the mechanical one in that electors do not want to waste votes by giving them to third parties, which are unlikely to win, so they so vote strategically for the lesser of two evils between the major parties. Similarly, politicians do not waste their energies running as third-party candidates because they cannot win.

Is the electoral college the basis of the two-party system? Nothing in the scholarly literature or our historical experience suggests that the electoral

college is a cause of the two-party system in America.[12] Americans fill
virtually every elected office in the country by directly electing officials in
single-member districts in plurality elections. This electoral protocol, not
the electoral college, is the real structural basis for our two-party system. In
other words, we have vast experience with direct election and have not
endured splintering, much less crippling, effects on the party system.

American political culture, with its pragmatism, consensus, and relative
lack of reinforcing cleavages, provides additional underpinnings for a two-
party system. As Gary Cox has shown, it takes more than the absence of
runoffs to create bipartisanism.[13] The electoral college is simply irrelevant.
As Clinton Rossiter has written, "The bounty of the American economy,
the fluidity of American society, the remarkable unity of the American
people, and, most important, the success of the American experiment have
all mitigated against the emergence of large dissenting groups that would
seek satisfaction of their special needs through the formation of political parties."[14]

In addition, the institution of the presidency encourages a two-party
system. According to V. O. Key, "The Presidency, unlike a multiparty
cabinet, cannot be parceled out among minuscule parties. The circumstances stimulate coalition within the electorate before the election rather
than in parliament after the vote. Since no more than two parties can for
long compete effectively for the Presidency, two contending groups tend to
develop, each built on its constituent units in each of the 50 states."[15] James
MacGregor Burns adds that parties focus around single executives, a pattern which forces third parties to amalgamate with major parties to achieve
some of their desired ends.[16]

There are other structural impediments to third parties. Federal campaign funding statutes require a third party to have obtained at least 5 percent of the vote in the previous presidential election to receive any funding
and 25 percent to receive full funding. The open and permeable nature of
American parties, as epitomized by the primary system, channels dissent
into the two major parties and works against the development of third
parties. State statutes ranging from restriction of ballot access to prevention
of primary losers from running in the general election under another party
label handicap third parties, as does the prohibition of "fusion" candidates
in most states.[17] According to Leon Epstein, state laws restricting third
parties have created an "institutionalized electoral duopoly."[18]

As several scholars concluded after studying the impact of abolishing the electoral college on the party system, there is "no reliable, convincing evidence to suggest that changing the presidential election system, in and of itself, would alter significantly the party system in a predictable manner. There are simply too many other factors that reinforce our system of two-party dominance beside Electoral College rules."[19]

The question remains, however, of whether the possibility of a runoff would change the structure of U.S. elections in a way that would encourage third parties.

ENCOURAGING THIRD PARTIES

A number of goals may motivate third parties to run in presidential elections. They may expect to win election or at least earn a position in a runoff. More cynically, a desire to deadlock the election or play a spoiler role may animate their efforts.

Would direct election of the president increase the probability of third-party presidential candidates with such goals? In the absence of a runoff provision, there is no question that direct election *discourages* third-party candidates. In a direct election, a party must win the entire country to gain the prize of the presidency. Coming in second or third gains a party no office and no leverage in the selection of the president. Moreover, under direct election, there would be no possibility of deadlocking an election. A third party could not leverage a few electoral votes to dictate the choice of president, because there would be no electoral votes to win. As a result, direct election would discourage third parties.

By contrast, the unit rule under the electoral college *encourages* third parties and provides incentive for regional candidates like Strom Thurmond in 1948 or George Wallace in 1968. Under the electoral college, prizes—states—are easier to win than is the entire country. Deadlocking a close election, and thus winning leverage in the choice of the president, may require a regional candidate to win only a few states, denying either major-party candidate a majority of the electoral vote. As we saw in some detail in Chapter 4, winning a few states may put a third party in a position to dictate the outcome of the election by either instructing its electors to support one of the major-party candidates in the electoral college or, in a contingent election in the House, by influencing the votes of representatives from the states that it won.

To put this analysis another way, consider two candidates, one contemplating running as a third-party candidate in a system of direct election, the other running under the electoral college. A potential candidate in a system of direct election risks his or her political future by running against the official party candidate. And there is no compensation. Such a candidate can win nothing at all coming in third, even if he takes a significant portion of the vote. So there is little incentive to run. Under the electoral college, however, a candidate finishing third might win some electoral votes and have leverage in determining the winner of the election. There is much more incentive for third-party candidates to run under the electoral college than under a system of direct election.

Larry Sabato implicitly recognizes that smaller electoral units encourage third parties when he argues against allocating electoral votes by congressional district because it would lower the winner-take-all bar from the state level to the district level and thus increase the probabilities of third parties winning electoral votes.[20] However, he misses the logical extension that raising the bar from the state level to the national level also will decrease the chances of third-party success.

Two other motivations may energize third parties. First, they may wish to illustrate the strength of the support for their cause, even if they have no hope of winning office. In such a case, the incentives to run are similar under the electoral college and direct election.

Second, it is theoretically possible that a third party may want to defeat a particular presidential candidate by drawing votes from that candidate. Because a third party is most likely to siphon votes from a party closer to it, it seems unlikely that this would be a compelling motivation for launching a candidacy.

Under the electoral college, however, there could be a situation such as occurred in 1948 and 1968, when some persons voting for Thurmond or Wallace might have followed their traditional habits and voted Democratic in their absence. The electoral college and the unit rule provide the opportunity for a party to win a few states and thus deny them to the disfavored candidate. Under direct election, by contrast, candidates do not win states and thus cannot deny them to another candidate.

In addition, no matter what its motivation for running, under the electoral college a third party can tip the balance in a closely contested state by siphoning a few votes from a major-party candidate.[21] There is little question, for example, that Ralph Nader cost Al Gore the election in 2000.[22] Most Nader voters would have voted for Gore in the absence of a Nader candidacy.[23] Gore lost Florida by 537 votes, whereas Nader received 97,488 votes in the state. (Pat Buchanan and Libertarian candidate Harry Browne received a total of only 33,899, which were more likely to go to Bush.) Similarly, Gore lost by 7,211 votes in New Hampshire, where Nader received 22,198 votes. (Buchanan and Browne together received 5,372 votes.)[24] Gore would have been elected if he had won either state.

The vote for Pat Buchanan exceeded the margin of victory of Gore over Bush in Iowa, New Mexico, Oregon, and Wisconsin. Yet we cannot attribute Bush's loss of these states to Buchanan without also considering the much larger vote that Nader received in each state. When we factor in the effects of both minor party candidates, it is highly likely that Gore would have still won the states in the absence of minor parties.

The electoral college, then, has not been successful in discouraging third parties. In presidential elections since the Civil War, third-party support has varied considerably between elections, but third parties have often received a substantial percentage of the vote *under the electoral college,* large enough to encourage future candidates and sometimes large enough to affect the outcome of the election (Table 8.1).

The electoral college has not discouraged candidates like Ross Perot and Ralph Nader with broad but less concentrated support than regional candidates. Moreover, the present system does not prevent many minor party candidates from qualifying for inclusion on ballots in many states. If we return to the quotations at the beginning of this section, one might wonder how Best could argue that a runoff would have encouraged Ross Perot in 1992, when he ran under the current system and won nearly 20 percent of the vote. He did not need the potential of a runoff for encouragement. As for Schlesinger's remarks, Perot, Nader, and Buchanan *did* run—under the electoral college.

The electoral college not only encourages rather than discourages third parties, it also discourages party competition in states that do not have close partisan divisions. As we saw in Chapter 6, the presidential candi-

Table 8.1
Third-Party Vote in Presidential Elections Since 1860

Year	Third Party % of Vote	Year	Third Party % of Vote
1864	0	1936	3
1868	0	1940	0
1872	1	1944	1
1876	1	1948	5
1880	4	1952	1
1884	3	1956	1
1888	4	1960	1
1892	11	1964	1
1896	3	1968	14
1900	3	1972	2
1904	6	1976	2
1908	5	1980	8
1912	35	1984	1
1916	5	1988	1
1920	6	1992	20
1924	17	1996	10
1928	1	2000	4
1932	3	2004	1
		2008	1

Sources: Congressional Quarterly's Guide to U.S. Elections, 6th ed. (Washington, DC: CQ Press, 2010); Jerrold G. Rusk, *A Statistical History of the American Electorate* (Washington, DC: CQ Press, 2001).

Note: Percentages are rounded to the nearest 1 percent.

dates of the main parties simply ignore these states because votes for the minority candidate do not count toward a national total. Counting every vote, regardless of where it is cast, in a direct election would foster two-party competition on a national scale. It would provide incentives for candidates to encourage all their supporters, no matter where they lived, to go to the polls and also encourage candidates to take their campaigns to these citizens. All of this would be a boon to two-party competition.

Party competition would not only encourage the second party but also discourage third parties. V. O. Key found that the unity of the Democratic

Party in the South was in almost direct proportion to the competition offered by Republicans. The more competition, the less splintered the Democrats.[25]

The evidence that the electoral college discourages third-party candidates is hardly compelling, whereas the evidence that it encourages third parties is strong. Moreover, in the absence of a runoff, the winner-take-all rule of a direct election would discourage third parties, and under any version, direct election would protect the country from the mischief of such third-party candidates as Strom Thurmond and George Wallace winning leverage to negotiate with the leading candidates or of a weakly supported third-party candidate like Ralph Nader determining the outcome of an election.

But would third parties receive more votes under a runoff system than under the electoral college? Would voters be discouraged from voting for third parties by the wasted-vote argument? John Ferejohn and Morris Fiorina have argued that rational voters should never engage in strategic voting—that is, voting for a major party candidate while actually favoring a third-party candidate.[26] Nevertheless, Paul Abramson, John Aldrich, Phil Paolino, and David Rohde conclude that George Wallace, John Anderson, and Ross Perot "were probably hurt somewhat by the wasted vote argument."[27]

Although the evidence is inherently circumstantial, there is reason to believe that a runoff feature in presidential elections between the top two contenders might encourage support for third parties in the first round of voting. We do not know whether such encouragement would be greater than the encouragement provided by the electoral college.

POLARIZING PARTIES

Opponents of direct election of the president fear that the threat of a runoff would not only splinter the party system but also more clearly define the ideological differences among the parties. If there were more parties, they would have to go to greater lengths to differentiate themselves and thus take clearer stands. Such stands, critics fear, would polarize politics in America.

There are three responses to such concerns. First, it is by no means clear that parties with clear stands are detrimental to democracy. For votes to be most effective in influencing public policy, the candidates must clearly differentiate themselves on the issues. Moreover, presidents cannot claim mandates for governing if they do not clarify their policy proposals during the campaign.

Second, the electoral college system has not prevented partisan polarization. One of the most important trends in American politics over the past four decades—*under the electoral college system*—has been the increasing homogeneity and polarization of the major parties.[28] As a result of decreasing diversity within the parties, there are fewer demands for compromise within each party.

Finally, there are limits on the fragmentation and polarization that would likely occur under direct election. It is true that each party in a multiparty system would have an incentive to differentiate itself. Yet the more seriously a party sought election, the more moderate it would have to become as long as voters were concentrated in the middle of the ideological spectrum, as they are in the United States. If a party made appeals to true believers alone, it would garner only a small number of votes.

V. O. Key found that factions within the one-party Democratic South were largely issueless. The potential of a runoff in the Democratic primaries did not polarize the factions. In fact, Key could not determine whether the possibility of a runoff encouraged factions at all. Some states that required majority election and runoffs if no candidate received a majority did not develop factions.[29]

There is also a theoretical possibility that candidates on the extremes could receive the bulk of the votes on the first ballot, eliminating middle-of-the-road candidates from the runoff. This could happen, however, only if the voters themselves were on the ideological extremes and were voting for candidates who gave them the options they desired. If the public was highly polarized, no party system could prevent extremist candidates from arising.

CORRUPT DEALS AMONG CANDIDATES

A runoff provision, advocates of the electoral college argue, would encourage those candidates who do not make the runoff to enter into secret and corrupt deals with the final two candidates in the period between the first ballot and the runoff. The deals that the winner might have made, they say, would diminish the president's ability to govern and decrease the legitimacy of the electoral verdict. Some authors also fear secret deals before the election to discourage (or encourage) a minor party.[30]

Once again, faulty premises lie at the base of these conclusions. Advocates of the electoral college fail to realize that the leaders of minor parties would have to make *open* bargains to serve as the basis for urging their followers to vote for a particular candidate. What good would a "secret" bargain do anyone? Supporters would want to know *why* they should support another candidate, what policy concessions a candidate has made to their views. Such concessions would have to be public.

The bargains that could be made would also be severely constrained. How could the leaders of minor parties deliver votes to other candidates if they bargained away the issue stances that attracted voters in the first place? If they made significant compromises, they could not deliver the votes. If they did not make such compromises, why would anyone bargain with them? Similarly, candidates from mainstream parties cannot compromise their issue stands with more extreme parties without alienating their own supporters, which they would be loath to do.

Because of a third party's concern for issues, moreover, its candidates would quite naturally endorse the party politically closer to the third party. The candidate's credibility would be lost if he or she endorsed the party farther from the third party's views. Could George Wallace really deliver votes to Hubert Humphrey? Could Ralph Nader deliver votes to George W. Bush? Or Patrick Buchanan to Al Gore? It is highly unlikely. Major-party candidates would understand the constraints on third parties, of course, limiting the ability of third-party candidates to extract much in the way of concessions from them. The limited benefits to be gained from bargaining between the first ballot and the runoff provide important disincentives to run in the first place.

Opponents of direct election of the president argue that politicians currently bargain in an open process before the national nominating conventions rather than in a closed process before the election or between the first ballot and a runoff. There is little evidence of such bargains, and advocates of the electoral college provide none. Actually, there is little need to bargain, because one of the candidates usually secures the nomination long before the convention. In 2000, for example, did George W. Bush make public concessions to John McCain? Did Al Gore make similar bargains with Bill Bradley? In 2008 did John McCain adopt Mitt Romney's policies? Or Mike Huckabee's? Did Barack Obama concede that Hillary Clinton was right on health care?

Not only is the premise of corrupt deals suspect, but the prospect of "secret" deals is also doubtful. In the age of 24/7 news coverage, just how long would any "secret" bargains remain secret?

As we saw in Chapter 4, the chances of secret and corrupt bargains are greatest in instances when no candidate receives a majority of the electoral vote. In such cases under the electoral college, minor-party candidates would have to deliver only a few electors, chosen for their loyalty, or a few representatives if the selection moved to the House. The potential for secret and corrupt deals is much greater under the electoral college than in a public runoff between leading candidates.

In addition, it is because third parties have the potential to play a complicating role in the electoral college that major-party candidates discourage them from running, as both parties did with Ross Perot, for example.

Related to the concern about corrupt and secret deals is the fear among advocates of the electoral college that the candidate who came in second on an initial ballot could win the runoff. Apparently, the fear is that the only way this could happen is if the second-place finisher made a corrupt deal with a third party for its votes. We have seen, however, that such a deal is highly improbable. Moreover, there is no evidence that the leader of a third party could deliver votes for anyone he or she chose, independent of issues.

There is no reason to be concerned if the candidate who came in second on the first ballot wins in the runoff. Indeed, this is exactly what should happen if voters prefer that candidate. Such an outcome can occur only if a majority of the public dislikes the candidate who came in first on the initial ballot and that candidate is the third or lower choice of supporters of the other parties. As a result, the voters would be choosing the candidate they can most support, or at least abide.

A RUNOFF?

Even though it would not encourage corrupt deals among political leaders, a runoff has a number of disadvantages. The runoff has some potential to fragment the party system. A runoff at the end of an already lengthy campaign would also place added burdens on the presidential candidates and especially on their depleted campaign treasuries. It would require a more rapid count and certification of ballots, including the resolution of disputes, than would otherwise be necessary. It is possible that a runoff would also result in a considerable vote drop-off from the initial ballot. By definition, a second ballot would delay the selection of the winner.

These costs of a runoff raise the question: Is it possible to institute direct election of the president without provision for a runoff? To answer this question we must first avoid falling into a logical trap. It is circular reasoning to argue that direct election will produce a plethora of candidates, which will force us to have a runoff, which will encourage candidates. In fact, direct election will not produce more general election candidates than the electoral college.

I have emphasized the importance of political equality throughout this book. It follows that the candidate who is most favored by the public ought to win the election. In more formal terms, the candidate who could beat all other candidates in a series of two-person races ought to become president. Such a candidate, whom the public most prefers, is known in game theory as the Condorcet winner.[31] For sake of presentation, I will typically refer to such a candidate as the "most preferred" candidate.

40 Percent Requirement

Would a runoff enhance the prospects of selecting the candidate most preferred by the public? The most common formulation is to require a runoff if no candidate receives at least 40 percent of the vote in the first round of voting. Since the beginning of popular voting in presidential elections, only one candidate, Abraham Lincoln, received less than 40 percent. He received 39.8 percent of the vote even though in ten states he did not run a slate of electors—a situation unlikely to recur. (It is rare for a winning gubernatorial candidate to receive less than 45 percent of the vote.[32] Even in the chaotic circumstances of the California recall election of 2003, with more than one hundred candidates on the ballot, the winner received 49 percent of the vote. Similarly, in the days of the one-party South, it was typical for the primary to produce a *majority* on the first ballot.)[33] A runoff thus seems unnecessary.

If the most preferred candidate won the most votes and more than 40 percent of the vote on the first ballot, no runoff would occur or be necessary to elect the most preferred candidate. If the candidate most preferred by the public finished third or lower on the initial ballot, a run-off would be irrelevant because that candidate would not be included in the runoff.

If the candidate most preferred by the public came in second on the initial ballot but another candidate received more than 40 percent, there would be no runoff and the most preferred candidate would lose the election. Thus, a runoff provision would not help to elect the most preferred candidate. In 1912 Theodore Roosevelt was probably the most preferred candidate because he would have received most of the vote for Republican William Howard Taft if Taft had not been running. However, Woodrow Wilson received more than 40 percent of the vote, so there would not have been a runoff anyway.

A runoff would produce the Condorcet winner only if the candidate most preferred by the public came in second on the initial ballot and the candidate who came in first failed to receive 40 percent of the vote. There has been only one presidential election since the beginning of popular voting in which a runoff might have been useful in electing the candidate most preferred by the public. This is the election of 1860, when Stephen A. Douglas would have beaten Abraham Lincoln with the support of the Solid South. We would hardly wish to generalize from this most deviant of elections.

A runoff with a trigger lower than 40 percent in the presidential election would thus produce few benefits for the country and would carry with it the risk of damaging the two-party system and exhausting the public and the candidates in an extended election. A plurality election encourages supporters of third parties to cast sophisticated votes for their second-favorite candidate, increasing the chance of electing the candidate most preferred by the public.

Majority Vote Requirement

Some reformers argue that only a president who has won with the support of a majority of voters possesses the legitimacy to govern. In a race of three or more candidates, a runoff may be necessary to produce a majority winner. Typically, these reformers advocate a runoff between the two candidates finishing with the greatest number of votes in the first round of voting.[34]

Yet there is no need to force artificially a majority vote for a candidate for the winner to govern. We saw in Chapter 7 that plurality winners are among the strongest presidents in U.S. history. We fill almost all elected offices in the United States by plurality election, so why should the presidency differ?

In both formal social choice theory and democratic theory more generally, Kenneth May's classic theorem occupies a prominent place as an argument for simple majority rule. The theorem states that in social decisions between two options, simple majority rule, uniquely among all aggregation procedures, satisfies the four normatively appealing conditions of being (1) open to all inputs ("universal domain"), (2) not biased in favor of any particular voter ("anonymity"), (3) not biased in favor of any particular option ("neutrality"), and (4) "positively responsive" to people's votes (if one or more voters change their votes in favor of one option and no others change theirs, then the social decision does not change in the opposite direction; and if the outcome was a tie before the change, then the tie is broken in the direction of the change).[35]

In its original form, however, May's theorem applies only to decisions between two options (for example, two candidates). Robert Goodin and Christian List have extended May's theorem to decisions where there are more than two choices and in which voters each cast a vote for one option or abstain. They prove that plurality rule uniquely satisfies May's conditions in single-vote balloting as we typically use in the United States.[36]

As the Gibbard-Satterthwaite theorem shows, the potential always exists of strategic manipulation in voting systems.[37] Under plurality rule, strategic voting is limited, however, because voters have an incentive to vote for their preferred option between those two options that they think are most likely to win. There is no incentive to vote insincerely in the hopes of manipulating a runoff.

Plurality rule can be criticized for focusing solely on voters' revealed "first choices" and not taking into account their full preferences, including their ranking of the candidates for whom they did not vote. Single-vote balloting does not solve the problems raised by standard social choice paradoxes, the most prominent of which is Arrow's impossibility theorem.[38] However, a runoff does not solve the problem either.

Instant Runoff Voting

It would be ideal to collect voters' full preferences on all presidential candidates. The normal means of doing so is to hold a runoff election. Is there any way to avoid the costs of such an election while obtaining the benefits of increased information on voters' preferences?

There is: instant runoff voting (IRV). A number of cities, including Minneapolis, San Francisco, Oakland, and Saint Paul, have adopted IRV to select mayors and city council members and sometimes other officials. Several states, including Arkansas, Louisiana, and South Carolina, employ the system for overseas voters. Australia uses IRV to elect members of Parliament in single-member districts and to elect members of most state and territory lower houses. The Republic of Ireland has used IRV to elect its president since 1922. London and several other British cities elect their mayors using IRV.[39]

Under this system, voters receive one vote and one ballot, but have the option of ranking candidates in order of preference (first, second, third, fourth, and so on). First choices are then tabulated, and if a candidate receives a majority of first choices, he or she is elected. If nobody has a majority of votes on the first count, one or more simulated runoffs is conducted, using each voter's preferences as indicated on the ballot. After the first count, the candidate with the lowest number of votes is eliminated, and the second preferences of the voters who supported the candidate are distributed to the remaining candidates in order. All other ballots are counted according to the top candidate of each. The weakest candidates are successively eliminated and their voters' ballots are redistributed to the highest remaining choices until a candidate earns a majority of votes.

A full discussion of IRV is beyond the scope of this volume. It is likely that the probability of the most favored candidate winning, and winning with a majority of the vote, would be greater under IRV than under the electoral college. IRV alleviates the "spoiler effect" whereby a third party with limited support can determine the outcome of an election, as in 2000, by taking a disproportionate number of votes from the candidate who is otherwise the favored candidate between the two major contenders. Moreover, because there is no second round of voting, there is no incentive for candidates to run in the hope of preventing a candidate from receiving a majority of the vote.[40]

However, IRV will not always select a Condorcet winner. Suppose, for example, that 40 percent of voters rank three candidates XYZ, another 40 percent rank them the reverse, ZYX, and the remaining 20 percent have Y as their first preference. Y will be eliminated in the first round of the count, despite being preferred by a (different) majority to each of X and Z. Such a scenario is not fanciful. One can easily imagine a centrist party that is the first preference of the fewest voters but the second preference of many more on both ends of the political spectrum and thus the preferred party overall.

IRV would be more difficult than plurality elections to implement with security and integrity because the votes cannot be simply summed.

Paradoxically, under some scenarios, ranking a candidate higher can actually cause the candidate to lose, and ranking a candidate lower can cause the candidate to win. Also possible is a scenario in which some voters, by turning out to vote rather than not voting, hurt the alternatives they rank highest. Thus IRV can be "nonmonotonic." In other words, a candidate may rise in the voting when she should go down, or vice versa. Whether a candidate who gets through the first round of counting will ultimately be elected may depend on which of her rivals she has to face in subsequent rounds, and some votes for a weaker challenger may do a candidate more good than a vote for that candidate herself. In short, a candidate might lose if certain voters back her, but would have won if they had not.[41]

Voters can also manipulate the rankings by strategic voting. If the candidate who is your second preference is a strong challenger to your first preference, you may be able to help your first preference by putting the challenger last.[42]

As in direct election without a runoff, there is only one prize in IRV. It is possible that, seeing that they have little chance of winning, small third parties would choose not to run candidates. However, IRV might encourage voters to support third parties in the first round, because voters have a backup of then supporting one of the established parties as a second choice. Votes for third parties would no longer be wasted.

Prudence dictates close scrutiny of IRV. There is much about it that we do not fully understand. Interestingly, a study of its use in three western Canadian provinces concluded, "On balance, it differed little from the single member plurality system."[43]

The electoral college is not essential for a two-party system and actually encourages third parties to run presidential candidates and discourages party competition in many states. There is no evidence that direct election of the president would polarize political parties. Similarly, there would be little incentive for secret deals under direct election and severe constraints on the bargains third parties could make. Moreover, there is much less chance of such deals under direct election than under the contingent election provision of the electoral college.

In addition, most critics of direct election of the president assume that it would require a runoff provision. Although it is possible that such a rule would encourage third-party candidacies, there is no need to institute a runoff under direct election of the president. Advocates of the electoral college are correct that America is better off without a second-ballot runoff election. They are incorrect, however, that the electoral college is the only way to avoid such a runoff. Although there is no voting system that guarantees that the most preferred candidate will win, both plurality election and IRV are more likely than the electoral college to produce the Condorcet winner. Neither system requires a second ballot.

Chapter 9 Conclusion

The electoral college is an extraordinarily complex system for electing a president, one that has the potential to undo the people's will at many points in the long journey from the selection of electors to counting their votes in Congress. Faithless electors may fail to vote as the people who elected them wish. Congress may find it difficult to choose justly between competing slates of electors. What is more significant, the electoral college violates political equality, favoring some citizens over others depending solely on the state in which they live. The unit rule, the allocation of electoral votes among the states, the differences in voter turnout among states, and the size of the House make the aggregation of votes for president inherently unjust.

Virtually no one is willing to defend the electoral college's provisions for contingent elections of the president and vice president. These provisions blatantly violate political equality, directly disenfranchise hundreds of thousands of Americans, have the potential to grossly misrepresent the wishes of the public, make the president dependent on Congress, give a few individuals extraordinary power to select the president, enable the selection of a president and vice president from different parties, and fail to deal with a tie for third in the electoral college.

For two centuries, supporters of the electoral college have built their arguments on a series of faulty premises. We cannot justify the electoral college as a result of the framers' coherent design based on clear political principles. The founders did not articulate a theory to justify political inequality. Instead, the electoral college was a jury-rigged improvisation formulated in a desperate effort to reach a compromise that would allow the Constitutional Convention to adjourn and take the entire Constitution to the people.

We have also seen that the electoral college does not protect important interests that would be overlooked or harmed under a system of direct election of the president. States—including states with small populations—do not embody coherent, unified interests and communities, and they have little need for protection. Even if they did, the electoral college does not provide it. Contrary to the claims of its supporters, candidates do not pay attention to most small states. The electoral college actually distorts the campaign such that candidates ignore many large and most small states and devote their attention to a few competitive states. Under the electoral college it makes no sense for candidates to allocate scarce resources to states they either cannot win or are certain to win, in which case the size of their victory is irrelevant.

Similarly, African Americans, Hispanics, and other minorities do not benefit from the electoral college because they are not well positioned to determine the outcomes in states. As a result, the electoral college system actually discourages attention to minority interests.

The electoral college also contributes little to maintaining the cohesion of the American polity by protecting it from alleged harms of direct election of the president. It does not contain the results of fraud and accidental circumstances within states. Instead, it magnifies their consequences for the outcome nationally. Similarly, under a system of direct popular election of the president, recounts would be *less* likely than under the electoral college.

The electoral college neither produces concurrent majorities around the country nor forces winning candidates to appeal successfully to all segments of society and all geographic locations. Nor does it encourage candidate moderation. Equally problematic is the view that the electoral college provides presidents with effective coalitions for governing. Moreover, the electoral college does not produce compromise within states, and it is fundamentally different from constitutional provisions that require super-majorities to take positive action.

Presidents frequently win election under the electoral college without a majority, and winning a majority of the vote in and of itself does not make a president more effective in dealing with Congress. Although the wide-spread perception of a mandate is an advantage for a president, election results do not reliably translate into such a perception.

The electoral college is not a safeguard of federalism. The electoral college is not based on federative principles and is unnecessary for a healthy federal system. Direct election of the president would not threaten the power of state and local parties and officials or presidential nominating conventions, and we should welcome national standards for elections.

The electoral college is not essential for a two-party system and does not promote it. Instead, it undermines it by encouraging third parties to run presidential candidates and discouraging party competition in states where one party has a significant advantage. There is no evidence that direct election of the president would polarize political parties. Similarly, there would be little incentive for secret deals among political leaders under direct election and severe constraints on the bargains third parties could make. Moreover, there is much less chance of such deals under direct election than under the contingent election provision under the electoral college. And there is no need for a runoff under direct election.

With its many flaws, it is not surprising that no other country uses such a system for selecting its chief executive. Indirect methods such as the electoral college are clearly on their way out. Recent reforms in democratic countries have replaced indirect procedures with direct popular voting. The United States is now the only country that elects a politically powerful president via an electoral college and the only one in which a candidate can become president without having obtained the highest number of votes in the sole or final round of popular voting.[1]

ALTERNATIVES TO THE ELECTORAL COLLEGE

Is there a method of selecting the president that would avoid the problems of faithless electors, competing slates of electors, selection of the president by Congress, violations of political equality, and distortions of political campaigns? Could that same system increase the impact of minorities, discourage fraud, encourage electoral turnout and party competition, and ultimately select the candidate most favored by the American people?

Over the decades, many reformers have offered plans to change the electoral college system. There is, for example, the Automatic Plan, which would award all electoral votes in each state directly to the candidate who obtained the most votes statewide. This alternative would constitutionally mandate the unit rule currently used to award electoral votes in forty-eight states and the District of Columbia. Although it would solve the problem of the faithless elector and to that extent be a worthwhile change, it would do nothing to remedy the much greater problems created by the electoral college that I have identified throughout this book.

Some plans focus primarily on the laudable goal of increasing the probability that the candidate who receives the most votes wins the election. The District Plan would award one electoral vote to the candidate who carries each congressional district within a state, with the two additional electoral votes in each state going to the candidate winning a plurality of the statewide vote. This alternative would constitutionally mandate the system currently used to award electoral votes in Maine and Nebraska. The Proportional Plan would apportion electoral votes in each state in proportion to the percentage of the statewide popular vote won by each ticket. Most versions of these plans would eliminate the office of elector and would award electoral votes directly to the candidates. In common with direct election, most would also require joint tickets of presidential and vice presidential candidates.

Each of these reforms would require a constitutional amendment, because it is unlikely that states would abandon the unit rule voluntarily. State officials believe (mistakenly, as we have seen) that it maximizes their power to cast votes as a block, especially if other states retain the unit rule. Perhaps the biggest problem with the Proportional Plan is that, other factors remaining the same, it would not have prevented an electoral college deadlock in 1960, 1968, 1992, 1996, and 2000, and the results for 1976 are unclear.[2] Allocating electoral votes in proportion to the vote a candidate receives would also encourage third parties, because it would be possible to win electoral votes by winning a relatively small percentage of the popular vote. We have seen the mischief that third parties can cause in contingent elections.

The District Plan would dramatically increase the significance of redistricting and create even more incentives for creative gerrymandering than there are now because presidential electors would be at stake. Redistricting has made approximately 90 percent of House districts noncompetitive and distorted the translation of votes into seats. The same problem would occur in presidential elections. It is impossible to project with certainty results under different methods of selecting the president. We cannot assume that candidates would have campaigned the same way and that voters would have responded to them in the same way, independent of the electoral system in place. Nevertheless, it is instructive to note that, assuming the same votes, the District Plan would have produced no winner in 1976 and would have elected George W. Bush in 2000.[3] Given the lack of competition within districts, there would inevitably be distortions in the campaign and in the attention different candidates pay to voters. The plan would do little to discourage fraud or encourage electoral turnout and party competition.

In the late 1970s a Twentieth Century Fund Task Force on Reform of the Presidential Election Process proposed a National Bonus Plan that would add a national pool of 102 electoral votes for the popular vote winner, balancing in theory the existing federal bonus (the two votes per state corresponding to its senators, plus two for the District of Columbia) with a national bonus.[4] The proposal would also eliminate electors. If no candidate received a majority of the electoral votes, there would be a runoff between the two candidates who received the most popular votes. There would be a mandatory recount and a rechecking of the tallies by an independent authority or agency.

The task force argued that the National Bonus Plan would make it impossible for the popular vote winner to lose the election, encourage voter participation and party competition, enhance voter equality, discourage regional candidates and third parties, lessen the likelihood of runoffs or of presidents winning without a plurality of the vote, and preserve the federal character of the election process. In other words, it would accomplish much of what would be accomplished by direct election of the president.

Although the National Bonus Plan would be an improvement over the electoral college, it would add layers to the already complex electoral college system, including a runoff, with all its disadvantages. The sole reason for this Rube Goldberg–like system seems to be to preserve the appearance of the federal aspect of the electoral college while actually eliminating its consequences. This cosmetic is purchased at a high price, for the fundamental inequality of the electoral college would remain, as would much of its distortion of the presidential campaigns. Candidates would still need to win states to receive the bulk of their electoral votes.

More recently, reformers have proposed a means of getting around the need to amend the Constitution. Under the U.S. Constitution (article II, section 1), the states have exclusive and plenary power to allocate their electoral votes, and they may change their state laws concerning the awarding of their electoral votes at any time. Under the National Popular Vote plan, states would enter into an interstate compact, agreeing that all of a state's electoral votes would be awarded to the presidential candidate who received the most popular votes nationwide.[5] The plan would take effect only when states cumulatively possessing a majority of the electoral votes— that is, enough to elect a president (270 of 538)—enacted identical bills embracing the plan.

Such a bill has been passed by state legislatures representing 61 electoral votes, 23 percent of the 270 necessary to activate the law—Hawaii, Illinois, Maryland, New Jersey, and Washington—and by at least one legislative chamber in Arkansas, California, Colorado, Connecticut, Delaware, Maine, Massachusetts, Michigan, Nevada, New Mexico, New York, North Carolina, Oregon, Rhode Island, and Vermont.

Although a state would be free to withdraw from the National Popular Vote compact at any time, the details of the compact postpone the effective date of a withdrawal occurring between July 20 of a presidential election year and the following January 20 inauguration date. In addition, as we have seen, federal law specifies that presidential electors may be appointed only on one specific day in every four-year period, namely the first Tuesday after the first Monday in November, and the impairments clause of the Constitution prohibits withdrawal from an interstate compact in any manner other than that specified in the contract. The real question for the National Popular Vote plan is whether a state, having cast its electoral votes contrary to the outcome in the state vote, would choose to repeal the contract for the next election.

DIRECT ELECTION

The Automatic, Proportional, District, and National Bonus plans all have limitations as remedies to the problems caused by the electoral college. The National Vote Plan is a commendable effort to achieve direct election of the president without amending the Constitution, but its sustainability is uncertain. There remains the system that Americans use to elect every member of Congress, every governor, and virtually every elected official in the country: direct election.

Any proposal to reform the electoral college must deal with its primary flaws. Direct election of the president remedies them all. Direct election of the president would eliminate all the problems caused by the selection and voting of electors themselves as well as the possibility of a contingency election in Congress. Direct election of the president assures political equality. Aggregating votes nationwide would decrease the incentives for and impact of electoral fraud, and it would strengthen the two-party system by discouraging third parties and, as we will see, giving parties an incentive to organize in areas in which they are weak. In addition, direct election would not diminish benefits from the electoral college that, as we have seen, do not exist.

Some critics of direct election mistakenly argue, in the words of Larry Sabato, that under direct election of the president, "candidates would be inclined to run airport 'tarmac' campaigns, jetting from population center to population center and focusing advertising dollars on large urban areas with many voters, virtually ignoring large swaths of the nation where there are relatively few voters."[6] Yet this is a myopic view, and only candidates wishing to lose the election would follow such a strategy. By investigating campaigns under direct election in more detail, we can see more clearly why it would have a wide range of benefits for the polity.

Campaigning

We know that candidates under the electoral college ignore most of the country, especially rural areas. Moreover, they do so because of the incentives of the electoral system. Because every vote counts in a direct election, candidates would have an incentive to appeal to all voters and not just those strategically located in swing states.[7] An extra vote—or a lost vote—in Massachusetts or Texas would count as much as one in Michigan or Florida.[8] Thus presidential candidates would be much more attentive to small states and minorities under direct election than they are under the electoral college. As Republican vice presidential and presidential candidate Robert Dole explained, "Were we to switch to a system of direct election, I think we would see a resulting change in the nature of campaigning. While urban areas will still be important campaigning centers, there will be a new emphasis given to smaller states. Candidates will soon realize that all votes are important, and votes from small states carry the same import as votes from large states. That to me is one of the major attractions of direct election. Each vote carries equal importance."[9]

With these incentives, candidates would find it easy to spread their attention more evenly across the country. Because the cost of advertising is mainly a function of market size, it does not cost more to reach ten thousand voters in Wyoming than it does to reach ten thousand voters in a neighborhood in Queens or Los Angeles. Actually, it might cost less to reach voters in smaller communities because larger markets tend to run out of commercial time, increasing the price of advertising. Moreover, advertisers pay a premium to reach television viewers in large metropolitan areas. Thus audiences in smaller population centers are more cost effective for political campaigns to target.[10]

Moreover, Goux and Hopkins found that the top 10 media markets contained 31.6 percent of the swing voters, and a prime-time campaign advertisement cost an aggregate of $14,859 per ratings point (or exposure to 1 percent of households). The bottom 155 markets, by contrast, had 35.8 percent of swing voters and cost in the aggregate just $10,737 per ratings point. In other words, there were more swing voters in the smaller markets, and it costs less to reach them than it does to reach swing voters in the large metropolitan markets.[11]

Politicians understand the cost effectiveness of advertising, even if advocates of the electoral college do not. That is why, in the election of 2000, for example, the candidates "devoted nearly as much advertising to Yakima as in Seattle, as much to Traverse City as to Flint, as much to Wausau as to Milwaukee" when they campaigned within states.[12]

Direct election of the president also would provide the incentive for candidates to encourage all of their supporters, no matter where they live, to go to the polls, because under direct election, every vote counts. Conversely, under the electoral college, it does not matter how many votes a candidate receives in a state as long as the number of votes surpasses that which any opponent receives. The goal is to win states, not voters. As Douglas Bailey, the media manager of the 1976 Ford-Dole campaign, put it, "There is a vast population [outside urban areas], with every vote counting, that you cannot ignore in a direct election."[13] Dole himself added, "Under direct election, candidates also would have to pay attention to areas within states that are now ignored because they are safe for one party or the other." Thus "the voters in the majority of States would receive greater attention and the objective of federalism would be served better."[14]

It is possible, but by no means certain, that under direct election some candidates would focus their visits on large urban areas where they would receive free television coverage before large audiences. Such actions would do nothing to undermine the argument against the electoral college, however. Small states cannot be worse off than they are now, because under the electoral college, candidates rarely visit or advertise in them. Direct election of the president cannot diminish campaign efforts that do not exist. Instead, direct election would provide *increased* incentives for candidates to campaign in most small states, as well as increased incentives to campaign in many large and medium-sized states. Moreover, the relative novelty of a visit to smaller media markets could stimulate more press and popular attention than the candidates receive in larger markets, providing an additional incentive to campaign in them. Direct election would disperse campaign efforts rather than deprive small states of them.

A perfect example is what occurred in 2004, when it appeared that one of Maine's electoral votes was up for grabs (Maine allocates two of its four electoral votes based on the popular vote in its two congressional districts). The campaigns sent a steady stream of surrogates to Maine's northern district.[15] In 2008 similar efforts were made to win the 2nd congressional district of Nebraska, the other state that allocates an electoral vote to the winner of each congressional district.

Similarly, there is no reason to be concerned that a national campaign would force candidates to rely more on technology. In the twenty-first century, candidates rely almost entirely on television and direct mail—under the electoral college—to reach voters. It is not clear whether it would cost more to campaign across the nation than in only a few battleground states. With every vote counting equally, candidates would have an incentive to distribute their campaign spending more equally across the country. There would be no need to concentrate on a few battleground states.

Consequences of Increased Competition

By making every vote in every state count toward electing the president, direct election would stimulate state party-building efforts in the weaker party, especially in less competitive states, and would encourage both parties to campaign actively. Most political scientists agree that one of the keys to increasing voting turnout levels in the United States is increased mobilization efforts on the part of the parties and candidates.[16] The impact is likely to be especially significant among lower-income voters.[17] Party competition is crucial to increasing voting turnout because competition stimulates interest in the electorate and induces the parties and candidates to expend resources to win the votes of potential supporters in states they could not win as a whole. The more media expenditures and candidate visits a state received in the 2000 presidential election, the higher the voter turnout.[18] Better-informed people are more likely to vote,[19] and their information levels, as well as focus on policy, in presidential elections reflect the high level of policy content in the candidates' political advertisements.[20] Moreover, people are more likely to vote if they think their vote matters,[21] and turnout levels affect election outcomes.[22]

By contrast, the electoral college reduces the incentives for voter participation in states that are safe for the locally dominant party's candidate. It also weakens the incentive for either the majority or minority party to attempt to persuade citizens to go to the polls and support its national ticket. Under the electoral college it makes no sense for candidates to allocate scarce resources to states they either cannot win or are certain to win, in which case, the size of their loss or victory is irrelevant.

Not only would more citizens participate in choosing the president under direct election, but they would also be better informed. Voters exposed to political advertising know more about the candidates and their issue stances.[23] Residents of battleground states are more likely than residents of other states to be interested in and follow the campaign in the news and more likely to discuss politics and think about the election.[24] There is also some evidence that increased campaigning can influence not only whether people vote but also how they vote.[25]

The electoral college encourages candidates to focus on areas of the country that are competitive and to ignore the rest of the country. In many instances, the lack of competition in areas such as the South and the large states such as California, Texas, and New York has the consequence of discouraging candidate attention to the interests of racial and ethnic minorities. Increased competition across the nation under direct election would reduce the power of sectionalism in politics and encourage candidates to focus their campaigns on the entire nation, including minorities.[26]

Given its many advantages of direct election of the president for the polity, the United States should adopt this system. The president and vice president are the only national officials who represent the people as a whole, and the candidate who wins the most votes best approximates the choice of the people. This is the essence of "the consent of the governed."

WHY NOT ELECT EVERYONE BY THE SAME RULES?

A common refrain from advocates of the electoral college goes something like this: "If you insist on majority—or at least plurality—rule, why don't you insist on abolishing the Senate, seats in which are allocated to states rather than population?" The answer is easy. The Senate is explicitly designed to represent states and the interests within them. The presidency is designed to do something quite different. The president is to rise above parochial interests and represent the nation as a whole, not one part of it.

Similarly, some defenders of the electoral college ask, "If you are so concerned about plurality rule in choosing the president, what about all the nonelected judges and other officials in government? Shouldn't we be electing them as well?" Of course not. It is not feasible to elect all these officials, no matter how we select the president. The issue is not the election of other officials. The issue is letting the greatest number of people select the president who nominates judges and executive officials.

PROSPECTS FOR CHANGE

At the core of the democratic process is the view that "all votes must be counted as equal."[27] In an election for a national officeholder, each voter has a right to expect that he or she will stand in the same relation to the national official as every other voter. Given its advantages for the polity, the United States should adopt direct election of the president.

A constitutional amendment is not a pipe dream. In 1969 the House passed a constitutional amendment to establish direct election of the president by a bipartisan vote of 338 to 70. The American Bar Association, the Chamber of Commerce, the AFL-CIO, the League of Women Voters, and other leading organizations backed the amendment. President Nixon endorsed it, and a poll of state legislatures indicated that the amendment would be approved by the requisite three-fourths of the states. The bill passed the Senate Judiciary Committee by a vote of 11 to 6 and reached the floor in September 1970. There it met a prolonged filibuster from southern senators, who did not want the president elected by a popular vote. After the Civil Rights revolution of the 1960s, they were trying to preserve the old order against any further national influence. Supporters of the amendment fell a few votes short of invoking cloture. And so the bill died. Its death was not the result of opposition from small states, however. Instead, it was the issue of race and the political power of the South that killed reform.[28]

The public has continuously supported abolishing the electoral college. The Gallup Poll reported in 2001 that "there is little question that the American public would prefer to dismantle the Electoral College system, and go to a direct popular vote for the presidency. In Gallup polls that stretch back more than fifty years, a majority of Americans have continually expressed support for the notion of an official amendment of the U.S. Constitution that would allow for direct election of the president."[29] Similarly, a series of state polls taken in the past three years have found that large majorities favor directly electing the president.[30]

In polls conducted on November 11–12 and December 15–17, 2000, Gallup asked about the electoral college system. Even at this highly charged political moment, about 60 percent of the American public favored amending the Constitution so that the candidate who receives the most total votes nationwide wins the election. Only about a third of the public favored keeping the electoral college, despite the apparent reluctance on the part of Republicans to support the change—which would have given the presidency that year to Democrat Al Gore rather than to Republican George W. Bush.

Despite the public's support for change, there is no question that instituting direct election of the president will be difficult.[31] In these times of extreme partisan polarization, it is interesting to note that defense of or opposition to the electoral college has traditionally not been a partisan issue. Over the years, Richard Nixon, Gerald Ford, Jimmy Carter, Robert Taft, Hubert Humphrey, and Robert Dole have supported abolition of the electoral college and direct election of the president.[32] Nevertheless, an obstacle to reform at present could be the stake some Republicans may feel they have in the electoral college in the wake of George W. Bush's 2000 electoral victory when he received fewer votes than his opponent.

Before election day in 2000, Republicans were actually much more concerned about the opposite scenario—that Bush would win the popular vote but lose the electoral vote—and the Bush campaign apparently prepared contingency plans in case this happened. CNN analyst Jeff Greenfield reported that "at least two conservative commentators were specifically briefed by the Bush campaign shortly before taking to the airwaves about the line of attack to be taken in the event that Bush wound up losing the Electoral count despite a popular vote lead."[33] Similarly, the *New York Daily News* reported before the election that the Bush campaign had prepared talking points about the essential unfairness of the electoral college and intended to run advertisements, encourage a massive talk radio operation, and mobilize local business leaders and the clergy against acceptance of a Gore victory if Bush won the popular vote. The goal was to persuade electors to cast their votes for the popular vote winner rather than be bound by the winner in their respective states.[34]

It would not be unprecedented for a political party to abandon a principled stance in favor of what it perceives to be political gain. In the case of the electoral college, however, there need not be a conflict between principle and pragmatism. The best evidence is that neither party has a lock on the electoral college.[35] If the Republicans had such a lock, Bill Clinton and Barack Obama would not have won the presidency. Our political history shows that party strength in various states ebbs and flows. Reliance on institutional arrangements to advantage a party is likely to backfire. Republicans do not need to rely on an antidemocratic relic of the eighteenth century to achieve power.

At least as great a challenge as obtaining bipartisan support will be amending the Constitution, appropriately a complex and time-consuming task. Although the public and many states and organizations support direct election, there are obstacles to change. Principal among them are officials who believe that their states or the members of their organizations (such as racial minorities) benefit from the electoral college. We now know that these officials are wrong. They have reached their conclusions on the basis of faulty premises.

It is more important than ever that we act on our best principles and not our worst instincts. Understanding the flawed foundations of the electoral college is the critical first step on the road to reforming the system of presidential selection. The culmination of this effort should be giving Americans the right to elect directly the presidents who serve them.

Appendix: U.S. Constitutional
Provisions Relating to Presidential Elections

ARTICLE II

Section 1. The executive Power shall be vested in a President of the United States of America. He shall hold his Office during the Term of four Years, and, together with the Vice President, chosen for the same Term, be elected, as follows.

Each State shall appoint, in such Manner as the Legislature thereof may direct, a Number of Electors, equal to the whole Number of Senators and Representatives to which the State may be entitled in the Congress; but no Senator or Representative, or Person holding an Office of Trust or Profit under the United States, shall be appointed an Elector.

[The Electors shall meet in their respective States, and vote by Ballot for two Persons, of whom one at least shall not be an Inhabitant of the same State with themselves. And they shall make a List of all the Persons voted for, and of the Number of Votes for each; which List they shall sign and certify, and transmit sealed to the Seat of the Government of the United States, directed to the President of the Senate. The President of the Senate shall, in the Presence of the Senate and House of Representatives, open all the Certificates, and the Votes shall then be counted. The Person having the greatest Number of Votes shall be the President, if such Number be a Majority of the whole Number of Electors appointed; and if there be more than one who have such Majority, and have an equal Number of Votes, then the House of Representatives shall immediately chuse by Ballot one of them for President; and if no Person have a majority, then from the five highest on the List the said House shall in like Manner chuse the President. But in chusing the President, the Votes shall be taken by States, the Representation from each State having one Vote; a quorum for this Purpose shall consist of a Member or Members from two thirds of the States, and a Majority of all the States shall be necessary to a Choice. In every Case, after the Choice of the President, the Person having the greatest Number of Votes of the Electors shall be the Vice President. But if there should remain two or more who have equal Votes, the Senate shall chuse from them by Ballot the Vice President.]*

The Congress may determine the Time of chusing the Electors, and the Day on which they shall give their Votes; which Day shall be the same throughout the United States.

No Person except a natural born Citizen, or a Citizen of the United States, at the time of the Adoption of this Constitution, shall be eligible to the Office of President; neither shall any person be eligible to that Office who shall not have attained to the Age of thirty five Years, and been fourteen Years a Resident within the United States.

In Case of the Removal of the President from Office, or of his Death, Resignation, or Inability to discharge the Powers and Duties of the said Office, the Same shall devolve on the Vice President, and the Congress may by Law provide for the Case of Removal, Death, Resignation or Inability, both of the President and Vice President, declaring what Officer shall then act as President, and such Officer shall act accordingly, until the Disability be removed, or a President shall be elected.

The President shall, at stated Times, receive for his Services, a Compensation, which shall neither be increased nor diminished during the Period for which he shall have been elected, and he shall not receive within that Period any other Emolument from the United States, or any of them.

Before he enter on the Execution of his Office, he shall take the follow-

*Paragraph in brackets superseded by Twelfth Amendment.

ing Oath or Affirmation—"I do solemnly swear (or affirm) that I will faithfully execute the Office of President of the United States, and will to the best of my Ability, preserve, protect and defend the Constitution of the United States."

Section 2. The President shall be Commander in Chief of the Army and Navy of the United States, and of the Militia of the several States, when called into the actual Service of the United States; he may require the Opinion, in writing, of the principal Officer in each of the executive Departments, upon any Subject relating to the Duties of their respective Offices, and he shall have Power to grant Reprieves and Pardons for Offenses against the United States, except in Cases of Impeachment.

He shall have Power, by and with the Advice and Consent of the Senate, to make Treaties, provided two thirds of the Senators present concur; and he shall nominate, and by and with the Advice and Consent of the Senate, shall appoint Ambassadors, other public Ministers and Consuls, Judges of the supreme Court, and all other Officers of the United States, whose Appointments are not herein otherwise provided for, and which shall be established by Law: but the Congress may by Law vest the Appointment of such inferior Officers, as they think proper, in the President alone, in the Courts of Law, or in the Heads of Departments.

The President shall have Power to fill up all Vacancies that may happen during the Recess of the Senate, by granting Commissions which shall expire at the End of their next Session.

Section 3. He shall from time to time give to the Congress Information of the State of the Union, and recommend to their Consideration such Measures as he shall judge necessary and expedient; he may, on extraordinary Occasions, convene both Houses, or either of them, and in Case of Disagreement between them, with Respect to the Time of Adjournment, he may adjourn them to such Time as he shall think proper; he shall receive Ambassadors and other public Ministers; he shall take Care that the Laws be faithfully executed, and shall Commission all the Officers of the United States.

Section 4. The President, Vice President and all Civil Officers of the United States, shall be removed from Office on Impeachment for, and Conviction of, Treason, Bribery, or other high Crimes and Misdemeanors.

AMENDMENT XII
(declared ratified September 25, 1804)

The Electors shall meet in their respective states and vote by ballot for President and Vice-President, one of whom, at least, shall not be an inhabitant of the same state with themselves; they shall name in their ballots the person voted for as President, and in distinct ballots the person voted for as Vice-President, and they shall make distinct lists of all persons voted for as President, and of all persons voted for as Vice-President, and of the number of votes for each, which lists they shall sign and certify, and transmit sealed to the seat of the government of the United States, directed to the President of the Senate;—The President of the Senate shall, in the presence of the Senate and House of Representatives, open all the certificates and the votes shall then be counted;—The person having the greatest number of votes for President, shall be the President, if such number be a majority of the whole number of Electors appointed; and if no person have such majority, then from the persons having the highest numbers not exceeding three on the list of those voted for as President, the House of Representatives shall choose immediately, by ballot, the President. But in choosing the President, the votes shall be taken by states, the representation from each state having one vote; a quorum for this purpose shall consist of a member or members from two-thirds of the states, and a majority of all the states shall be necessary to a choice. [And if the House of Representatives shall not choose a President whenever the right of choice shall devolve upon them, before the fourth day of March next following, then the Vice-President shall act as President, as in the case of the death or other constitutional disability of the President]*—The person having the greatest number of votes as Vice-President, shall be the Vice-President, if such number be a majority of the whole number of Electors appointed, and if no person have a majority, then from the two highest numbers on the list, the Senate shall choose the Vice-President; a quorum for the purpose shall consist of two-thirds of the whole number of senators, and a majority of the whole number shall be necessary to a choice. But no person constitutionally ineligible to the office of President shall be eligible to that of Vice-President of the United States.

*Sentence in brackets superseded by the Twentieth Amendment.

AMENDMENT XIV
(declared ratified July 28, 1868)

Section 1. All persons born or naturalized in the United States and subject to the jurisdiction thereof, are citizens of the United States and of the State wherein they reside. No State shall make or enforce any law which shall abridge the privileges or immunities of citizens of the United States; or shall any State deprive any person of life, liberty, or property, without due process of law; nor deny to any person within its jurisdiction the equal protection of the laws.

Section 2. Representatives shall be apportioned among the several States according to their respective numbers, counting the whole number of persons in each State, excluding Indians not taxed. But when the right to vote at any election for the choice of electors for President and Vice President of the United States, Representatives in Congress, the Executive and Judicial officers of a State, or the members of the Legislature thereof, is denied to any of the male inhabitants of such State, being twenty-one years of age, and citizens of the United States, or in any way abridged, except for participation in rebellion, or other crime, the basis of representation therein shall be reduced in the proportion which the number of such male citizens shall bear to the whole number of male citizens twenty-one years of age in such State.*

Section 3. No person shall be a Senator or Representative in Congress, or elector of President and Vice President, or hold any office, civil or military, under the United States, or under any State, who, having previously taken an oath, as a member of Congress, or as an officer of the United States, or as a member of any State legislature, or as an executive or judicial officer of any State, to support the Constitution of the United States, shall have engaged in insurrection or rebellion against the same, or given aid or comfort to the enemies thereof. But Congress may by a vote of two-thirds of each House, remove such disability. . . .

Section 5. The Congress shall have power to enforce, by appropriate legislation, the provisions of this article.

---

*The sections of this amendment which would reduce a state's congressional representation (and thus its votes in the electoral college) have never been enforced.

AMENDMENT XV
(declared ratified March 30, 1870)

Section 1. The right of citizens of the United States to vote shall not be denied or abridged by the United States or by any State on account of race, color, or previous condition of servitude.

Section 2. The Congress shall have power to enforce this article by appropriate legislation.

AMENDMENT XVII
(declared ratified May 31, 1913)

The Senate of the United States shall be composed of two Senators from each State, elected by the people thereof, for six years, and each Senator shall have one vote. The electors in each State shall have the qualifications requisite for electors of the most numerous branch of the State legislatures. . . .

AMENDMENT XIX
(declared ratified August 26, 1920)

The right of citizens of the United States to vote shall not be denied or abridged by the United States or by any State on account of sex. Congress shall have power to enforce this article by appropriate legislation.

AMENDMENT XX
(declared ratified February 6, 1933)

Section 1. The terms of the President and Vice President shall end at noon on the 20th day of January, and the terms of Senators and Representatives at noon on the 3rd day of January, of the years in which such terms would have ended if this article had not been ratified; and the terms of their successors shall then begin.

Section 2. The Congress shall assemble at least once in every year, and such meeting shall begin at noon on the 3rd day of January, unless they shall by law appoint a different day.

Section 3. If, at the time fixed for the beginning of the term of the

President, the President elect shall have died, the Vice President elect shall become President. If a President shall not have been chosen before the time fixed for the beginning of his term, or if the President elect shall have failed to qualify, then the Vice President elect shall act as President until a President shall have qualified; and the Congress may by law provide for the case wherein neither a President elect nor a Vice President elect shall have qualified, declaring who shall then act as President, or the manner in which one who is to act shall be selected, and such person shall act accordingly until a President or Vice President shall have qualified.

Section 4. The Congress may by law provide for the case of the death of any of the persons from whom the House of Representatives may choose a President whenever the right of choice shall have devolved upon them, and for the case of the death of any of the persons from whom the Senate may choose a Vice President whenever the right of choice shall have devolved upon them . . .

AMENDMENT XXII
(declared ratified February 26, 1951)

Section 1. No person shall be elected to the office of the President more than twice, and no person who has held the office of President, or acted as President, for more than two years of a term to which some other person was elected President shall be elected to the office of the President more than once. But this Article shall not apply to any person holding the office of President when this Article was proposed by the Congress, and shall not prevent any person who may be holding the office of President, or acting as President, during the term within which this Article becomes operative from holding the office of President or acting as President during the remainder of such term. . . .

AMENDMENT XXIII
(declared ratified March 29, 1961)

Section 1. The District constituting the seat of Government of the United States shall appoint in such manner as the Congress may direct:

A number of electors of President and Vice President equal to the whole number of Senators and Representatives in Congress to which the District would be entitled if it were a State, but in no event more than the least populous State; they shall be considered, for the purposes of the election of President and Vice President, to be electors appointed by a State; and they shall meet in the District and perform such duties as provided by the twelfth article of amendment.

Section 2. The Congress shall have power to enforce this article by appropriate legislation.

AMENDMENT XXIV
(declared ratified January 23, 1964)

Section 1. The right of citizens of the United States to vote in any primary or other election for President or Vice President, for electors for President or Vice President, or for Senator or Representative in Congress, shall not be denied or abridged by the United States or any State by reason of failure to pay any poll tax or other tax.

Section 2. The Congress shall have the power to enforce this article by appropriate legislation.

AMENDMENT XXV
(declared ratified February 10, 1967)

Section 1. In case of the removal of the President from office or of his death or resignation, the Vice President shall become President.

Section 2. Whenever there is a vacancy in the office of the Vice President, the President shall nominate a Vice President who shall take office upon confirmation by a majority vote of both houses of Congress.

Section 3. Whenever the President transmits to the President pro tempore of the Senate and the Speaker of the House of Representatives his written declaration that he is unable to discharge the powers and duties of his office, and until he transmits to them a written declaration to the contrary, such powers and duties shall be discharged by the Vice President as Acting President.

Section 4. Whenever the Vice President and a majority of either the principal officers of the Executive departments or of such other body as Congress may by law provide transmit to the President pro tempore of the Senate and the Speaker of the House of Representatives their written declaration that the President is unable to discharge the powers and duties of his office, the Vice President shall immediately assume the powers and duties of the office as Acting President.

Thereafter, when the President transmits to the President pro tempore of the Senate and the Speaker of the House of Representatives his written declaration that no inability exists, he shall resume the powers and duties of his office unless the Vice President and a majority of either the principal officers of the executive departments or of such other body as Congress may by law provide transmits within four days to the President pro tempore of the Senate and the Speaker of the House of Representatives their written declaration that the President is unable to discharge the powers and duties of his office. Thereupon Congress shall decide the issue, assembling within forty-eight hours for that purpose if not in session. If the Congress, within twenty-one days after receipt of the latter written declaration, or, if Congress is not in session, within twenty-one days after Congress is required to assemble, determines by two-thirds vote of both houses that the President is unable to discharge the powers and duties of his office, the Vice President shall continue to discharge the same as Acting President; otherwise, the President shall resume the powers and duties of his office.

Notes

1. RAISING QUESTIONS

1. Gallup Poll, news release, January 5, 2001.
2. Gary C. Jacobson, "The Bush Presidency and the American Electorate," *Presidential Studies Quarterly* 33 (December 2003): 701–729.
3. CBS/*New York Times* poll, May 9–12, 2003.
4. Thomas E. Patterson, *The Vanishing Voter* (New York: Knopf, 2002), 140.
5. James A. Baker III, *"Work Hard, Study . . . and Keep Out of Politics!"* (New York: Putnam, 2006), 71.
6. Federal Election Commission at www.fec.gov.
7. Gallup poll, November 6–8, 2008.
8. Gallup poll, October 31–November 2, 2008.
9. Tara Ross, *Enlightened Democracy: The Case for the Electoral College* (Los Angeles: World Ahead, 2004), 79.
10. U.S. Census Bureau, 2008 population estimates.
11. Quoted in Jerry Hagstrom, "Obama's Polling and Media Teams Went All In," *National Journal,* November 8, 2008.
12. David Plouffe, *The Audacity to Win* (New York: Viking, 2009), 247.
13. Nielsen data found at blog.nielsen.com/nielsenwire/media_entertainment/how-obamas-local-buys-added-up/.

14. If independent leaners are included as partisans, the figure rises to 8.0 percent; only John F. Kennedy attracted fewer (7.1 percent). These figures are from Gary C. Jacobson, "Legislative Success and Political Failure: The Public's Reaction to Barack Obama's Early Presidency," *Presidential Studies Quarterly* 41 (June 2011), 221.

15. Ibid., 221–222.

16. Jay Cost, "Electoral Polarization Continues Under Obama," RealClearPolitics HorseRaceBlog, November 20, 2008, www.realclearpolitics.com/horseraceblog/2008/11/polarization_continues_under_o.html.

17. Ibid.

18. Gallup Daily tracking averages for February 9–15, 2009.

19. Gallup Daily tracking averages for April 20–26, 2009.

20. Jeffrey M. Jones, "Obama's Approval Most Polarized for First-Year President," Gallup Poll, January 25, 2010.

21. For more on the conditions that encourage perceptions of a mandate, see George C. Edwards III, *At the Margins: Presidential Leadership of Congress* (New Haven: Yale University Press, 1989), chapter 8; Lawrence J. Grossback, David A. M. Peterson, and James A. Stimson, *Mandate Politics* (New York: Cambridge University Press, 2006, chapter 2.

22. ABC News/ *Washington Post* poll, January 13–16, 2009.

23. See George C. Edwards III, *Overreach* (Princeton: Princeton University Press, 2012), chapter 3.

2. HOW THE ELECTORAL COLLEGE WORKS

1. Robert Alexander, David Brown, and Jason Kaseman, "Pinning a Face on the Electoral College: A Survey of the Class of 2000," *PS: Political Science and Politics* 37 (October 2004): 833.

2. *Senate Report* no. 22, 19th Cong., 1st sess., January 19, 1826 (hereafter cited as 1826 Senate *Report*), 4.

3. Lucius Wilmerding Jr., *The Electoral College* (New Brunswick, NJ: Rutgers University Press, 1958), 175.

4. James A. Michener, *Presidential Lottery: The Reckless Gamble in Our Electoral System* (New York: Random House, 1969), 9.

5. Dane Smith, "Vote for Edwards an Electoral Shock," *Minneapolis Star Tribune*, December 14, 2004.

6. Alexander, Brown, and Kaseman, "Pinning a Face on the Electoral College," 834–835.

7. Robert G. Dixon Jr., "Electoral College Procedure," *Western Political Quarterly* 3 (June 1950): 216.

8. Alexander, Brown, and Kaseman, "Pinning a Face on the Electoral College"; U.S. Congress, Senate, Committee on the Judiciary, Subcommittee on Constitutional Amendments, *Hearings, Nomination, and Election of President and Vice President and Qualifications for Voting,* 87th Cong., 1st sess., 1961, 546 (hereafter cited as 1961 Senate *Hearings*).

9. These are available at www.archives.gov/federal-register/electoral-college/certificates.html.

10. Article II, sec. 1, cl. 2.

11. *Williams v. Rhodes,* 393 U.S. 23 (1968), at 44–45.

12. Michael J. Glennon, *When No Majority Rules* (Washington, DC: Congressional Quarterly, 1992), 12.

13. Quoted in *McPherson v. Blacker,* 146 U.S. 1 (1892), at 34–35.

14. 146 U.S. 1, at 27 and 35.

15. U.S. Congress, *Register of Debates,* 2:1405, cited by Wilmerding, *Electoral College,* 43.

16. *Bush v. Gore,* 531 U.S. 98 (2000), at 104.

17. *Ex parte Yarbrough,* 110 U.S. 651 (1884); *Burroughs and Cannon v. United States,* 290 U.S. 534 (1934); *Buckley v. Valeo,* 424 U.S. 1 (1976).

18. See James C. Kirby Jr., "Limitations on the Power of State Legislatures over Presidential Elections," *Law and Contemporary Problems* 25 (Spring 1962): 497–504.

19. 393 U.S. 23.

20. Glennon, *When No Majority Rules,* 27–30.

21. Article II, sec. 1, cl. 3.

22. Charles A. O'Neil, *The American Electoral System* (New York: Putnam, 1887), 41–43.

23. Ibid., 43–44.

24. This information was provided by Richard Winger, editor, *Ballot Access News,* www.ballot-access.org/.

25. J. Hampden Dougherty, *The Electoral System of the United States* (New York: Putnam, 1906), 392–393.

26. Dixon, "Electoral College Procedure," 217.

27. "The Electoral College: Operation and Effect of Proposed Amendments," Memorandum prepared by the staff of the Senate Judiciary Committee, Subcommittee on Constitutional Amendments, Oct. 10, 1961, 16 (hereafter cited as 1961 Senate Committee *Memorandum*).

28. Dixon, "Electoral College Procedure," 217; Wilmerding, *Electoral College,* 74; Glennon, *When No Majority Rules,* 68.

29. Rufus King in 1824. See *Annals of Congress,* 18th Cong., 1st sess., 1:355.

30. Dougherty, *Electoral System of the United States,* 226.

31. Section 7 of Chapter 1 of Title 3, United States Code (62 Stat. 672, as amended).

32. The rules regarding meetings of the electors and their voting are available at www.archives.gov/federal-register/electoral-college/state_responsibilities.html #meeting. See also, Dixon, "Electoral College Procedure," 218–219.

33. Section 6 of Chapter 1 of Title 3, United States Code (62 Stat. 672, as amended).

34. *Ann Arbor News,* December 14, 1948, cited in *Congressional Record,* April 13, 1949, 4449.

35. Dixon, "Electoral College Procedure," 219–221.

36. Lawrence D. Longley, "Why the Electoral College Should Be Abolished," Speech to the 1976 Electoral College, Madison, Wisconsin, December 13, 1976. In 1988 the Wisconsin electoral college voted overwhelmingly to adopt a similar resolution: "Resolved: That the 1988 Wisconsin Presidential Electoral College goes on record as calling upon Congress to act to abolish the Electoral College—including the office of Elector; The U.S. President instead should and must be elected directly and equitably by a vote of the American people."

37. Dixon, "Electoral College Procedure," 220–221.

38. James Cheetham to Thomas Jefferson, December 10, 1801, in *Proceedings of the Massachusetts Historical Society,* 3d ser., 1:47; cited by Wilmerding, *Electoral College,* 183.

39. William Purcell, cited by Dougherty, *Electoral System of the United States,* 253.

40. Wilmerding, *Electoral College,* 38–40.

41. Section 11 of Chapter 1 of Title 3, United States Code (62 Stat. 672, as amended). The signed Certificates of Vote are available at www.archives.gov/federal-register/electoral-college/certificates.html.

42. David A. McKnight, *The Electoral System of the United States* (Philadelphia: Lippincott, 1878), 15. See also William Josephson and Beverly J. Ross, "Repairing the Electoral College," *Journal of Legislation* 22, no. 9 (1996): 145–193.

43. Bruce Ackerman, *The Failure of the Founding Fathers* (Cambridge: Harvard University Press, 2005), 55–76, 250–253, 311n24, 312n26.

44. Ibid., chapter 3.

45. Glennon, *When No Majority Rules,* 36–37.

46. Dougherty, *Electoral System of the United States,* 51–57, 86–87; U.S. Congress, House Committee on the Judiciary Subcommittee no. 5, *Hearings, Amending the Constitution with Respect to Election of President and Vice President,* 81st Cong., 1st sess., 1949, 15.

47. U.S. Congress, House Select Committee on the Election of the President and the Vice President, H.R. Rep. 1638, 49th Cong., 2d sess., 18 *Congressional Record,* 30 (1886). Cited in Glennon, *When No Majority Rules,* 39.

48. 531 U.S. 98 (2000).

49. Eric Schickler, Terri L. Bimes, and Robert W. Mickey, "Safe at Any Speed:

Legislative Intent, the Electoral Count Act of 1887, and *Bush v. Gore,*" *Journal of Law and Politics* 16 (Fall 2000): 717–764; Robert W. Bennett, *Taming the Electoral College* (Stanford: Stanford University Press, 2006), 37, 152; Stephen A. Siegel, "The Conscientious Congressman's Guide to the Electoral Count Act of 1887," *Florida Law Review* 56, no. 3 (2004): 541–658.

50. Schickler, Bimes, and Mickey, "Safe at Any Speed."

51. "Joint Session of Congress Finds Nixon Elected President, Agnew Elected Vice President," *Congressional Quarterly Weekly Report,* January 10, 1969, 49, 54–55. Congressional Quarterly, *Guide to Congress,* 2d ed. (Washington, DC: Congressional Quarterly, 1976), 8–9.

52. Charles Babington and Brian Faler, "Congress Makes Reelection Official," *Washington Post,* January 7, 2005; Sheryl Gay Stolberg and James Dao, "Congress Ratifies Bush Victory After Challenge," *New York Times,* January 7, 2005.

53. This discussion relies on U.S. Library of Congress, Congressional Research Service, *Overview of Electoral College Procedure and the Role of Congress,* CD00785 (Nov. 17, 2000).

54. Ibid.

55. For a more recent examination of issues arising in the case of the death of a presidential candidate or president-elect, see U.S. Congress, Senate Judiciary Committee, Subcommittee on the Constitution, *Hearings on Presidential Succession Between the Popular Election and the Inauguration,* 103d Cong., 2d sess., February 2, 1994 (hereafter cited as the February 1994 Senate *Hearings*).

56. See the Republican National Committee Rules, 2000, Rule No. 9; The Charter and By Laws of the Democratic Party of the U.S., Sept. 25, 1999, Article III, sec. 1, cl. c.

57. John D. Feerick, *From Failing Hands: The Story of Presidential Succession* (New York: Fordham University Press, 1965), 161, 271.

58. Ibid., 271–272.

59. Akhil Reed Amar, "Presidents, Vice Presidents, and Death: Closing the Constitution's Succession Gap," *Arkansas Law Review* 48 (1995): 215.

60. Corwin, *The President,* 339–340; Edward Stanwood, *A History of the Presidency from 1788 to 1897* (Boston: Houghton Mifflin, 1898), 353–354.

61. Feerick, *From Failing Hands,* 274. The 1873 precedent, in which Congress refused to count the Greeley votes, would not be binding because Greeley was already dead when the electors cast their votes.

62. House of Representatives, Committee on Election of President and Vice President, and Representatives in Congress, *Proposing an Amendment to the Constitution of the United States,* Report to Accompany Senate Joint Resolution 14, 72nd Cong., 1st sess., H. Report 72-345 (Washington, Government Printing Office: 1932).

63. Walter Berns, ed., *After the People Vote* (Washington, DC: American Enterprise Institute, 1992), 26–27.

64. Carl Becker, "The Will of the People," *Yale Review*, March 1945, 389.

3. THE ELECTORAL COLLEGE AND POLITICAL EQUALITY

1. Robert A. Dahl, *On Democracy* (New Haven: Yale University Press, 2000), 37. See also Robert A. Dahl, *Democracy and Its Critics* (New Haven: Yale University Press, 1989), 110.

2. For examples of those who support the view of the centrality of political equality to democracy, see Barry Holden, *The Nature of Democracy* (London: Nelson, 1974), 19; Giovanni Sartori, *Democratic Theory* (New York: Praeger, 1965), chapter 14; and Ivor Brown, *The Meaning of Democracy*, 3d ed. (London: R. Cobden Sanderson), 1926), 44.

3. James S. Fishkin, *Democracy and Deliberation* (New Haven: Yale University Press, 1990), 29.

4. Jon Elster, Introduction to Jon Elster and Rune Slagstad, eds., *Constitutionalism and Democracy* (Cambridge: Cambridge University Press, 1993), 1.

5. Dahl, *On Democracy,* 65.

6. This discussion follows Dahl in *On Democracy,* 66–68.

7. Joseph A. Schumpeter, *Capitalism, Socialism, and Democracy* (New York: Harper, 1942), 265–266.

8. John Rawls, *A Theory of Justice,* rev. ed. (Cambridge: Belknap Press of Harvard University Press, 1999).

9. Frank Newport, "Americans Support Proposal to Eliminate Electoral College System," Gallup Poll, news release, January 5, 2001.

10. Gallup polls of November 11–12, 2000, and October 11–14, 2004.

11. 376 U.S. 8 (1964).

12. Robert A. Dahl, *A Preface to Democratic Theory* (Chicago: University of Chicago Press, 1963), 118.

13. Quoted in Stanley Elkins and Eric McKitrick, *The Age of Federalism: The Early American Republicanism, 1788–1800* (New York: Oxford University Press, 1993), 267. From Madison's essay, "Parties," in the *National Gazette,* January 23, 1792.

14. In Marvin Meyers, ed., *The Mind of the Founder: Sources of the Political Thought of James Madison,* rev. ed. (Hanover, NH: Brandeis University Press, 1981), 416.

15. In the nineteenth century, a few states followed the practice of averaging the number of votes received by the various members of an electoral slate, rather than taking the highest electoral vote. The practice has since been discontinued. The only difficulty in the prevailing method arises in rare instances, like that of

Alabama in 1960, when the members of the same electoral slate in a particular state favor different candidates (see the discussion later in this chapter).

16. Congressional Quarterly, *Guide to U.S. Elections,* 6th ed. (Washington, DC: CQ Press, 2010); Jerrold G. Rusk, *A Statistical History of the American Electorate* (Washington, DC: CQ Press, 2001).

17. One calculation found that in the eleven presidential elections from 1908 through 1948, a total of 372 million votes were cast for president, but 163 million (44 percent) of these votes were cast by supporters of losing candidates in various states who failed to see a single electoral vote cast representing their votes. Figures presented by former Representative Clarence F. Lea of California in U.S. Congress, House, Committee on the Judiciary, Subcommittee No. 5, *Hearings on Amending the Constitution with Respect to Election of President and Vice President,* 81st Cong., 1st sess., 1949, 28 (hereafter cited as 1949 House *Hearings*).

18. See, e.g., the discussion in Lawrence D. Longley and Neal R. Peirce, *The Electoral College Primer 2000* (New Haven: Yale University Press, 1999), 149–154.

19. George Rabinowitz and Stuart Elaine MacDonald, "The Power of the States in U.S. Presidential Elections," *American Political Science Review* 80 (March 1986): 77–78.

20. James Madison to George Hay, August 23, 1823, in Max Farrand, ed., *The Records of the Federal Convention of 1787,* rev. ed., vol. 3 (New Haven: Yale University Press, 1966), 459.

21. Edward J. Larson, *A Magnificent Catastrophe: The Tumultuous Election of 1800, America's First Presidential Campaign* (New York: Free Press, 2007).

22. Madison to Hay, August 23, 1823.

23. Lucius Wilmerding Jr., *The Electoral College* (New Brunswick, NJ: Rutgers University Press, 1958), 57–67. See also Madison to Hay, August 23, 1823; Farrand, *Records of Federal Convention,* 1:77, 80; and Jack N. Rakove, "The E-College in an E-Age," in Rakove, *The Unfinished Election of 2000* (New York: Basic, 2001), 215–220.

24. John Ferling, *Adams v. Jefferson: The Tumultuous Election of 1800* (New York: Oxford University Press, 2004), 156–157.

25. J. Hampden Dougherty, *The Electoral System of the United States* (New York: Putnam, 1906), 73.

26. U.S. Census Bureau, 2010 census results.

27. Jeffrey W. Ladewig and Mathew P. Jasinski, "On the Causes and Consequences of and Remedies for Interstate Malapportionment of the U.S. House of Representatives," *Perspectives on Politics* 6 (March 2008): 89-107.

28. David W. Abbott and James P. Levine, *Wrong Number: The Coming Debacle in the Electoral College* (New York: Praeger, 1991), 82–83.

29. U.S. Census Bureau, 2010 census results. Another way to measure the weight of a vote is to compare the voting-age populations of states (rather than the total population) at the time of the election. In a study based on projections of the voting-age populations as of November 7, 2000, William Frey found that in the 2000 presidential election, an elector represented 471,000 voting-aged persons in Florida but only 119,000 in Wyoming. See William H. Frey, "Regional Shifts in America's Voting-Aged Population: What Do They Mean for National Politics?" Institute for Social Research, University of Michigan, 2000, app. D. The electors in 2000 were allocated on the basis of the 1990 census.

30. These turnout rates are based on the percent of voting-eligible population in each state who vote rather than on the percentage of the voting-age population. The inclusion of large numbers of noncitizen residents and others who are ineligible to vote in the base for measuring turnout lowers turnout rates in some states. The data come from Michael McDonald and can be accessed at http:// elections.gmu.edu/Turnout_2008G.html.

31. Michael G. Neubauer and Joel Zeitlin, "Outcomes of Presidential Elections and the House Size," *PS: Political Science and Politics* 36 (October 2003): 721–725. These results assume that the one elector who abstained from casting an electoral vote in 2000 would have done so in the hypothetical elections.

32. Ladewig and Jasinski, "Interstate Malapportionment."

33. Charles A. O'Neil, *The American Electoral System* (New York: Putnam, 1887), 48.

34. Wilmerding, *Electoral College*, 174.

35. 1826 Senate *Report*, 4.

36. Cited by J. Hampden Dougherty, *The Electoral System of the United States* (New York: Putnam, 1906), 250, 251.

37. *Ray v. Blair*, 343 U.S. 232 (1952).

38. 1961 Senate *Hearings*, 446 (in transcript of *CBS Reports* program).

39. James Madison to Robert Taylor, January 30, 1826, in Gaillard Hunt, ed., *The Writings of James Madison*, vol. 9 (New York: Putnam, 1910), 150.

40. 1826 Senate *Report*, 5.

41. Source for 1948 example: U.S. Congress, House Committee on the Judiciary Subcommittee no. 5, *Hearings, Amending the Constitution with Respect to Election of President and Vice President*, 81st Cong., 1st sess., 1949, 148 (hereafter cited as 1949 House *Hearings*). Source for the 1972 example: presidential campaign involvement of Larry Longley. Source for 1992 example: Timothy Noah, "Perot Could Face Hurdle of Reversals in Electoral College: Some Electors No Longer Back Texan, Threaten Attempt to Give His Race Meaning," *Wall Street Journal*, October 28, 1992. Source for 1980 example: Lawrence D. Longley and Neal R. Peirce, *The Electoral College Primer 2000* (New Haven: Yale University Press, 1999), 115.

42. L. Paige Whitaker, *State Statutes Binding Electors' Votes in the Electoral College* (Washington, DC: Library of Congress, Congressional Research Service, 2000).

43. 343 U.S. 214 (1952). The Court also determined that state imposition of such pledge requirements does not violate the Twelfth Amendment, nor does it deny equal protection and due process under the Fourteenth Amendment.

44. Kirby, "Limitations on the Power of State Legislatures," 509.

45. Akhil Reed Amar, "Presidents, Vice Presidents, and Death: Closing the Constitution's Succession Gap," *Arkansas Law Review* 48 (1995): 230; see also 215. However, Beverly J. Ross and William Josephson, "The Electoral College and the Popular Vote," *Journal of Law and Politics* 12, no. 4 (1996): 665–747, conclude that "state statute–based direct or party pledge binding legislation is valid and should be enforceable."

46. Cited by Edward S. Corwin, *The President: Office and Powers* (New York: New York University Press, 1957), 41.

47. James Russell Lowell to Leslie Stephen, quoted in Horace Elisha Scudder, *James Russell Lowell: A Biography*, vol. 1 (Boston: Houghton Mifflin, 1901), 217.

48. Everett S. Brown, ed., *William Plumer's Memorandum of Proceedings in the United States Senate, 1803–1807* (New York: Macmillan, 1923), vii, cited by Wilmerding, *Electoral College*, 176.

49. John Bach McMaster, *A History of the People of the United States from the Revolution to the Civil War*, vol. 5 (New York: Appleton, 1891), 74–75; A. R. Newsome, *The Presidential Election of 1824 in North Carolina* (Chapel Hill: University of North Carolina Press, 1939), chapter 8, cited in Wilmerding, *Electoral College*, 177–178.

50. Wilmerding, *Electoral College*, 178–179.

51. "Democratic Elector Deserts Stevenson," *New York Times,* December 18, 1956.

52. Later, Republican National Chairman Morton said that if Irwin "had the support of the Republican National Committee, I knew nothing about it."

53. 1961 Senate *Hearings,* 622.

54. 1961 Senate *Hearings,* 445–446, 634. The program, a transcript of which was printed in the *Hearings,* was the *CBS Reports* telecast of January 5, 1961.

55. See also Congressional Quarterly, *Guide to Congress,* 2d ed. (Washington, DC: Congressional Quarterly, 1976), 240–241, and Congressional Quarterly, *Guide to U.S. Elections* (Washington, DC: Congressional Quarterly, 1975), 211–212.

56. "Reagan Nudges His Electors," *Newsweek,* November 10, 1980, 33.

57. Interview on *Democracy NOW!* December 19, 2000, Pacifica Radio Network.

58. Dane Smith, "Vote for Edwards an Electoral Shock," *Minneapolis Star Tribune,* December 14, 2004.

59. Chris Stirewalt, "Robb's Vote May Not Go to Bush," *Charleston Daily Mail,* September 8, 2004.

60. *Rotarian* magazine, July 1949.

61. Elizabeth P. McCaughey, "Democracy at Risk," *Policy Review* 63 (Winter 1993): 80.

62. Jerrold G. Rusk, *A Statistical History of the American Electorate* (Washington, DC: CQ Press, 2001), 132, updated by author.

63. William W. Freehling, *The Road to Disunion: Secessionists at Bay, 1776–1854* (New York: Oxford University Press, 1990), 146–148; James R. Sharp, *American Politics in the Early Republic* (New Haven: Yale University Press, 1993), 247; Garry Wills, *"Negro President": Jefferson and the Slave Power* (Boston: Houghton Mifflin, 2003), 2–5, 234; John Ferling, *Adams v. Jefferson: The Tumultuous Election of 1800* (New York: Oxford University Press, 2004), 168.

64. Eugene H. Roseboom, *A History of Presidential Elections* (New York: Macmillan, 1957), 243–245. For a full treatment of the election, see William H. Rehnquist, *Centennial Crisis* (New York: Knopf, 2004); and Michael F. Holt, *By One Vote: The Disputed Presidential Election of 1876* (Lawrence: University Press of Kansas, 2008).

65. Edward Stanwood, *A History of the Presidency from 1788 to 1897* (Boston: Houghton Mifflin, 1898), 381; Roseboom, *History of Presidential Elections,* 245.

66. Dougherty, *Electoral System of the United States,* 110–116.

67. Roseboom writes that "fortune seemed to reserve her smiles for the Republicans during these years, but in this case asinine blundering by the Illinois Democrats would seem to be a more logical explanation" (*History of Presidential Elections,* 247).

68. See James A. Michener, *Presidential Lottery,* 78–91; and Paul L. Haworth, *The Hayes-Tilden Disputed Election of 1876* (New York: Russell and Russell, 1966).

69. Stanwood, *History of the Presidency,* 390–391.

70. Roseboom, *History of Presidential Elections,* 248–249.

71. Stanwood, *History of the Presidency,* 393.

72. Charles W. Calhoun, *Minority Victory: Gilded Age Politics and the Front Porch Campaign of 1888* (Lawrence: University Press of Kansas, 2008).

73. The commonly accepted practice in determining popular votes for president is to credit the candidate with the number of votes received by the highest-polling elector pledged to him in the state.

74. See also Brian J. Gaines, "Popular Myths About Popular-Vote Electoral College Splits," *PS: Political Science and Politics* 34 (March 2001): 71–75.

75. "1960 Vote Analysis," *Congressional Quarterly Weekly Report,* February 17, 1961, 285–288; "Hypothetical Effects of Proposed Reforms on 1960 Presidential Election," *Congressional Quarterly Weekly Report,* February 17, 1961, 286–287. See also U.S. Congress, Senate Committee on the Judiciary, Subcommittee on Constitutional Amendments, *Hearings on Nomination and Election of President and*

Vice President and Qualifications for Voting, 87th Cong., 1st sess., 1961, 391–399 (hereafter cited as 1961 Senate *Hearings*).

An alternative method of reporting the Alabama vote, adopted by Neal Peirce for Congressional Quarterly, reported the vote for the highest Kennedy elector (318,303) as part of his national count and the vote for the highest unpledged elector (324,050) as part of the national unpledged elector vote (eventually credited to Byrd). The result was a Kennedy plurality nationwide of 112,827 votes. In reporting this result, Congressional Quarterly took care to note, however, that it was actually reporting the votes of the citizens who supported Democratic electors in Alabama twice—once for Kennedy, once for unpledged electors. The result involved a serious distortion, since the votes of the Democratic voters in Alabama were counted twice, whereas the Republican voters in the state—and the votes of citizens in every other state—were reported but once.

76. These figures are from the Clerk of the House of Representatives, Jeff Trandahl, *Statistics of the Presidential and Congressional Election of November 7, 2000*, U.S. House of Representatives, 2001.

77. Neal R. Peirce and Lawrence D. Longley, *The People's President* (New Haven: Yale University Press, 1981), 116–119; Samuel Merrill III, "Empirical Estimates for the Likelihood of a Divided Verdict in a Presidential Election," *Public Choice* 33, no. 2 (1978): 127–133; John F. Banzhaf, "One Man, 3.313 Votes: A Mathematical Analysis of the Electoral College," *Villanova Law Review* 13 (Winter 1968): 303–346.

78. This analysis assumes the nondefection of Republican elector Mike Padden of Washington. If he had nevertheless declined to vote for Ford, the election would have been inconclusive and would have gone to the House in January 1977.

79. For some simulations regarding the impact of the winner-take-all and two votes per state for senators provisions of the electoral college, see Jack E. Riggs, Gerald R. Hobbs, and Todd H. Riggs, "Electoral College Winner's Advantage," *PS: Political Science and Politics* 42 (April 2009): 353–357.

80. 377 U.S. 567–568 (1964).

4. CONTINGENT ELECTIONS

1. John Ferling, *Adams v. Jefferson: The Tumultuous Election of 1800* (New York: Oxford University Press, 2004), 132.

2. Ibid., 192–195; Bruce Ackerman, *The Failure of the Founding Fathers* (Cambridge: Harvard University Press, 2005), 104–108; Edwards J. Larson, *A Magnificent Catastrophe* (New York: Free Press, 2007), 267; James Roger Sharp, *The Deadlocked Election of 1800: Jefferson, Burr, and the Union in the Balance* (Lawrence: University Press of Kansas, 2010), 161–162.

3. The Twelfth Amendment also provided that if an election was thrown into the House, the choice would be from the top three candidates rather than from the top five as previously; that if by Inauguration Day no president had been selected, the new vice president would become president; that a vice president would need a majority of electoral votes (previously he only needed the second-highest number); and that age, citizenship, and residency requirements would be the same for vice president as for president.

4. Jefferson to George Hay, August 17, 1823, in Paul L. Ford, ed., *The Works of Thomas Jefferson,* vol. 12 (New York: Putnam, 1905), 303.

5. What House action might have been in 1825 had its widely revered and very powerful Speaker been among the candidates that could be considered is unknown. Clay received only 13 percent of the popular vote, but institutional and personal loyalty among House members toward their Speaker might have been a potent influence on their votes.

6. Edward Stanwood, *A History of the Presidency from 1788 to 1897* (Boston: Houghton Mifflin, 1898), 139; Eugene H. Roseboom, *A History of Presidential Elections* (New York: Macmillan, 1957), 84.

7. Cited by Roseboom, *History of Presidential Elections,* 88. See also Stanwood, *History of the Presidency,* 138–139; and Theodore G. Venetoulis, *The House Shall Choose* (Margate, NJ: Elias, 1968), 130–135.

8. Samuel Eliot Morison and Henry Steele Commager, *The Growth of the American Republic,* 4th ed., vol. 1 (New York: Oxford University Press, 1950), 464.

9. Joseph B. Gorman, *Election of the President by the House of Representatives and the Vice President by the Senate: Relationship of the Popular Vote for Electors to Subsequent Voting in the House of Representatives in 1801 and 1825 and in the Senate in 1837,* U.S. Library of Congress, Congressional Research Service (Washington, DC, November 20, 1980), 13–22.

10. Richard C. Baker, "On Becoming President by One Vote," *American Bar Association Journal,* May 1962, 455; Roseboom, *History of Presidential Elections,* 86.

11. Cited by John B. Andrews, "Should the President Be Elected by Direct Popular Vote? Yes!" *Forum,* October 1949, 231.

12. Sidney Hyman, *The American President* (New York: Harper, 1954), 145; Lucius Wilmerding, *The Electoral College* (New Brunswick, NJ: Rutgers University Press, 1958), 209.

13. Stanwood, *History of the Presidency,* 187–188.

14. "Six Electors Bar Kennedy Support," *New York Times,* December 11, 1960.

15. "14 Unpledged Electors to Meet," *Washington Evening Star,* December 12, 1960.

16. Associated Press dispatch, December 12, 1960.

17. See "Independent Electors," *Congressional Quarterly Weekly Report,* June 14,

1963, 969; and "Unpledged Electors," *Congressional Quarterly Weekly Report,* September 13, 1963, 1572.

18. See "Wallace Tailors Campaign to Varied State Election Laws," *Congressional Quarterly Weekly Report,* July 17, 1964, 1499; and "Wallace Withdrawals," *Congressional Quarterly Weekly Report,* July 24, 1964, 1547. For further background on the 1960 effort, see "South Considers Independent Elector Plan," *Congressional Quarterly Weekly Report,* April 1, 1960, 569; and U.S. Congress, Senate Committee on the Judiciary, Subcommittee on Constitutional Amendments, *Hearings on Nomination and Election of President and Vice President and Qualifications for Voting,* 87th Cong., 1st sess., 1961, 562 ff., esp. 622–625 (hereafter cited as 1961 Senate *Hearings*), describing plans to mobilize independent electors for subsequent elections.

19. As discussed in Chapter 1, Wallace's electoral vote was later increased by one and Nixon's decreased by a like number by the actions of a faithless Nixon elector. See also Paul R. Abramson, John H. Aldrich, Phil Paolino, and David W. Rohde, "Third-Party and Independent Candidates in American Politics: Wallace, Anderson, and Perot," *Political Science Quarterly* 110 (Summer 1995): 349–367.

20. An electoral college majority in 1968 was 270 votes out of a total of 538, while in 1960 it was 269 votes out of a total of 537. The reason for this change was that the total electoral college vote rose temporarily for the 1960 election to 537 to accommodate the new states of Alaska and Hawaii, while by 1968 the total electoral college vote had increased permanently to 538 electoral votes when the Twenty-third Amendment gave the District of Columbia 3 electoral votes.

21. Quoted in Neal R. Peirce, *The People's President,* rev. ed. (New Haven: Yale University Press, 1981), 75.

22. Elizabeth P. McCaughey, "Democracy at Risk," *Policy Review* 63 (Winter 1993): 80.

23. Quoted in Peirce, *The People's President,* 75.

24. Among the nastiest rumors of the 1968 election was that if electoral college deadlock appeared imminent and if the new House appeared likely to elect Nixon, outgoing president Lyndon Johnson might reconvene the old Congress for the purpose of moving the meeting time of the new Congress back beyond January 6 so that the old Congress could choose the new president. This rumor never had any substance but illustrates both the suspicions generated by threatened deadlock and the frightening possibilities under the contingent proceedings.

25. Quoted in "The Electoral College," *Congressional Quarterly Guide to Current American Government,* Spring 1970, 144.

26. "House Candidates Pledges," *Congressional Quarterly Weekly Report,* October 25, 1968, 2956. The representatives made the pledges in response to widespread

speculation that the election might go to the House and that in such a situation members would vote for the nominee of their party. For Democrats in districts that were expected to go to Nixon or Wallace, this was a potentially hazardous campaign issue. To protect themselves, candidates pledged to follow the mandate of their districts and to vote in the House for the winner of their districts regardless of party affiliation.

27. This analysis of possible voting alignments in the House following the 1968 presidential election highlights another aspect of the inequality of the contingent election scheme. One man, representing the 285,278 citizens of Nevada, would cast one-fiftieth of the vote for president. At the same time, had the Illinois, Maryland, Montana, and Oregon delegations voted along party lines, they would have been split and would have lost their vote; more than 15 million people would, therefore, have been disenfranchised. In addition, the 700,000 residents of the District of Columbia had no vote in the House.

28. "Testimony of Honorable Robert Dole, U.S. Senator from the State of Kansas," *The Electoral College and Direct Election: Hearings Before the Committee on the Judiciary, United States Senate,* 95th Cong., 1st sess., January 27, February 1, 2, 7, 10, 1977, 37.

29. Wilmerding, *The Electoral College,* 184–185.

30. James Madison to George Hay, August 23, 1823, in Gaillard Hunt, ed., *The Writings of James Madison,* vol. 9 (New York: Putnam's Sons, 1910), 147–155.

31. Quoted in J. Hampden Dougherty, *The Electoral System of the United States* (New York: Putnam, 1906), 23–24.

32. Dougherty, *Electoral System of the United States,* 23–24.

33. Clerk of the House of Representatives Jeff Trandahl, *Statistics of the Presidential and Congressional Election of November 7, 2000* (U.S. House of Representatives, 2001), 61.

34. Harold W. Stanley and Richard G. Niemi, *Vital Statistics on American Politics, 2001–2002* (Washington, DC: CQ Press, 2001), 46.

35. Paul J. Piccard, "The Resolution of Electoral Deadlocks by the House of Representatives," in *Selecting the President: The 27th Discussion and Debate Manual (1953–54),* vol. 1, reprinted in 1961 Senate *Hearings,* 826–843.

36. Judith A. Best, *The Choice of the People? Debating the Electoral College* (Lanham, MD: Rowman and Littlefield, 1996), 13.

5. THE ORIGINS OF THE ELECTORAL COLLEGE

1. Max Farrand, ed., *The Records of the Federal Convention of 1787,* rev. ed., 4 vols. (New Haven: Yale University Press, 1966), 2:501.

2. Spoken in the Pennsylvania Convention, December 11, 1787, ibid., 3:166.

3. See Shlomo Slonim, "Designing the Electoral College," in Thomas E. Cronin, ed., *Inventing the American Presidency* (Lawrence: University Press of Kansas, 1989), 33–60.

4. See, for example, Pauline Maier, *Ratification: The People Debate the Constitution, 1787–1788* (New York: Simon and Schuster, 2010).

5. *The Federalist Papers,* No. 68.

6. Farrand, *Records of the Federal Convention,* 1:80, 91, 2:29–30, 109–111, 500–501, 511.

7. See, e.g., ibid., 2:500.

8. See Richard Beeman, *Plain, Honest Men: The Making of the American Constitution* (New York: Random House, 2010), 135, 136, 231.

9. Farrand, *Records of the Federal Convention,* 2:30–32, 103–104, 403–404, 500, 522–525; Richard C. Welty, "Who *Really* Elects Our Presidents?" *Midwest Quarterly* 2 (Autumn 1960): 23.

10. Farrand, *Records of the Federal Convention,* 2:525.

11. Beeman, *Plain, Honest Men,* pp. 135–136, 232.

12. Farrand, *Records of the Federal Convention,* 2:29, 31–32, 57, 114, 501, 511.

13. Ibid., 2:111, 511. This first assessment of the probable consequences of a direct vote for the president seems reasonably accurate for this historical period. What was not anticipated, of course, was the later development of political parties able to popularize national contenders, inform the nation's electorate about them, and actively engage in aggregating support for candidates across state lines.

14. Farrand, *Records of the Federal Convention,* 2:30, 57, 114.

15. See, e.g., Farrand, *Records of the Federal Convention,* 1:68–69, 2:29–31, 56–57, 109, 111, 114–115.

16. Michael J. Glennon, *When No Majority Rules: The Electoral College and Presidential Succession* (Washington, DC: Congressional Quarterly, 1992), 7.

17. Farrand, *Records of the Federal Convention,* 2:29, 31, 501.

18. Ibid., 2:30.

19. Slonim, "Designing the Electoral College," 55. Oliver Ellsworth, Luther Martin, and Roger Sherman also opposed popular election of the president.

20. Lucius Wilmerding Jr., *The Electoral College* (Boston: Beacon, 1958), 21.

21. Beeman, *Plain, Honest Men,* 135, 232.

22. John Dickinson to George Logan, January 16, 1802, in James H. Hutson, *Supplement to Max Farrand's The Records of the Federal Convention of 1787* (New Haven: Yale University Press, 1987), 300–301.

23. Jonathan Elliott, *The Debates in the Several State Conventions on the Adoption of the Federal Constitution,* 2d ed., 5 vols. (Salem, NH: Ayer, 1987), 3:487, 494.

24. Ibid., 2:512.

25. Wilmerding, *Electoral College,* 171, 174.

26. Glennon, *When No Majority Rules,* 8, 13.

27. Joseph Story, *Commentaries on the Constitution of the United States* (Durham, NC: Carolina Academic Press, 1987), 531.

28. 146 U.S. 1 (1892).

29. 343 U.S. 214 (1952) at 232.

30. 393 U.S. 23 (1968) at 43–44.

31. Elliott, *Debates in the Several State Conventions,* 3:486, 488.

32. Charles A. O'Neil, *The American Electoral System* (New York: Putnam, 1887), 3–4; J. Hampden Dougherty, *The Electoral System of the United States* (New York: Putnam, 1906), 1.

33. See, e.g., Farrand, *Records of the Federal Convention,* 2:30, 111, 403, 527.

34. Ibid., 2:119. The Society of the Cincinnati was founded in 1783 to preserve the ideals and fellowship of Revolutionary War officers and to pressure the government to honor pledges made to them.

35. See ibid., 2:403.

36. John P. Feerick, "Electoral College: Why It Was Created," *American Bar Association Journal* 54 (March 1968): 254. See also William Josephson and Beverly J. Ross, "Repairing the Electoral College," *Journal of Legislation* 22, no. 9 (1996): 145–193.

37. Farrand, *Records of the Federal Convention,* 2:404.

38. The change in the contingent procedure from the Senate to the House resulted from fears that the Senate, which had already been given treaty ratification powers and confirmation responsibilities, was accumulating too much authority in comparison with the House of Representatives. See, e.g., ibid., 2:501–502, 511–513, 522–526.

39. As Madison later put it, voting by states in the House was "an accommodation to the anxiety of the smaller States for their sovereign equality, and to the jealousy of the larger towards the cumulative functions of the Senate." Madison to George Hay, August 23, 1823, ibid., 3:458. See also similar comments by Rufus King and Roger Sherman, ibid., 2:512–514.

40. John P. Roche, "The Founding Fathers: A Reform Caucus in Action," *American Political Science Review* 55 (December 1961): 811. See also Farrand, *Records of the Federal Convention,* 2:29–30, 500–501, 511–512, 525.

41. Jack N. Rakove, *Original Meanings: Politics and Ideas in the Making of the Constitution* (New York: Vintage, 1997), 266. See also Beeman, *Plain, Honest Men,* 301–304.

42. Quoted in Elliott, *Debates in the Several State Conventions,* 2:495, 464. See also Feerick, "Electoral College," 254; and Farrand, *Records of the Federal Convention,* 2:512–514.

43. Farrand, *Records of the Federal Convention*, 2:536; see also 514 for another concern about minority election.

44. Elliott, *Debates in the Several State Conventions*, 3:492–493.

45. Farrand, *Records of the Federal Convention*, 1:486. For an analysis of the context and consequences of this argument by Madison in the Great Compromise, see Rosemarie Zagarri, *The Politics of Size: Representation in the United States, 1776–1850* (Ithaca, NY: Cornell University Press, 1987), 78–81.

46. See, e.g., Farrand, *Records of the Federal Convention*, 2:32.

47. Ibid., 2:56–57; see also 111.

48. For more on slavery and the electoral college, see Paul Finkelman, "The Pro-slavery Origins of the Electoral College," *Cardozo Law Review* 23 (March 2002): 1145–1157.

49. William T. Gossett, "Electing the President: New Hope for an Old Ideal," *American Bar Association Journal* 53 (December 1967): 1103.

50. John Dickinson, quoted in Roche, "The Founding Fathers," 799. Roche describes the convention delegates as "first and foremost superb democratic politicians who *made* history and did it within the limits of consensus," and the convention itself as "a *nationalist* reform caucus that had to operate with great delicacy and skill in a political cosmos full of enemies to achieve the one definitive goal—popular approbation."

51. Neal R. Peirce and Lawrence D. Longley, *The People's President*, rev. ed. (New Haven: Yale University Press, 1981), 22.

52. Madison to Hay, August 23, 1823.

53. Farrand, *Records of the Federal Convention*, 2:516.

54. Felix Morley, "Democracy and the Electoral College," *Modern Age* 5 (Fall 1961): 377.

55. Farrand, *Records of the Federal Convention*, 2:111; Madison to Hay, August 23, 1823.

56. Bartholomew H. Sparrow and Sanford Levinson, Introduction to Bartholomew H. Sparrow and Sanford Levinson, eds., *The Louisiana Purchase and American Expansion, 1803–1898* (Rowman and Littlefield 2005), 13–14.

57. Farrand, *Records of the Federal Convention*, 2:403.

58. Ibid., 1:149, 156, 174–175, 2:57, 109.

59. Martin Diamond, *The Electoral College and the American Idea of Democracy* (Washington, DC: American Enterprise Institute, 1977), 4.

60. Farrand, *Records of the Federal Convention*, 2:500.

61. Jack Rakove, "The Accidental Electors," *New York Times,* December 19, 2000.

62. Roche, "Founding Fathers," 811.

63. Robert A. Dahl, *How Democratic Is the Constitution?* (New Haven: Yale University Press, 2001), 66.

6. PROTECTING INTERESTS

1. Tara Ross, *Enlightened Democracy: The Case for the Electoral College* (Los Angeles: World Ahead, 2004), 79.

2. Darshan J. Goux and David A. Hopkins, "The Empirical Implications of Electoral College Reform," *American Politics Research* 36 (November 2008): 860–864; Daron Shaw, *The Race to 270* (Chicago: University of Chicago Press, 2007); Daron R. Shaw, "The Methods Behind the Madness: Presidential Electoral College Strategies, 1988–1996," *Journal of Politics* 61 (November 1999): 893–913; Scott C. James and Brian L. Lawson, "The Political Economy of Voting Rights Enforcement in America's Gilded Age: Electoral College Competition, Partisan Commitment, and the Federal Election Law," *American Political Science Review* 93 (March 1999): 115–131; Raymond Tatalovich, "Electoral Votes and Presidential Campaign Trails, 1932–1976," *American Politics Quarterly* 7 (October 1979): 489–497.

3. For examples of these assertions, see Judith A. Best, *The Choice of the People? Debating the Electoral College* (Lanham, MD: Rowman and Littlefield, 1996), chapter 3; Curtis Gans, "Electoral College Reform: How to Keep, but Improve, the Current System," *Congressional Digest,* January 2001, 12; James R. Stone Jr., "Federalism, the States, and the Electoral College," in Gary L. Gregg, ed., *Securing Democracy: Why We Have an Electoral College* (Wilmington, DE: ISI, 2001), 52; Paul A. Rahe, "Moderating the Political Impulse," ibid., 68; and Michael M. Uhlman, "Creating Constitutional Majorities: The Electoral College After 2000," ibid., 105–106.

4. Jack Rakove, "The Accidental Electors," *New York Times,* December 19, 2000, A35.

5. James Madison to George Hay, August 23, 1823, in Gaillard Hunt, ed., *The Writings of James Madison,* vol. 9 (New York: Putnam Sons, 1910), 47–55.

6. Max Farrand, ed., *The Records of the Federal Convention of 1787,* rev. ed., 4 vols. (New Haven: Yale University Press, 1966), 2:111.

7. Best, *Choice of the People?* 37.

8. Ibid., 35.

9. See Robert A. Dahl, *How Democratic Is the American Constitution?* (New Haven: Yale University Press, 2001), 50–53, 84.

10. Farrand, *The Records of the Federal Convention,* 1:483, 1:447–449, 2:403.

11. Stoner, "Federalism, States, and Electoral College," 52. Stoner somewhat contradictorily also agrees that campaigns for national office ought to focus on national issues and feature candidates of national stature.

12. Uhlman, "Creating Constitutional Majorities," 109.

13. Steve Vogel, "Controversy over Yucca Mountain May Be Ending," *Washington Post*, March 4, 2009.

14. Farrand, *Records of the Federal Convention*, 1:447–449.

15. U.S. Department of Agriculture, *2007 Census of Agriculture*, vol. 1 (Washington, DC: National Agricultural Statistics Service, 2009), chapter 2, table 2, 294–310. This census occurs every five years.

16. Clea Benson, "Rural Sophistication," *CQ Weekly Online*, October 5, 2009.

17. Uhlman, "Creating Constitutional Majorities," 106; Larry J. Sabato, *A More Perfect Constitution* (New York: Walker, 2007), 139; Ross, *Enlightened Democracy*, 79; Rahe, "Moderating the Political Impulse," 63.

18. The results were published by Stanford University on a CD entitled *In Their Own Words: Sourcebook for the 2000 Presidential Election*. Five additional speeches obtained after the CD was made can be found at http://pcl.stanford.edu. The Stanford team edited out remarks at the beginning of some speeches, generally those thanking the organizers of the event.

19. *Annenberg / Pew Archive of Presidential Campaign Discourse* (CD-ROM).

20. Michael Hagen, Richard Johnston, and Kathleen Hall Jamieson, "Effects of the 2000 Presidential Campaign," paper delivered at the Annual Meeting of the American Political Science Association, August 29–September 1, 2002, 3.

21. "How Would They Campaign?" *National Journal*, November 18, 2000, 3653.

22. For work on elections before 1976, see Steven J. Brams and Morton D. Davis, "The 3/2's Rule in Presidential Campaigning," *American Political Science Review* 68 (March 1974): 113–134; Claude S. Colantoni, Terrence J. Levesque, and Peter C. Ordeshook, "Campaign Resource Allocations Under the Electoral College," *American Political Science Review* 69 (March 1975): 141–154; Steven J. Brams and Morton D. Davis, "Comment on 'Campaign Resource Allocations Under the Electoral College,'" *American Political Science Review* 69 (March 1975): 155–156.

23. See also Larry M. Bartels, "Resource Allocation in a Presidential Campaign," *Journal of Politics* 47 (August 1985): 928–936.

24. Stanley Kelley Jr., "The Presidential Campaign," in Paul T. David, ed., *The Presidential Election and Transition, 1960–1961* (Washington, DC: Brookings Institution, 1961), 70–72.

25. Daron R. Shaw, "The Effect of TV Ads and Candidate Appearances on State-wide Presidential Votes, 1988–96," *American Political Science Review* 93 (June 1999): 359–360. See also F. Christopher Arterton, "Campaign '92: Strategies and Tactics of the Candidates," in Gerald M. Pomper, *The Election of 1992* (Chatham, NJ: Chatham House, 1993), 87.

26. *Annenberg / Pew Archive of Presidential Campaign Discourse*.

27. Data for 2004 were collected by the author.

28. *Congressional Record,* July 10, 1979, 17748.

29. Hagen, Johnston, and Jamieson, "Effects of the 2000 Presidential Campaign," 1, 3–4.

30. The data were obtained from a joint project of the Brennan Center for Justice at New York University School of Law and Professor Kenneth Goldstein of the University of Wisconsin–Madison and include media tracking data from the Campaign Media Analysis Group in Washington, DC. The Brennan Center–Wisconsin project was sponsored by a grant from the Pew Charitable Trusts. The opinions expressed in this article are those of the author and do not necessarily reflect the views of the Brennan Center, Professor Goldstein, or the Pew Charitable Trusts.

31. Craig B. Holman and Luke P. McLoughlin, *Buying Time 2000: Television Advertising in the 2000 Federal Elections* (New York: Brennan Center for Justice, 2002), 85.

32. Hagen, Johnston, and Jamieson, "Effects of the 2000 Presidential Campaign," 6.

33. "Testimony of Hon. Hubert H. Humphrey, U.S. Senator from the State of Minnesota," *The Electoral College and Direct Election: Hearings Before the Committee on the Judiciary, United States Senate,* 95th Cong., 1st sess., January 27, February 1, 2, 7, 10, 1977, 25, 35; "Testimony of Douglas Bailey," *Electoral College and Direct Election,* July 20, 22, 28, August 2, 1977, 267, 258–273; as well as the testimony at the same hearings by Sen. Robert Dole, "Testimony of Hon. Robert Dole, U.S. Senator from the State of Kansas," *The Electoral College and Direct Election: Hearings Before the Subcommittee on the Constitution of the Committee on the Judiciary, Supplement,* 30, who also stressed the campaign distortions created by the electoral college.

34. Shaw, "The Effect of TV Ads and Candidate Appearances on Statewide Presidential Votes, 1988–96"; Shaw, *The Race to 270,* chapter 4. See also Bartels, "Resource Allocation in a Presidential Campaign"; Arterton, "Campaign '92," 87.

35. *Presidential Election Inequality* (Washington, DC: FairVote, 2006).

36. Fair Vote, "2008's Shrinking Battleground and Its Stark Impact on Campaign Activity," December 4, 2008. Accessed at archive.fairvote.org/tracker/?page=27&pressmode=showspecific&showarticle=230.

37. Nielsen data found at blog.nielsen.com/nielsenwire/media_entertainment/how-obamas-local-buys-added-up/.

38. See, e.g., Best, *Choice of the People?* 24; Judith A. Best, "Should the Current Electoral College System Be Preserved?" *Congressional Digest,* January 2001, 22; Rahe, "Moderating the Political Impulse," 63; Alexander M. Bickel, "Wait a Minute!" *New Republic,* May 10, 1969, 11–13; "Prepared Statement of Cur-

tis Gans on Behalf of Americans for Democratic Action," *The Electoral College and Direct Election: Hearings Before the Subcommittee on the Constitution of the Committee on the Judiciary, Supplement, United States Senate,* 95th Cong., 1st sess., July 20, 22, 28, August 2, 1977, 95th Cong., 1st sess., 398; Wallace S. Sayre and Judith H. Parris, *Voting for President: The Electoral College and the American Political System* (Washington, DC: Brookings Institution, 1970), 72–73.

39. U.S. Bureau of the Census, Population Division, *Estimates of Resident Population by Race and Hispanic Origin for the United States: July 1, 2009* (June 2010).

40. Robert L. Lineberry, Darren Davis, Robert Erikson, Richard Herrera, and Priscilla Southwell, "The Electoral College and Social Cleavages: Ethnicity, Class, and Geography," in Paul D. Schumaker and Burdett A. Loomis, eds., *Choosing a President* (New York: Chatham, 2002), 168–169.

41. Edward G. Carmines and Robert Huckfeldt, "Party Politics in the Wake of the Voting Rights Act," in Bernard Grofman and Chandler Davidson, eds., *Controversies in Minority Voting: The Voting Rights Act in Perspective* (Washington, DC: Brookings Institution, 1992), 120–125.

42. Goux and Hopkins, "The Empirical Implications of Electoral College Reform."

43. On the lack of centrality of black voters, see Larry M. Bartels, "Where the Ducks Are: Voting Power in a Party System," in John G. Geer, ed., *Politicians and Party Politics* (Baltimore: Johns Hopkins University Press, 1998), 53, 57, 59, 63–68.

44. For an argument that the electoral college seriously dilutes the votes of minorities, see Matthew M. Hoffman, "The Illegitimate President: Minority Vote Dilution and the Electoral College," *Yale Law Journal* 105 (1996): 935–1021.

45. James and Lawson, "Political Economy of Voting Rights Enforcement."

46. Best, *Choice of the People?* 36.

47. U.S. Bureau of the Census, Population Division, *Estimates of Resident Population by Race and Hispanic Origin for the United States: July 1, 2009* (June 2010).

48. Ross, *Enlightened Democracy,* 41.

49. Farrand, *Records of the Federal Convention,* 2:111.

7. MAINTAINING COHESION

1. Judith A. Best, *The Choice of the People? Debating the Electoral College* (Lanham, MD: Rowman and Littlefield, 1996), 57; see also 14.

2. See, e.g., Alexander M. Bickel, "Direct Election of the President," *New Republic,* September 26, 1970, 9; Theodore H. White, "Direct Elections: An Invitation to National Chaos," *Life,* January 30, 1970, 4; Martin Diamond, *The Electoral College and the American Idea of Democracy* (Washington, DC: American Enterprise Institute, 1977), 16; Paul A. Rahe, "Moderating the Political Impulse," in

Gary L. Gregg, ed., *Securing Democracy: Why We Have an Electoral College* (Wilmington, DE: ISI, 2001), 68–69; Tara Ross, *Enlightened Democracy: The Case for the Electoral College* (Los Angeles: World Ahead, 2004), 102–109.

3. Best, *Choice of the People?* 58.

4. Robert Wiedrich, "Connell Says Dems 'Stole' 100,000 Votes: Charges Looting in 12 City Wards," *Chicago Tribune,* November 14, 1960.

5. *New York Herald Tribune,* July 14, 1961. Cited in Neil R. Peirce and Lawrence D. Longley, *The People's President,* rev. ed. (New Haven: Yale University Press, 1981), 68.

6. Associated Press, "3 Chicagoans Admit Guilt in Vote Fraud," *New York Times,* March 4, 1962.

7. Eric Lipton and Ian Urbina, "In 5-Year Effort, Scant Evidence of Voter Fraud," *New York Times,* April 12, 2007.

8. U.S. Election Assistance Commission, *Election Crimes: An Initial Review and Recommendations for Future Study,* December 2006. The commission also found that there have been no studies of voter fraud based on a comprehensive, nationwide study, survey, or review of all allegations, prosecutions, or convictions of state or federal crimes related to voting fraud or voter intimidation in the United States. Most reports have focused on a limited number of case studies or instances of alleged voting fraud or voter intimidation.

9. Mitchell McConnell, Introduction to Gregg, *Securing Democracy,* xv. See also "Three Cheers for the Electoral College," *American Enterprise,* January–February 2001, 6.

10. Vincent Merlin and Jack H. Nagel, "The U.S. Electoral College and the Probability of Disputable Outcomes Under Direct and Indirect Elections," unpublished paper, November 2008.

11. Monideepa Talukdar and Rob Richie, *A Survey and Analysis of Statewide Election Recounts, 1980–2006,* FairVote Research Report, July 27, 2007.

12. See, e.g., Best, *Choice of the People?* 14, 58; Wallace S. Sayre and Judith H. Parris, *Voting for President: The Electoral College and the American Political System* (Washington, DC: Brookings Institution, 1970), 84.

13. Gallup polls of November 26–27 and December 15–17, 2000.

14. See, e.g., Daniel Patrick Moynihan, "The Electoral College and the Uniqueness of America," in Gregg, *Securing Democracy,* 95; Michael M. Uhlman, "Creating Constitutional Majorities," ibid., 109–110; Rahe, "Moderating the Political Impulse," ibid., 63; James A. Baker III, *"Work Hard, Study . . . and Keep Out of Politics!"* (New York: Putnam, 2006), 388; Ross, *Enlightened Democracy,* 34, 76, 142, 170; George F. Will, "From Schwarzenegger, a Veto for Voters' Good," *Washington Post,* October 12, 2006.

15. Best, *Choice of the People?* 23; see also 21, 27.

16. Ibid., 14, 24, 27, 36–37. For another view, see Lucius Wilmerding Jr., *The Electoral College* (New Brunswick, NJ: Rutgers University Press, 1958), xi. See also Rahe, "Moderating the Political Impulse," 72–73; Ross, *Enlightened Democracy*, 34, 41, 79, 87, 109, 142, 170, 182, 187–188.

17. John C. Calhoun, *A Disquisition on Government and a Discourse on the Constitution and Government of the United States* (Indianapolis: Bobbs-Merrill, 1953).

18. Best, *Choice of the People?* 24, 38.

19. Ross, *Enlightened Democracy*, 109, 182, 187–188.

20. Voter News Service exit polls; Gallup News Service, "Candidate Support by Subgroup," news release, November 6, 2000 (based on six-day average, October 31–November 5, 2000).

21. For such an argument, see George Grant, *The Importance of the Electoral College* (San Antonio: Vision Forum Ministries, 2004).

22. See, for example, Ross, *Enlightened Democracy*, 80, 93–94, 99.

23. A point made by Alexander M. Bickel, "Direct Election of the President," *New Republic,* September 26, 1970, 9.

24. See, for example, Ross, *Enlightened Democracy*. See also Samuel Issacharoff, "Law, Rules, and Presidential Selection," *Political Science Quarterly* 120 (Spring 2005): 113–129.

25. George C. Edwards III and Andrew Barrett, "Presidential Agenda Setting in Congress," in Jon R. Bond and Richard Fleisher, eds., *Polarized Politics: Congress and the President in a Partisan Era* (Washington, DC: Congressional Quarterly, 2000).

26. See, e.g., Diamond, *Electoral College and American Idea of Democracy,* 22; and Best, *Choice of the People?* 68.

27. See, e.g., Sayre and Parris, *Voting for President,* 85–86.

28. See, e.g., Best, *Choice of the People?* 66–67.

29. George C. Edwards III and Stephen J. Wayne, *Presidential Leadership,* 6th ed. (Belmont, CA: Wadsworth, 2003), 115–116.

30. See, e.g., George C. Edwards III, *At the Margins: Presidential Leadership of Congress* (New Haven: Yale University Press, 1989), chapter 8; Robert E. Goodwin, "The Importance of Winning Big," *Legislative Studies Quarterly* 2 (November 1977): 399–407.

31. Lawrence J. Grossback, David A. M. Peterson, and James A. Stimson, *Mandate Politics* (New York: Cambridge University Press, 2006).

32. David R. Mayhew, *Congress: The Electoral Connection* (New Haven: Yale University Press, 1974), 70–71.

33. Quoted in Everett Carll Ladd, *The Ladd Report #1* (New York: Norton, 1985), 3.

34. See Grossback, Peterson, and Stimson, *Mandate Politics,* chapter 2; Edwards, *At the Margins,* chapter 8.

35. Gallup poll, January 30–February 2, 1981.

36. See, e.g., CBS News/ *New York Times* Poll, news release, January 21, 1985, tables 1–3; "Opinion Roundup," *Public Opinion,* December–January 1985, 37.

37. Gallup poll, January 25–28, 1985.

38. See Grossback, Peterson, and Stimson, *Mandate Politics,* chapter 2; Edwards, *At the Margins,* chapter 8.

39. See, e.g., "The Myth of the Presidential Mandate," *Political Science Quarterly* 105 (Fall 1990): 355–372; George C. Edwards III, *The Public Presidency* (New York: St. Martin's, 1983), 18–23.

40. Stanley Kelley Jr., *Interpreting Elections* (Princeton: Princeton University Press, 1983), 72–125.

41. *Los Angeles Times* poll, October 12–15, 1984; Martin P. Wattenberg, *The Decline of American Political Parties, 1952–1984* (Cambridge: Harvard University Press, 1986), 154.

42. Gallup poll, September 24–27, 2007.

43. *Los Angeles Times* poll, October 12–15, 1984; Wattenberg, *Decline of American Political Parties,* 154.

44. Benjamin I. Page, *Choices and Echoes in Presidential Elections* (Chicago: University of Chicago Press, 1978), 168–169; Gerald M. Pomper with Susan S. Lederman, *Elections in America,* 2d ed. (New York: Longman, 1980), 134–135.

45. George C. Edwards III, "Interview with President Jimmy Carter," *Presidential Studies Quarterly* 38 (March 2008): 5–6.

46. Best, *Choice of the People?* 55.

47. William C. Kimberling, "The Electoral College," on the Federal Election Commission Web site, www.fec.gov/pdf/eleccoll.pdf.

48. For other examples, see James R. Stoner Jr., "Federalism, States, and Electoral College," in Gregg, *Securing Democracy,* 51–52; Larry J. Sabato, *A More Perfect Constitution* (New York: Walker, 2007), 139; Ross, *Enlightened Democracy,* 53.

49. Richard Beeman, *Plain, Honest Men: The Making of the American Constitution* (New York: Random House, 2010), 135, 232–233.

50. Diamond, *The Electoral College and the American Idea of Democracy,* 4.

51. Neal R. Peirce, "A Partial Dissent," *Winner Take All* (New York: Holmes and Meier, 1978), chapter 6.

52. Diamond, *Electoral College and American Idea of Democracy,* 21. See also Charles Fried, "Should the Current Electoral College System Be Preserved?" *Congressional Digest,* January 2001, 30; Stoner, "Federalism, the States, and the Electoral College," 46; Uhlman, "Creating Constitutional Majorities," 107; Curtis Gans, "Electoral College Reform: How to Keep, But Improve, the Current System," *Congressional Digest,* January 2001, 12; and Sayre and Parris, *Voting for President,* 78–79.

53. Reported in Peirce and Longley, *The People's President*, 223.
54. See, e.g., Uhlman, "Creating Constitutional Majorities," 107.
55. See Richard G. Niemi and Paul S. Herrnson, "Beyond the Butterfly: The Complexity of U.S. Ballots," *Perspectives on Politics* 1 (June 2003): 317–326.
56. *Voting: What Is, What Could Be* (2003).
57. Remarks of President George W. Bush at signing ceremony for the Help America Vote Act of 2002, White House, October 29, 2002.
58. "Testimony of Honorable Robert Dole, U.S. Senator from the State of Kansas," *The Electoral College and Direct Election: Hearings Before the Committee on the Judiciary, United States Senate,* 95th Cong., 1st sess., January 27, February 1, 2, 7, 10, 1977, 39.

8. PRESERVING THE PARTY SYSTEM

1. See, for example, Tara Ross, *Enlightened Democracy: The Case for the Electoral College* (Los Angeles: World Ahead, 2004), 84, 96–97; Larry J. Sabato, *A More Perfect Constitution* (New York: Walker, 2007), 138; George F. Will, "From Schwarzenegger, a Veto for Voters' Good," *Washington Post,* October 12, 2006.
2. See, e.g., Martin Diamond, *The Electoral College and the American Idea of Democracy* (Washington, DC: American Enterprise Institute, 1977), 20; Michael Barone, "The Electoral College and the Future of American Political Parties," in Gary L. Gregg, ed., *Securing Democracy: Why We Have an Electoral College* (Wilmington, DE: ISI, 2001), 82–83, 85; Arthur M. Schlesinger Jr., *The Cycles of American History* (Boston: Houghton Mifflin, 1986), 319–320; Paul A. Rahe, "Moderating the Political Impulse," in Gregg, *Securing Democracy,* 69; Wallace S. Sayre and Judith H. Parris, *Voting for President: The Electoral College and the American Political System* (Washington, DC: Brookings Institution, 1970), 73–82, 146–147.
3. Judith A. Best, *The Choice of the People? Debating the Electoral College* (Lanham, MD: Rowman and Littlefield, 1996), 56.
4. Arthur M. Schlesinger Jr., "Not the People's Choice," *American Prospect,* March 25, 2002, 275.
5. See, e.g., Sayre and Parris, *Voting for President,* 78.
6. See, e.g., Michael M. Uhlman, "Creating Constitutional Majorities," in Gregg, *Securing Democracy,* 111–112; Best, *Choice of the People?* 58.
7. See, e.g., Rahe, "Moderating the Political Impulse," 68; Sayre and Parris, *Voting for President,* 85.
8. See, e.g., Arend Lijphart, *Patterns of Democracy: Government Forms and Performance in Thirty-Six Countries* (New Haven: Yale University Press, 1999), 168–170; Gary W. Cox, *Making Votes Count: Strategic Coordination in the World's*

Electoral Systems (New York: Cambridge University Press, 1997), chapter 10, p. 190. See also Peter Ordeshook and Olga Shvetsova, "Ethnic Heterogeneity, District Magnitude, and the Number of Parties," *American Journal of Political Science* 38 (February 1994): 100–123.

9. See, e.g., Frank J. Sorauf, *Party Politics in America* (Boston: Little, Brown, 1968), 35–37.

10. Maurice Duverger, *Political Parties* (New York: Wiley, 1954), 217–218, 239. See also Maurice Duverger, "Duverger's Law: Thirty Years Later," in Arend Lijphart and Bernard Grofman, eds., *Choosing an Electoral System: Issues and Alternatives* (New York: Praeger, 1986).

11. See, e.g., G. Bingham Powell, *Contemporary Democracies: Participation, Stability, and Violence* (Cambridge: Harvard University Press, 1982), 205; William H. Riker, "The Two-Party System and Duverger's Law: An Essay on the History of Political Science," *American Political Science Review* 76 (December 1982): 753–766; Giovanni Sartori, *Comparative Constitutional Engineering* (New York: New York University Press, 1994); Rein Taagepera and Matthew Soberg Shugart, *Seats and Votes: The Effects and Determinants of Electoral Systems* (New Haven: Yale University Press, 1989); Douglas W. Rae, *The Political Consequences of Electoral Laws* (New Haven: Yale University Press, 1967), 67–129; Lijphart, *Patterns of Democracy*, 226.

12. An exception is an assertion written more than fifty years ago by Alexander Heard in *A Two-Party South?* (Chapel Hill: University of North Carolina Press, 1952), 169.

13. Cox, *Making Votes Count,* esp. 96.

14. Clinton Rossiter, *Parties and Politics in America* (Ithaca, NY: Cornell University Press, 1962), 8.

15. V. O. Key Jr., *Politics, Parties, and Pressure Groups,* 5th ed. (New York: Crowell, 1964), 209.

16. James MacGregor Burns, "A New Course for the Electoral College," *New York Times Magazine,* December 18, 1960, 28.

17. John F. Bibby and L. Sandy Maisel, *Two Parties—or More?* (Boulder, CO: Westview, 1998), 56–64.

18. Leon D. Epstein, *Political Parties in the American Mold* (Madison: University of Wisconsin Press, 1986), 173.

19. Allan Cigler, Joel Paddock, Gary Reich, and Eric Uslaner, "Changing the Electoral College: The Impact on Parties and Organized Interests," in Paul D. Schumaker and Burdett A. Loomis, *Choosing a President* (New York: Chatham, 2002), 87.

20. Sabato, *A More Perfect Constitution,* 143–144.

21. See, e.g., Samantha Luks, Joanne M. Miller, and Lawrence R. Jacobs, "Who

Wins? Campaigns and the Third Party Vote," *Presidential Studies Quarterly* 33 (March 2003): 9–30.

22. See, e.g., Barry C. Burden, "Minor Parties in the 2000 Presidential Election," in Herbert F. Weisberg and Clyde Wilcox, eds., *Models of Voting in Presidential Elections: The 2000 U.S. Election* (Stanford: Stanford University Press, 2003); Michael C. Herron and Jeffrey B. Lewis, "Did Ralph Nader Spoil a Gore Presidency? A Ballot-Level Study of Green and Reform Party Voters in the 2000 Presidential Election," *Quarterly Journal of Political Science* 2 (August 2007): 205–226.

23. Stephen J. Wayne, *The Road to the White House 2004* (Belmont, CA: Thomson/Wadsworth, 2004), 291.

24. These figures are from *Congressional Quarterly's Guide to U.S. Elections,* 6th ed. (Washington, DC: CQ Press, 2010).

25. V. O. Key Jr., *Southern Politics* (New York: Vintage, 1949), 300, 420.

26. John A. Ferejohn and Morris P. Fiorina, "The Paradox of Not Voting: A Decision Theoretic Analysis," *American Political Science Review* 68 (June 1974): 525–536; "Closeness Counts Only in Horseshoes and Dancing," *American Political Science Review* 69 (September 1975): 920–925. William H. Riker defines strategic voting as "voting contrary to one's immediate tastes in order to obtain an advantage in the long run." See Riker, *The Art of Political Manipulation* (New Haven: Yale University Press, 1986), 78.

27. Paul R. Abramson, John H. Aldrich, Phil Paolino, and David W. Rohde, "Third Party and Independent Candidates in American Politics: Wallace, Anderson, and Perot," *Political Science Quarterly* 110 (Autumn 1995): 349–367.

28. See, for example, Nolan McCarty, Keith T. Poole, and Howard Rosenthal, *Polarized America: The Dance of Ideology and Unequal Riches* (Cambridge: MIT Press, 2006); Gary C. Jacobson, *A Divider, Not a Uniter: George W. Bush and the American Public,* 3rd ed. (New York: Longman, 2010).

29. Key, *Southern Politics,* 37–41, 47, 89–91, 110–114, 131–135, 223–224, 248, 251–253, 259, 302–310, 419–423.

30. See, e.g., Best, *Choice of the People?* 14, 56; Rahe, "Moderating the Political Impulse," 70; Diamond, *Electoral College and American Idea of Democracy,* 20; and Sayre and Parris, *Voting for President,* 75.

31. A good discussion of the relation of a runoff to selecting Condorcet winners can be found in Theodore S. Arrington and Saul Brenner, "The Advantages of a Plurality Election of the President," *Presidential Studies Quarterly* 10 (Summer 1980): 476–482.

32. Donald Stokes, Testimony Before the U.S. Senate Judiciary Committee's Subcommittee on Electoral College Reform, July 18, 1967. Cited in Neal R. Peirce and Lawrence D. Longley, *The People's President,* rev. ed. (New Haven: Yale University Press, 1981), 222.

33. Cortez A. M. Ewing, *Primary Elections in the South* (Norman: University of Oklahoma Press, 1953), 96.

34. For one example, see Robert A. Dahl, *How Democratic Is the American Constitution?* (New Haven: Yale University Press, 2001), 86.

35. Kenneth O. May, "A Set of Independent, Necessary and Sufficient Conditions for Simple Majority Decision," *Econometrica* 20 (October 1952): 680–684.

36. Robert E. Goodin and Christian List, "A Conditional Defense of Plurality Rule: Generalizing May's Theorem in a Restricted Informational Environment," *American Journal of Political Science* 50 (October 2006): 940–949.

37. Allan Gibbard, "Manipulation of Voting Schemes: A General Result," *Econometrica* 41 (July 1973): 587–601; Mark A. Satterthwaite, "Strategy-Proofness and Arrow's Conditions: Existence and Correspondence Theorems for Voting Procedures and Social Welfare Functions," *Journal of Economic Theory* 10 (April 1975): 187–217.

38. Kenneth J. Arrow, *Social Choice and Individual Values*, 2nd ed. (New Haven: Yale University Press, 1963).

39. For advocacy for IRV, see www.fairvote.org/instant-runoff-voting.

40. For more on IRV, see Jack H. Nagel, "The Burr Dilemma in Approval Voting," *Journal of Politics* 69 (February 2007): 43–58.

41. See Stephen J. Brams and Peter C. Fishburn, *Approval Voting*, 2nd ed. (New York: Springer, 2010).

42. See ibid.

43. Harold J. Jansen, "The Political Consequences of the Alternative Vote: Lessons from Western Canada," *Canadian Journal of Political Science* 27 (September 2004): 647–669.

9. Conclusion

1. Matthew Soberg Shugart, "The American Process of Selecting a President: A Comparative Perspective," *Presidential Studies Quarterly* 34 (September 2004): 632–655.

2. Robert Dudley and Alan R. Gitelson, *American Elections: The Rules Matter* (New York: Longman, 2000), 149–152.

3. Ibid., 149–152.

4. Twentieth Century Fund, *Winner Take All* (New York: Holmes and Meier, 1978). A useful discussion of this plan can be found in Thomas E. Cronin, "The Direct Vote and the Electoral College: The Case for Meshing Things Up!" *Presidential Studies Quarterly* 9 (Spring 1979): 144–158.

5. The plan is fully discussed in John R. Kosa et al., *Every Vote Equal: A State-Based*

Plan for Electing the President by National Popular Vote, 2nd ed. (Los Altos, CA: National Popular Vote Press, 2009).

6. Larry J. Sabato, *A More Perfect Constitution* (New York: Walker, 2007), 142. See also Tara Ross, *Enlightened Democracy: The Case for the Electoral College* (Los Angeles: World Ahead, 2004), 81, 83.

7. See Eric R. A. N. Smithy and Peverill Squire, "Direct Election of the President and the Power of the States," *Western Political Quarterly* 40 (March 1987): 29–44.

8. Electoral college supporter James Stoner seems to recognize this but misses the point of how this would advance democracy in America. See James R. Stoner Jr., "Federalism, the States, and the Electoral College," in Gary L. Gregg, ed., *Securing Democracy: Why We Have an Electoral College* (Wilmington, DE: ISI, 2001), 46.

9. *Congressional Record,* January 14, 1979, 309.

10. Darshan J. Goux and David A. Hopkins, "The Empirical Implications of Electoral College Reform," *American Politics Research* 36 (November 2008), 870–873.

11. Ibid. See also Daron Shaw, *The Race to 270* (Chicago: University of Chicago Press, 2007).

12. Michael Hagen, Richard Johnston, and Kathleen Hall Jamieson, "Effects of the 2000 Presidential Campaign," paper delivered at the Annual Meeting of the American Political Science Association, August 29–September 1, 2002, 3.

13. Quoted in U.S. Congress, Senate, Committee on the Judiciary, *Report on Direct Popular Election of the President and Vice President of the United States,* 95th Congress, 1st session, 1967, 124.

14. Senator Robert Dole, "Testimony of Hon. Robert Dole, U.S. Senator from the State of Kansas," *The Electoral College and Direct Election: Hearings Before the Subcommittee on the Constitution of the Committee on the Judiciary, Supplement,* 40. See also, *Congressional Record,* January 14, 1979, 309.

15. "Maybe They Go for the L.L. Bean Sales," *National Journal,* October 30, 2004; Dan Balz and Jim VandeHei, "Candidates Debut Closing Themes," *Washington Post,* October 15, 2004.

16. See, for example, Tasha S. Philpot, Daron R. Shaw, and Ernest B. McGowen, "Winning the Race: Black Voter Turnout in the 2008 Presidential Election," *Public Opinion Quarterly* 73, no. 5 (2009): 995–1022; Seth E. Masket, "Did Obama's Ground Game Matter? The Influence of Local Field Offices During the 2008 Presidential Election," *Public Opinion Quarterly* 73, no. 5 (2009): 1023–1039; Kevin Arceneaux and David W. Nickerson, "Who Is Mobilized to Vote? A Re-Analysis of 11 Field Experiments," *American Journal of Political Science* 53 (January 2009): 1–16; Daniel E. Bergan, Alan S. Gerber, Donald P. Green, and Costas Panagopoulos, "Grassroots Mobilization and Voter Turnout in 2004," *Public Opinion Quarterly* 69, no. 5 (2005): 760–777; D. Sunshine Hillygus,

"Campaign Effects and the Dynamics of Turnout Intention in Election 2000," *Journal of Politics* 67 (February 2005): 50–68; Thomas E. Patterson, *The Vanishing Voter* (New York: Knopf, 2002), 137, 142; Thomas M. Holbrook and Scott D. McClurg, "The Mobilization of Core Supporters: Campaigns, Turnout, and Electoral Composition in United States Presidential Elections," *American Journal of Political Science* 49 (October 2005): 689–703.

   For some debate on the impact of advertising, see Jonathan S. Krasno and Donald P. Green, "Do Televised Presidential Ads Increase Voter Turnout? Evidence from a Natural Experiment," *Journal of Politics* 70 (January 2008): 245–261; Michael M. Franz, Paul Freedman, Ken Goldstein, and Travis N. Ridout, "Understanding the Effect of Political Advertising on Voter Turnout: A Response to Krasno and Green," *Journal of Politics* 70 (January 2008): 262–268; Jonathan S. Krasno and Donald P. Green, "Response to Franz, Freedman, Goldstein, and Ridout," *Journal of Politics* 70 (January 2008): 269–271.

17. James G. Gimpel, Karen M. Kaufman, and Shanna Pearson-Merkowitz, "Battleground States Versus Blackout States: The Behavioral Implications of Modern Presidential Campaigns," *Journal of Politics* 69 (August 2007): 786–797.

18. David Hill and Seth C. McKee, "The Electoral College, Mobilization, and Turnout in the 2000 Presidential Election," *American Politics Research* 33 (September 2005): 700–725.

19. David Dreyer Lassen, "The Effect of Information on Voter Turnout: Evidence from a Natural Experiment," *American Journal of Political Science* 49 (January 2005): 103–118.

20. Martin Gilens, Lynn Vavreck, and Martin Cohen, "The Mass Media and the Public's Assessments of Presidential Candidates, 1952–2000," *Journal of Politics* 69 (November 2007): 1160–1175.

21. Jens Großer and Arthur Schram, "Public Opinion Polls, Voter Turnout, and Welfare: An Experimental Study," *American Journal of Political Science* 54 (July 2010): 700–717; John Duffy and Margit Tavits, "Beliefs and Voting Decisions: A Test of the Pivotal Voter Model," *American Journal of Political Science* 52 (July 2008): 603–618; Seth McKee and David Hill, "The New Democratic Majority: Who Voted in the 2008 Presidential Election," paper presented at 2009 Annual Meeting of the American Political Science Association, Toronto, September 3–6.

22. Thomas G. Hansford and Brad T. Gomez, "Estimating the Electoral Effects of Voter Turnout," *American Political Science Review* 104 (May 2010): 268–288.

23. Darrell West, *Air Wars: Television Advertising in Election Campaigns,* 5th ed. (Washington, DC: CQ Press, 2010); Gilens, Vavreck, and Cohen, "The Mass Media and the Public's Assessments of Presidential Candidates, 1952–2000"; Markus Prior, "News vs. Entertainment: How Increasing Media Choice Widens

Gaps in Political Knowledge and Turnout," *American Journal of Political Science* 49 (July 2005): 577–592; Patterson, *The Vanishing Voter,* 144; Stephen Ansolabehere and Shanto Iyengar, *Going Negative* (New York: Free Press, 1995); Thomas E. Patterson and Robert D. McClure, *The Unseeing Eye: The Myth of Television in National Elections* (New York: Putnam, 1976), 116–120.

24. Jennifer Wolak, "The Consequences of Presidential Battleground States for Citizen Engagement," *Political Research Quarterly* 59 (September 2006): 353–361; Patterson, *The Vanishing Voter,* 143–144.

25. Costas Panagopoulos, "Campaign Dynamics in Battleground and Nonbattleground States," *Public Opinion Quarterly* 73 (Spring 2009): 119–129.

26. Although it might seem reasonable to expect that smaller electoral units would have higher levels of turnout due to a more highly developed sense of community, the evidence is that there is little relationship between the size of a voting population and the turnout rates of its citizens. See Martin P. Wattenberg, *Where Have All the Voters Gone?* (Cambridge: Harvard University Press, 2002), 41.

27. Robert A. Dahl, *On Democracy* (New Haven: Yale University Press, 2000), 37.

28. Alexander Keyssar, "Peculiar Institution," *Boston Globe,* October 17, 2004.

29. Gallup Poll, news release, January 5, 2001.

30. A list of these polls and a report on each can be found at www.nationalpopular vote.com/pages/polls.php.

31. For the most thorough evaluation of the prospects for change, see Gary Bugh, ed., *Electoral College Reform* (Burlington, VT: Ashgate, 2010).

32. Arthur M. Schlesinger Jr., *The Cycles of American History* (Boston: Houghton Mifflin, 1986), 318.

33. Jeff Greenfield, *Oh Waiter! One Order of Crow!* (New York: Putnam, 2001), 14.

34. Michael Kramer, "Bush Set to Fight an Electoral College Loss," *New York Daily News,* November 1, 2000, 6.

35. See, e.g., I. M. Destler, "The Myth of the 'Electoral Lock,'" *PS: Political Science and Politics* 29 (September 1996): 491–494; Thomas Brunell and Bernard Grofman, "The 1992 and 1996 Presidential Elections: Whatever Happened to the Republican Electoral College Lock?" *Presidential Studies Quarterly* 27 (Winter 1997): 134–138.

Index